Selfless-Sufficient:

Growing in Love by the Power

of God

Sarah, you are precious to God and I know He is proud of you and all the charitable work you've done. I can tell He's doing a good work in you, and He's not finished yet! I hope you are blessed by this book, which is a big piece of my heart.

Benjamin P. Olson

Selfless-Sufficient: Growing in Love by the Power of God

Copyright © 2019 by Benjamin P. Olson

www.benjaminpolson.com

Paperback ISBN 978-1-7338065-0-3

eBook ISBN 978-1-7338065-1-0

Library of Congress Control Number: 2019903064

All rights reserved. No portion of this book may be reproduced in any form without permission from the publisher, except as permitted by U.S. copyright law. For permission, contact: authorbpo@gmail.com

Unless otherwise indicated, all Scripture quotations are taken from the Holy Bible, New International Version®, NIV® Copyright ©1973, 1978, 1984, 2011 by Biblica, Inc.® Used by permission. All rights reserved worldwide.

Scripture quotations marked NKJV are taken from the New King James Version®. Copyright © 1982 by Thomas Nelson. Used by permission. All rights reserved.

Scripture quotations marked NASB are taken from the New American Standard Bible® (NASB), Copyright © 1960, 1962, 1963, 1968, 1971, 1972, 1973, 1975, 1977, 1995 by The Lockman Foundation. Used by permission. www.Lockman.org.

Scripture quotations marked KJV are taken from the King James Version of the Bible. Public domain.

All emphasis in Scripture is that of the author.

Author photo: Sarah Pierce Photography LLC www.sarahpiercephotography.com

Cover design: Miladinka Milic www.milagraphicartist.com

Cover images: Kseniakrop/Shutterstock.com, rolandtopor/Shutterstock.com, Anna Kutukova/Shutterstock.com, De-V/Shutterstock.com

Contents

Introduction	1
Stage One: Seedling	11
Chapter 1: Self-Sufficient?	13
Chapter 2: Selfless-Sufficient	23
Chapter 3: Kingdom VIP	35
Stage Two: Primary Growth	61
Chapter 4: How Faith Works	63
Chapter 5: The Cocoon of Communion	71
Chapter 6: Yeah, But What If …	103
Stage Three: Secondary Growth	141
Chapter 7: The New You	143
Chapter 8: Loving Every Person	171
Chapter 9: Who Is the Greatest?	205
Stage Four: Maturity	231
Chapter 10: Coming Out of Hiding	233
Chapter 11: Making Disciples	263
Chapter 12: Love Anthem	283
Conclusion: Who Will Rise Up?	301
Appendix: If You're Not a Christian	311
Acknowledgments	313
About the Author	317
References	319

Introduction

I am God. *Look* at me. *Watch* me take my selfie. Tell me I look *amazing*.

I get what I want when I want it. Not even my parents could tell me what to do. I am my own master. You think you've got a lot of stuff, but I've got even more. If you have what I want, I will take it from you. I dare you to slap me; I will make you wish you weren't born. Do you know where I graduated from? Do you know where I work, and how much I get paid? Do you know where I've been and how much I get laid? You can't keep up with me.

I don't care what you think. You're a victim I hate, and I will laugh while you sink. I'll smear you with my words and beat you with my fists. Don't tell me about God as if he isn't me. I am self-made; no one ever helped me. I had to do life myself, and I determine to stop at nothing. Get in my way and I'll throw you under the bus.

What can I say? Only the fittest survive. Life isn't fair. It's your fault you lost, and my fault I'm the boss. While you're crying, don't mind me lying while I'm making bank on your blindness. Where is God's power? I'm lifting more than you. Fool, go ahead and try measuring what isn't real, while I have fun with winning and things I can feel.

Where Is the Love?

What you just read is my rendition of 2 Timothy 3:1–7, which expresses the terrible reality of a darkened world littered with hardened hearts. A place filled with bitter people, highly disturbed in thought, word, and deed. It's a glimpse of self-centered language, which we learned from Adam through the fall of man. Though harsh sounding, it's the battle cry of the loveless world we live in.

Obviously, our world has many problems. But if Jesus has overcome the world, which He has (John 16:33), then where are the overcomers? Perhaps these messengers of God are covering their light under a basket (Matthew 5:15). If so, how unfortunate! The light of God is what the world *needs*. Our refusing to invest with what we've been given is not unlike the wicked and lazy man who buried his talents—to nobody's benefit (see Matthew 25:14–30).

Everyone needs the life-changing light of God's love, to shine in this dark world. But where is it? And if we have it, how do we uncover it?

Jesus rightly predicted that in the times prior to His second coming, "the love of many will grow cold" (Matthew 24:12 NKJV). Do we need to hear any more stories of war, murder, betrayal, thievery, rape, and racism to agree that we're living in the times Jesus mentioned? He predicted these stormy times. You may wonder what hope we have for a better future when so much damage has already been done.

Fortunately, Jesus has given us the antidote to this chaos. It isn't about survival of the fittest, but revival of the selfless.

What Are Christians to Be Known For?

Even Christians fall prey to selfishness. This may not come as a surprise, but really, isn't it surprising? There's an undeniable element of confusion for both Christians and non-Christians alike: How is it that God is love but Christians are not? Sure, God is God, and the Holy Spirit lives within the believer, but it doesn't stop there. The Bible says, "He who does not love does not know God, for God is love" (1 John 4:8 NKJV). In other words, if love is missing, in *large* part, such as in my life and relationships, then I don't have much of a relationship with God, if any.

Ironically, I can go to church, sing Christian songs, do Bible studies, put a "Christians aren't perfect, just forgiven" bumper sticker on my car, wear a Christian T-shirt, and *still not know the Lord.* If I'm not loving people the way Jesus does, selflessly and unconditionally, then the Bible, my actions, and the world agree there's a peculiar disconnect.

Jesus said, "By this all will know that you are My disciples, if you have love for one another" (John 13:35 NKJV). *All* will know … *if* … you have love.

If love is missing, what are we known for? Doing church, putting up with people, and struggling to get through life? Having the same issues as everyone else? Passing people by? Where is the Good Samaritan in any of that?

Love is what Christians are known for. It is about connecting with God and helping people. Love is the heart of the Bible, Jesus, and born-again Christians. We would do well to understand it.

What Is Love?

The Bible makes it clear that now is the prime time to love, but what *exactly* is love?

It's such a broad term. Or is it? Maybe it's more simple and specific than we think. So simple a child can grasp it. What if it's so simple we can reduce it to one word? A word we don't use much: *selfless*.

Such simplicity is not to be confused with familiarity, or any watered-down versions of Scripture such as "God is love," or, "For God so loved the world," and so on. I don't wish to keep Him at bay as an abstract concept having no particular relevance to the life I live now. There's no time like the present to dig in deep and come up with the treasures of a life lived in connection to God.

The trouble is, God remains an abstract concept for many. Maybe even for some of you reading this. Truthfully, I haven't always understood what love is, let alone how God is relevant to my real life. However, I can confidently say I'm secure in my understanding now, and this "growing in knowing" has revolutionized the way I live. It's only getting better. If this is possible for me, it's possible for you too. After all, why would Jesus instruct us to love like He does if it isn't possible? (John 13:34–35).

The life of Jesus holds all the clues we need. Following Him = finding and becoming selfless love.

Why Is Love Important?

The evidence is in: Love has grown cold. Non-lukewarm Christians are needed now more than ever. Many people are looking for Jesus and they don't even know it. Pray that God will bring such people to you. Many who don't know Him are dying, *daily*. In fact, someone in your sphere of influence may not have a chance, outside of you, of experiencing the love of God.

I frequently have productive conversations about God with non-Christians, but they often seem (keyword: *seem*) to lead them nowhere near the Lord. My heart hurts for them! I yearn for their reconciliation to God; I know there's no greater satisfaction and life-transforming power than that of knowing Jesus. In these types of situations, we would do well to avoid the notion of failing someone and instead put our trust in God. Naturally, He is the one who does the best work through our words and actions. He works on the hearts of those around us, as we love them. And if we've loved them, we've done right—even if they don't respond with hands raised in praise to the Lord.

Love doesn't say, "Oh no! They're going to hell and it's all my fault!" No. This isn't about worry, fear, or assuming we are somehow in control of someone's eternal destiny. God saves—not us. People fail people, but "love never fails" (1 Corinthians 13:8 NKJV). God is always faithful, and He shows kindness to both the righteous and the unrighteous (Matthew 5:45). He wants everyone to know Him so their joy may be complete, and He patiently and persistently gives them chance after chance, wishing that no one would perish. He even loves His enemies because He can't help but love—it's His essence. Therefore, it's my privilege, as a Christian, to know God (i.e., be like Him) and love people without letting the old me (filled with anger, frustration, anxiety, and discouragement) get in the way.

One thing is for sure: The world needs to see the love of God in your life. So get to know Jesus. If you already know Him, get closer. Spend *quality* time with Him. There are easy ways to do this (more on that later). Only then can you truly love others, selflessly. Help people find Jesus, and teach them how to follow Him. We don't know how much time we have with the people we know. Consider Jesus' last words in Revelation: "Surely I am coming quickly" (Revelation 22:20 NKJV). Time is running out.

I am excited for Jesus's return. Even so, I've learned that love says, "Don't come yet!" Because there's so much love left to do. Many souls still need our Savior. They need to hear about Jesus and see His selfless love in action. We must prepare for His return. You know that exhilarating feeling you get when company is about to come over, and you need to get everything ready before company arrives? Feeling pressed on time and doing your best to make the most of the time you have? Then, *boom*! They come fifteen minutes early. The same urgency applies here, but it's of infinitely greater consequence.

If you're reading this, we still have time. Don't worry about not having enough, which will only discourage you. Discouragement doesn't come from God. Instead, get excited about this fresh revelation. It will motivate you to get on with love. Be encouraged! He will accomplish His purposes through you, on His time, which is the *right* time. For now, cling to Him and learn to live a life of love. Watch His Spirit cover you with fruitfulness as He blesses everyone coming into contact with you. Each act of love matters.

Amazingly, just one encounter with truth—one act of love—can change the entire course of a person's life. I'm a firsthand witness of a massive chain reaction that love has sparked in my own life, causing a ripple effect and literally changing everything, from how I pray to what I eat and everything in between. Whether I'm driving, shopping, budgeting, or with my family, I've been learning how to do all things to the glory of God—in a way that isn't exhausting, rigid, or legalistic. Yay! In case you can't tell, I'm seriously having fun. The Christian life *should* be filled with great joy—regardless of the circumstances (James 1:2).

If you're burned out, love will help you. A refresher, or a complete overhaul, on love is most likely what you need to ascend from the rut. Coming to know and learning to show the love of God is what you're after. If you want to discover how this can happen in your life, have I got the book for you!

As you read these pages, the truth may resonate with you on a visceral level. You may feel your heart racing with excitement, energy coursing through your veins, a special kind of laugh, or a smile that only freedom in Christ can bring. A few aha moments may come and peel away layers of deception. You may find a surge of strength to do what you couldn't do before. Hopefully eyes will be opened, and the world will be seen through a strikingly clear lens of love.

Instead of missing people, you will see them. Prayer will become a pleasure, not a chore. You may feel God for the first time. If you don't feel Him, you'll be at peace with that because truth will take root, and faith will put feelings in their proper place. You may see—really see—your spouse for the first time, and feel a compassion that moves you to tears. Maybe you'll have an epiphany and realize you believe for the first time that you are precious to God, and that He is proud of you and smiling over you—He's not mad at you. And much, much more. I can't limit your experiences to my list. Basically, Jesus wants to give you the best life you can possibly have. This can't happen unless you know Him and receive His Holy Spirit.

Most importantly: Love is the evidence of our intimate relationship with God. The world would benefit from such evidence!

The goal of this book is to spread God's love all over the earth, one heart at a time. One person can make a huge difference. This is your time. God is calling *you*. If this book serves to help you know Jesus better, receive and give forgiveness, live free from addiction, hold your spouse's hand more often, show kindness to those that persecute you, give your children a few extra hugs, eat a little healthier, or all of the above—it's worth it. Christians are in the love-building business. They ought to be the most passionate lovers and the happiest, most generous helpers, making the best of individuals, families, society, and all countries across the world. It's our privilege, as citizens of heaven, to establish more heaven on earth. Love is God's flag on the land. Will you claim your territory—your sphere of influence—for Him? Let's cover the earth with His glory!

All of that sounds great, but ...

How Can I Become Love?

I'm happy to announce it's not even hard to begin growing in the right direction. In a short time, loving people becomes rather easy, even effortless. But I realize many people can't say the same; there was a time when I didn't care much about anyone but myself. That's why I'm writing this—things change! Now the joy of the Lord is welling up within me. It's springing up and onto these pages, to God's glory.

Just take in these words and, rest assured, it will feel like you're running high and light by the end of this book. That's what God's love does—it sets you free. Things are about to change for you. For the better. Why else would God have directed your eyes to land here?

As you follow His lead, in this way—His way—I'm confident you'll enjoy the move from burned out to energized (no caffeine or sugar required); from inconsistent to consistent; from up and down to steadily up; from complaining to praising; from depressed to joyous; from discouraged to encouraged; from insecure to confident; from confused to clear; from feelings to faith; from selfish to selfless; from confession to celebration; from trying to relaxing; from sin-conscious and self-conscious to Jesus Christ-conscious; from living alone to living with Him, and so on. The more you abide in Him, the more you will notice this (don't worry, I'll soon explain what I mean by abiding in Him).

The Lord has blessed me with an analogy to explain how this works. This isn't a method or a formula, so to speak, but a model illustrating how love works.

The Four Stages of Tree Growth

Introducing the four stages of tree growth, with their spiritual counterparts in parentheses: **1) Seedling** (T1: Truth), **2) Primary Growth** (T2: Thankfulness), **3) Secondary Growth** (T3: Transformation), and **4) Maturity** (T4: Thoughtfulness). We'll unpack these throughout the book.

When I first discovered these stages, I was struck by the spiritual parallels concerning the growth of love in the life of a Christian. It's not surprising that God reveals Himself through nature, and it sure is fun to see the signs. Watch this.

"Trees are essential to human existence, because they produce oxygen, cleanse the air, provide shade, clean the soil and control noise pollution. The growth of trees begins with a single seed that must compete with others for water, nutrients and space to grow. Not many seeds reach all four stages of tree growth; many are destroyed by insects or disease before reaching maturity."[1]

Likewise, Christians are essential to human existence because they reproduce the image of God, who cleanses us of our sins, provides for our needs, cleans our hearts, and manages our lives and the rhythms of the universe. The growth of love in Christians begins with a single seed of self, which must stop competing (with itself and others) and die in order to make room for the Holy Spirit to grow us from seed to fruitful tree. Not many Christians reach all four stages of tree growth; many are defeated by themselves and the Enemy before reaching spiritual maturity (because they refuse to die to self, or keep running the rat race).

From Seed to Tree

If we're going to grow from seed to tree, there's something we should know: Self is the seed that must die in order for God to grow His character within us. Only then can the seed of self become unlike it*self*—something much larger, stronger, and useful.

How does the seed of self die? By asking Jesus for the deposit of His Holy Spirit. (If you've never done this, please see the appendix for help asking and believing in the receiving of Jesus's Holy Spirit.) Doing this effectively indicates that our sin-ridden seed with poor potential has been swapped out for His seed of righteousness with tremendous potential—"the planting of the LORD" (Isaiah 61:3 NKJV).

The Word of God is the seed we need!

In the Parable of the Sower (Luke 8:4–15), Jesus tells of the dangers of seeds sown on their own, in the shallow soil of self, versus the productivity of seed sown "on good ground." He then explains the parable in certain terms:

> "Now the parable is this: The seed is the word of God. Those by the wayside are the ones who hear; then the devil comes and takes away the word out of their hearts, lest they should believe and be saved. But the ones on the rock are those who, when they hear, receive the word with joy; and these have no root, who believe for a while and in time of temptation fall away. Now the ones that fell among thorns are those who, when they have heard, go out and are choked with cares, riches, and pleasures of life, and bring no fruit to maturity. But the ones that fell on the good ground are those who, having heard the word with a noble and good heart, keep it and bear fruit with patience." (vv. 11–15).

Here's what I want us to take away from this: the ones who heard the Word of God—heard it with a noble and good heart—kept it, and bore fruit with patience. Whoa! They held onto the word of truth, *patiently,* then the fruit showed up. It takes time for fruit to appear. But don't worry, you don't have to wait twenty-five years to see the love of God at work in your life. God can do a lot in twenty-five years, but He can also do a lot in one day. What matters most is that we abide in Him daily.

Jesus said, "If you abide in My word, you are My disciples indeed. And you shall know the truth, and the truth shall make you free" (John 8:31–32 NKJV). Come on, friend! It is time for us to take care of the Lord's planting and grow by the power of His indwelling Spirit.

Stage One:

Seedling

(T1: Truth—Gaining Understanding)

*"The seedling represents the first stage in tree growth; this stage begins once the tree seed is put into the ground. The seedling begins to grow as it **receives** the proper **sunlight** and adequate **water**. As the tree begins to sprout, it is weak and much of its energy is spent growing **deeper roots** and thicker stems. During this stage, parts of the tree begin to develop, including the parts that carry sap and nutrients and grow bark."*[2]

Chapter 1:

Self-Sufficient?

There's a reason you don't see your face when you open your eyes: you weren't designed to focus on yourself. You were made to love, and love isn't about you. If you close your eyes, you miss out on opportunities. When you see, however, you have an opportunity to do what needs to be done.

For instance, I grabbed the almond milk off the top shelf of the fridge because I can see it's not on the bottom. Since I can see it, I know where to reach. Because my sight, or perspective, gave me the knowledge I needed to act. Likewise, when we look for God we'll find Him (Jeremiah 29:13), and once we do, we'll behold His love and know where to reach—out to others (1 John 4:8).

Ironically, when you drink Him in, you're pouring yourself out (becoming selfless). You'll lose yourself in the process, but you're never empty. On the contrary, you're full because He is full and His Spirit lives in you. He simply replaces what shouldn't be there (selfishness) with what should (selflessness). It's like He is water and we are soda. If you keep pouring water into a dark glass of soda, what happens? Eventually, there won't be any more soda in the glass—it got washed out!

Likewise, when we get filled with the Holy Spirit, His love fills our hearts until there's no trace left of who we were, but only who we are now that He came (Romans 5:5). Consequently, this filling causes us to empty, or "wash out," so we become full of Him and people can tell (that glass of dark soda looks awfully clear). After all, "He must become greater; I must become less" (John 3:30). For without Him, we can do nothing (John 15:5); we need Him to survive and thrive.

If only living a pure life was as simple as pouring water into a glass. Perhaps it's not as hard as we think. But what happens if we consciously or subconsciously keep our eyes closed and refuse the water we need? In that case, things won't be very clear, and these words might describe us: "they may be ever seeing but never perceiving, and ever hearing but never understanding" (Mark 4:12). And just like that, we've fallen victim to religious delusions.

But we're not about to settle for that, because we mean well and know we're better than that. So we try hard, fail hard, and wonder why. Why is it so difficult to be Christlike? Is the Christian life supposed to be a struggle? How do some people make it look so easy? But let's be honest, is *anyone* doing it well?

If you're anything like I was, you went through a time, or are currently going through a time, of spiritual exhaustion. Tired of trying to grow in Christ. Maybe you're going to church, doing Bible study, praying, and trying to weed out bad habits, but secretly feel like a failure with rotten fruit to show for it. To make matters worse, you've got some people fooled; they think your plastic fruit is real. You want to keep them at a safe distance because if they get too close, your dirty secret will be revealed: you're not as clean as you look. A taste of your plastic fruit will make that disgustingly obvious.

Or perhaps you're not doing any of those things. You want to be a better Christian, but you don't know how to make that a reality. So you live ashamed and discouraged. Carrying a spirit of heaviness. Moping in defeat, like you'll never overcome. You live victoriously for a moment, but soon relapse into the same old guilt. You take inventory of your sins and confess them, but you just can't break free. You'll never be like that *other* Christian. It just isn't working, so you wonder, *What's the use?*

You might even feel like it's time to give up on trying so hard to live like a saint. Finding solace in platitudes like, "We all make mistakes," "Nobody's perfect," or "I'm not perfect, just forgiven." Getting permission for anything less than a transformed life. You don't have all the answers, but that's fine because you have faith that things will work out somehow. Until then, life is filled with misery. You can't wait to go to heaven and escape this hell on earth.

Maybe you're smart. Gifted with a keen intellect. Convinced you're uncovering the mysteries of God. A proof-texting professional. Ready to enlighten, correct, and debate. You might even feel a sense of superiority (one might rather call it giftedness). Nevertheless, it's the idea that you know something they don't. You know God's Word and have a degree, books, or a thesis to prove it. A true Christian apologist. Persuaded by the necessity to have an intelligent response to every question hurled and every charge leveled.

You find it essential that our beliefs stand up to the world's scrutiny. You long to become better versed in the Word, occupy positions in academia, and fight for political rights that mesh with our values. You want opponents of the faith to submit to the reasonableness of God, and to repent at the mercy of the soundness of our arguments. This is your active service for God.

Some of you wouldn't say so but are actually quite proud of yourself. You do your best. Overcame some bad habits. Are helping others do the same, perhaps through *your* ministry. You've been in the soup kitchens, given to charity, and done some other volunteer work. Maybe you've got a few problems, but not compared to other people—now, *they* have problems! You find it astonishing that people could be so blind to their own faults, calling themselves Christians but acting like hypocrites. They're not going to fool your high-level discernment. At church, you know you're shaking hands with dirty hands.

You know they've been sleeping around. Still swearing. Looking at porn. Wearing a fake smile. You know better. You won't be tricked by their façade. You remember what it's like to make mistakes. But thank God for how far you've come! You're not like them, right? You're convinced your reward is great in heaven—rightfully so.

Then again, maybe you've altogether rebelled against all things Christian. You see through it all. You grew up in a Christian home with parents behaving anything but Christlike, and no one is going to fool you anymore. You know what goes on behind the scenes of that movie, so you know it's all an act. You know how parents tell their children, "Don't worry, it's not real. It's just a movie." But you aren't fooled by that sentiment when you see them going to church arguing, getting there smiling, and leaving arguing again—every Sunday.

You've had enough of people saying one thing but doing another. Clearly, the Christian life doesn't work, so you're going to find something that does. Something that makes you feel alive. Like everything you were told *not* to do. Yet the possibility of an authentic Christianity gnaws at you deeply, in the recesses of your soul: *What if I'm wrong? Maybe there's something I've been missing all along.* Raising contentious questions and playing the devil's advocate mask this fearful wonderment. Really, your heart is pure and you just want to taste and see something real.

Whatever your narrative is, you're not alone. Some are excelling, some are not, and some things are not as they seem. Many can attest to this, including myself. Sometimes it seems like things *are* working, but often it doesn't. For instance, I worked hard at building a fine Christian out of myself—"by His grace," *of course*—only to see a poor return on my investment and a lack of validation from my superiors. Some fine Christian. Fortunately, God's guiding hand specializes in redeeming what's lost. He actively works through His people to help those in trouble.

Please notice something here. All of the aforementioned scenarios have one thing in common: they're self-absorbed. None speak of having a personal relationship with God and laying down our lives for others, putting their interests above our own, and loving one another as Jesus loved us. In other words, I was describing how we fall into the trap of thinking and doing "Christian stuff" *without* God. *Self-sufficient*, as I define it (in a Christian-living context), is trying to live the Christian life in your own power, independently of God, with or without help from others.

The truth is, people can't make me succeed, and I'm not self-made. God made me. It took me some time, but now I finally realize I can do nothing worthwhile without Jesus (John 15:5). After all, I'm clay. And guess what: Clay can't do *anything* but be formed by the potter. God is the Potter, we are the clay. We are the work of *His* hand—not ours (Isaiah 64:8). *His* works produce real fruit. Our hands produce fake, plastic fruit.

I know I would rather live on the real stuff.

Help from a Mentor

I've tried to be fruitful on religious terms. I even sought help from several respectable Christians. The first startling account that comes to mind is when I sought help from a man of God: a professor of New Testament and practical theology, John Kilde.

I wanted him to know my heart and give me practical advice on how I could better glorify God. So I brought in stacks of my journals, with select entries for him to read. He studiously paged through them as I eagerly awaited his response. I was hoping for praise. He seemed impressed.

When he closed my journal, he looked up in surprise. Weighing his words carefully, he said, "I see how much you want to do for God. You're very diligent. That's a good thing, *but* I would like to see you *rest*—just rest—in God's love for you. To think about how much He loves you, and how there's nothing you can do to make Him love you more than He already does. Just try that for a while and see how it feels. You might find it feels ... light."

He continued, "I've been studying Philippians for my sermon this Sunday [he was also an associate pastor], and there's a particular passage that spoke to me, and I think it might speak to you too." Then he quoted the passage: "But whatever were gains to me I now consider loss for the sake of Christ. What is more, I consider everything a loss because of the surpassing worth of knowing Christ Jesus my Lord, for whose sake I have lost all things. I consider them garbage, that I may gain Christ and be found in him, not having a righteousness of my own that comes from the law, but that which is through faith in Christ—the righteousness that comes from God on the basis of faith" (Philippians 3:7–9).

Once again, he reiterated the importance of simply knowing God, resting in His love for me. I felt disappointed and left wanting. *That's all? That's all he has to say? What about my desires, plans, and efforts? I know God loves me. I want to love him back! Let's be practical here. What about the things I need to do?*

My expectations weren't met. I felt misunderstood, as if my good intentions went underappreciated. I got that God loves me and I should "rest" in that, but what about the battle plan? What was I doing right, and what could use some work?

I left his office disheartened, trying to mask my displeasure. I'd poured out my heart concerning my valiant efforts to please the Lord, I'd sought wise counsel and practical advice, and yet I came away with "rest in the Lord"? That didn't mean anything to me. It wasn't the kind of feedback I'd expected, or appreciated (until several years later).

It felt like a tease, which I may have fancied for only a moment, thinking, *Wouldn't it be great* to not *have to try so hard?* I know rest feels amazing—especially after long periods of labor—but let's face it, rest is not exactly a mission accomplished; buildings won't get built if the workers stay in bed or sit on the couch. Clearly, or so I thought, John didn't get through to me. Things quickly fizzled out between us, and I had no intention of meeting with him again.

I left feeling heavy and helpless. It was like I went to his office for a splash of cold water to the face. I didn't find this refreshing until several years later. Okay, so he didn't literally splash me in the face, but he just as well could have. Here I'd made myself vulnerable, poured out my heart, and what he wanted me to do was listen to Someone Else's heart! My attention-starved self protested, *What about me? I know you said rest, but really, what am I supposed to do?*

Now it's obvious to me: I was completely self-centered.

This simple fact slipped by me for years, merely because I was preoccupied with doing religion—having an *appearance* of wisdom. I just wanted to honor God, right? Not exactly. But I did want to know what God could do for me. I wanted to make "the cut" and go to heaven. I wanted to feel better and do better so I'd have valid reason to be prouder. To be able to say, "Look at what I've done. See what I've accomplished." Or I could put on some false humility and talk about how insignificant I am, how others are rightfully better, and how I'll never be good enough: "Look at all these sins of mine. I'm more in need of a Savior than anyone. I'm a poor excuse of a Christian. I'm not worthy." And so on.

Please don't be fooled. Whining is just as selfish as bragging!

Whichever way you swing it, selfish ambition is the biggest problem in the church, because all evil can be traced back to selfishness in the human heart (James 3:16). Sadly, slavery to selfishness is common within the church. It's the condition of the fallen heart that seeks its own and lacks a life-transforming knowledge of God. Lack of understanding opens the door to all kinds of deception, teaching things like "give more to so *you* can get more." You can have the best intentions and know *about* God but still remain utterly selfish.

No wonder love has grown cold. Deception is running rampant. But take heart, there's a huge tide of love on the horizon, and it's moving in fast. God exists, and His love is setting people free! A revelation of love is here, and it's absolutely changing lives, mine included. Your life is fair game too. No one is out of God's reach. Selfishness may have stolen the show, but love is taking it back.

Growing up, I don't ever remember hearing a sermon on love. It's time to talk about Jesus and experience a revelation of His love for us and others. Not only to receive it, but *live* it *because* we've received it! Living a life of love is the evidence of properly receiving God's love.

Receiving is for giving. For instance, God is love, mercy, kindness, and forgiveness. He wants us to know that, but it doesn't stop there. We're supposed to *become* these things, bearing the nature of our Father. It's natural for a child to resemble his father, and we are children of God (Galatians 3:26). If we don't bear any resemblance to Him, there's a problematic disconnect. Furthermore, if we claim to know God, why do we still make life all about us, take things personally, ignore others, and withhold love?

All of the narratives we ran through (though there are more) are equally detrimental because they're equally self-absorbed. All of the things mentioned can be done *without* knowing God personally and without showing genuine love to others (1 Corinthians 13 and 1 John makes this clear). We can do many good-appearing things without having true love in our hearts. But that's not an automatic win, because if we miss the heart of love, we miss the meaning of our existence.

I eventually realized that what John Kilde said about "resting in God's love" was one of the most profound things anyone had ever told me. Understanding God's love unlocks the meaning of life, stares self in the eye, and makes selfishness die. There's so much we can't do in our own power. So why not do the best thing we can? Enough trying to live the Christian life in vain. Why not rest in His love and good works, and enjoy the lightness of being a child of God? Ironically, by giving up on our "self-sufficiency," we can easily begin to grow in Christ by abiding, or resting in Him. Gaining a biblically sound understanding of the truth about love is the water and sunshine our seedling needs for growing in the transformative strength of God's grace.

Resting in God's love sounds nice, but what does that even mean? What does this kind of rest look like, and how will it impact everyday life? There is an answer, and I'm going to share it with you. What took several years for me to discover you can have within hours since the message has been boiled down to the contents of this book.

Continue reading for a revelation of love.

Chapter 2:

Selfless-Sufficient

In a selfish world, selflessness stands out.

Selfless-Sufficient is the term the Lord gave me to describe a biblically based, out-of-this-world-but-in-it lifestyle of Christlike love. It's all about love—His love, in us and through us. There are many forces to reckon with in life, but love is the greatest thing (1 Corinthians 13:13).

The world has countless definitions of love, but the Bible has one: God. "God is love" (1 John 4:8). So if we're going to gain an understanding about the *truth* of love, I suppose we better get to know God. What better way to start than looking at Jesus? He is exactly what God looks like, in a body (Colossians 2:9; Hebrews 1:3). This is great, because having a body is something we can relate to. Furthermore, the fullness of God dwells in Jesus, and we can be filled with the same fullness by the indwelling power of His Holy Spirit (Colossians 2:9; Ephesians 3:14–19). Transformation is possible. He will sustain our growth, in each and every stage, by His powerful word, if only we remain in Him (Hebrews 1:3; John 15:4).

We can remain in Him. We can get to know Him by receiving His truth about love through His Word. Seeing how His Word reveals love is foundational to growing in it. It's time to zoom in on love. This chapter flips it all around, from the dead end of ~~self-help~~ self-hell to the open road of heaven on earth: selflessness. Gaining understanding is the gateway to greater things. The more we know God—understand and experience being loved by Him—the better prepared we are to naturally become love.

Proverbs 4:7 tells us, "In all your getting, get understanding" (NKJV).

Let's get into it!

Defining Selfless-Sufficient

What does *selfless-sufficient* mean?

Two things.

First, it means *love is enough*.

Selfless is my favorite word for describing ultimate love as demonstrated in the life of Jesus, and *sufficient* implies there's nothing more. Pair them together and you've got "there's nothing greater than the selfless love of Jesus." Like Dr. Kilde told me, "There's nothing you can do that would make God love you more." It's not about my works, because it's a finished work in Christ (John 19:30). *He* is enough. That's the broader sense of the term.

Second, it means living the Christian life by depending on God's power. Or, as Dr. Kilde described it, "resting in God's love." I previously described self-sufficiency as trying to live the Christian life in my power—a fallen power with twisted perspectives and religious behaviors. Try as I might, my own right hand cannot save me. Ultimately, I brought a heavier load upon myself.

Fortunately, Jesus removes heavy burdens; His load is light, just as Dr. Kilde said it would be. Matthew 11:28–30 confirms this: "Come to me, all you who are weary and burdened, and I will give you rest. Take my yoke upon me and learn from me, for I am gentle and humble in heart, and you will find rest for your souls. For my yoke is easy and my burden is light." This lightness is found when we say goodbye to self and hello to Jesus.

The selfless-sufficient life is based on the finished work of Jesus. It's one of resting, not stressing; thriving, not striving; being, not doing; trusting, not fussing. Putting confidence not in what I've done, but in Jesus and what He has accomplished.

Defining Love

It's time to hear the gentle voice of Jesus and let Him narrate your life. Things are different now. Part of being a believer is understanding that "if anyone is in Christ, he is a new creation; old things have passed away; behold, all things have become new" (2 Corinthians 5:17 NKJV).

Following Jesus moves us from selfish living to selfless loving. Because we've been with Him, and getting to know Him is changing everything about our perspective. It's no longer about who we are because of what we've done, but who we are because of what He has done. It's no longer about what I've gone through, but what He has been through. It's no longer about what I'm doing by my willpower, but what He's doing through me according to His good will. I no longer have a reason to boast about what I've accomplished; I can rest only in what He's accomplished. It's all about His love—the selfless, unconditional love of Jesus Christ.

Relying on God invites the power of His transforming grace into our lives. Anything other than that is a counterfeit. But I don't need to worry about getting into legalism, sin, or even doing the right thing, because seeking first the kingdom of God (which I'm describing throughout this book) makes everything fall into its proper place. Basically, when you get to know God, you look more like Him. If you don't look like Him, who were you with?

Love looks like selflessness. Jesus shows us the selfless nature of perfect love. He was always helping people. He was present. Relational. He ate, walked, talked, asked questions, and taught. He fed the hungry, opened blind eyes, cast out demons, forgave sins, gave hope to the downtrodden, freed captives from the prison of self-centeredness, and called us out of the darkness and into the light, coming not to be served but to serve. He washed His disciples' feet, setting an example for them to love as He loved—selflessly. The apostle Paul said, "I am not seeking my own good but the good of many, so that they may be saved. Follow my example, as I follow the example of Christ" (1 Corinthians 10:33–11:1). Furthermore,

> In your relationships with one another, have the same mindset as Christ Jesus: Who, being in very nature God, did not consider equality with God something to be used to his own advantage; rather, he made himself nothing by taking the very nature of a servant, being made in human likeness. And being found in appearance as a man, he humbled himself by becoming obedient to death—even death on a cross! Therefore God exalted him to the highest place and gave him the name that is above every name, that at the name of Jesus every knee should bow, in heaven and on earth and under the earth, and every tongue acknowledge that Jesus Christ is Lord, to the glory of God the Father. (Philippians 2:5–11)

The Heart of a Christian

Jesus said, "If anyone desires to come after Me, let him deny himself, and take up his cross daily, and follow Me" (Luke 9:23 NKJV). Jesus calls us to, "Love one another. As I have loved you, so you must love one another. By this everyone will know that you are my disciples, if you love one another" (John 13:34–45).

The heart of a Christian is love—Christlike, out-of-this-world-but-in-it love.

The wisdom of the world tells you to love those who love you and support your interests, and to forget those who don't. It says you deserve respect, so if you don't get it from someone, show them the door. It teaches you to "think for yourself." If anyone dares to insult you, let them know how you feel—speak your mind. Wear your heart on your sleeve. Don't back down! You've had a hard life. Remember all the ways you've been beaten down and mistreated—the people who have done you wrong? Don't let them win! Stand tall now—be the bigger person. Go from rags to riches.

People who didn't believe in you, prove them wrong and show them you can do it. Go higher than they are. When they come crawling back to you, treat them how they treated you and remind them, "What goes around comes around. That's karma for you. Tough luck!" Beat out the competition and get that promotion. You've been answering to people your whole life; it's their turn to answer to you. Be proud of your hard work—of the degree you achieved despite the odds stacked against you. Remember, most people haven't come this far. Tell the less fortunate how you did it so they can hope to rise where you are. Remind your critics that you don't care what they think. It's a tough world, so get tougher. Protect yourself and your best interests. People will try to stop you, but the success of your life depends on you. Let people bolster your success, not derail it. You can do it.

This makes sense to the world. But the wisdom of heaven doesn't understand such self-centered language (1 Corinthians 3:19). As far as heaven is concerned, there's *one* language of love: selflessness. God's ways are higher than our ways (Isaiah 55:8–9). Jesus demonstrates the sharp difference, as do His faithful followers.

His ways may seem lower from the world's point of view, but that's because the world doesn't understand the language of God's love. It operates by different values. What the world says is up, God says is down, and vice versa.

Fortunately, God has made provision to lift the veil and set us free from the bondage of our confused worldview, which is based on deception and set in motion by the devil. For every truth of God, the devil devises a clever counterfeit in an attempt to rob us of the truth.

Why does Satan bother? Because he's jealous of God. Because heaven on earth is a threat to the rule of his sinister system. He doesn't want to see the image of God in anyone; he hates anything and everything that resembles more than himself. If people know the truth, he knows they'll no longer remain under his control. And "he is filled with fury, because he knows that his time is short" (Revelation 12:12). He's going down and trying to take as many people with him as he can, especially the weak and vulnerable with shallow roots. Like a lion looking for an easy meal, he prowls around, on a mission to take life (1 Peter 5:7–9).

But Jesus won't have that. He said, "The thief comes only to steal and kill and destroy; I have come that they may have life, and have it to the full" (John 10:10). Focusing on oneself leads to dysfunction and destruction, not transformation. Jesus shows us the way to the Father—through Himself. Not to get us to heaven, but to get heaven back into us! If you're still here reading this, it's not your appointed time to be with Jesus in heaven; it's your time to participate in His grand mission on earth, shining the light and seeing to it that the needy are helped and the lost are saved. Jesus says, "Follow me. Love as I have loved you."

First Corinthians 13 paints a colorful picture of love. Love isn't self-seeking—it seeks to help people. Love doesn't envy—it celebrates the successes of others and wishes for their promotion. Love is patient—not hurried or upset when things aren't happening faster. Love does no harm to its neighbor, but protects all.

The love of heaven believes the best about people, and doesn't think everyone is out to get them. It sees people for their potential—not as a product of their past, destined to fail again and again, as if their future can't be any different. Love keeps no record of wrongs—it doesn't hold people hostage to mistakes they've made. Nor does it keep one trapped under the weight of their own sin; rather it frees them from it.

Love doesn't focus on sin. Love focuses on Jesus.

Don't Focus on Sin—Focus on Him

Many years ago I would take an "inventory" of my sins and pray over each area. I was following a system to freedom as if freedom in Christ was a formula as opposed to a Person to follow. Freedom in Christ is based on a relationship, not a set of rules. Christ's love compels us, not our shortcomings (2 Corinthians 5:14–15).

Love calls me to no longer live for myself. I shouldn't be impressed and obsessed with my sin. It bothered me so much I wanted to change it ~~now~~ yesterday. I knew all too well I would just mess up again. I was heavily sin-conscious when I needed to be Son-conscious. I couldn't move onward until I became impressed with Jesus and His ability to wash me clean in His presence.

He buries my sin and lifts me out of the dirt. Like a seedling, I reach to the skies in praise of the One who made me new. He justified me and clothes me in the robe of His righteousness and purifies my heart, letting me tag along for the fun ride of glory to glory. I needed to put my confidence in Christ, not my flesh.

Love doesn't gratify the desires of the flesh. In the world, we snap at the smallest things. Spewing things like, "I'll wait one minute for my coffee, but don't you dare make me wait two," or "I ordered before they did. How come they get their food first?" If someone is nice to us, we'll be nice back, but if we get crossed, that person better watch their back. We might even one-up them, just to get the point across that "you don't mess with me."

But love isn't easily offended. It's secure because it lacks nothing in Christ. It doesn't need to prove itself. It doesn't need you to treat me a certain way. It doesn't need you to speak to me a certain way for me to be okay. It can still thrive if I don't get a *please, thank you* or *I'm sorry*. Like Pastor Dan Mohler of Neck Ministries says, "Love doesn't say, 'I love you—do you love me?' It says, 'I love you.' Period."[3]

In other words, if I'm in it for what you can do for me, then I've made you Lord of my life and you have the power to make me or break me. Not to mention, if I have expectations of you, then I set you up to fail me. Then I feel justified in seeing you as the perpetrator and me as the victim. My hatred toward you feels warranted on the basis of how you've failed me. Then I may consider you my enemy.

But where is the love in any of that? In the spirit of Christlike love, nobody owes me anything. After all, if I put my trust in you, you can fail me. But if I put my trust in God, He won't fail me because God is love and love never fails. You can't fail me when Jesus is Lord of my life. What the world calls enemies, heaven refers to as people we love unconditionally.

Consider Luke 6:32–36:

"If you love those who love you, what credit is that to you? Even sinners love those who love them. And if you do good to those who are good to you, what credit is that to you? Even sinners do that. And if you lend to those from whom you expect repayment, what credit is that to you? Even sinners lend to sinners, expecting to be repaid in full. But love your enemies, do good to them, and lend to them without expecting to get anything back. Then your reward will be great, and you will be children of the Most High, because he is kind to the ungrateful and wicked. Be merciful, just as your Father is merciful."

Love supernaturally transcends the natural ways of the world. Some people may harbor ill will toward us, but love wishes them well. Not even trials, tribulations, and persecution can prevent love from rejoicing, because its joy is dependent on our immovable Lord and not ever-changing circumstances. God is our inexhaustible strength. Our present security and future hope in Him are the reasons we can laugh at the temporary trials of this world, because our present suffering cannot compare with the future glory that awaits (Romans 8:18).

Love overcomes retaliation by not retaliating (Matthew 5:38–41). It forgives, protects, and blesses. Love takes things to the highest level, not looking for what it can get but what it can give. It goes the extra mile. It doesn't condemn, judge, or show favoritism by treating one person better than another. There is no ranking system or partiality in love. God sends his rain on the just and on the unjust (Matthew 5:45). All are loved by God and equally in need of His presence. His reach extends to all. Love doesn't consider anyone out of reach.

Love isn't hungry for status symbols like a huge house, a lucrative career, the finest designer clothing, a degree from a prestigious university, the latest luxury car, or the sexiest partner. Love doesn't try to amass wealth for itself, but it isn't afraid of it either. In fact, love welcomes it because it desires to give generously, wherever there is a need, such as to a church, charity, single mother or father, or struggling family. Love calls all of us to action.

Romans 13:8–14 reminds us:

Let no debt remain outstanding, except the continuing debt to love one another, for whoever loves others has fulfilled the law. The commandments, "You shall not commit adultery," "You shall not murder," "You shall not steal," "You shall not covet," and whatever other command there may be, are summed up in this one command: "Love your neighbor as yourself." Love does no harm to a neighbor. Therefore love is the fulfillment of the law. And do this, understanding the present time: The hour has already come for you to wake up from your slumber, because our salvation is nearer now than when we first believed. The night is nearly over; the day is almost here. So let us put aside the deeds of darkness and put on the armor of light. Let us behave decently, as in the daytime, not in carousing and drunkenness, not in sexual immorality and debauchery, not in dissension and jealousy. Rather, clothe yourselves with the Lord Jesus Christ, and do not think about how to gratify the desires of the flesh.

The day of Jesus's second coming is closing in quickly. It's time for love to awaken in Christians (Ephesians 5:14). Lukewarm is over. The light under the basket is out. Let your light shine brightly! Overcome darkness with light; be a star in the night. "Clothe yourselves"... In other words, *wear* the Lord Jesus Christ, as He wears you. Yes, if the Spirit of Christ is inside a believer, He is wearing us. We are His arms, hands, and feet. Designed to spread love everywhere we go. His life is made manifest through our bodies, just as the Spirit of God manifested love through Jesus when He walked the earth. We are carriers of His glory—living out the revelation we have received (in proportion to our faith).

God's love shone through His people in Bible times, and it still shines now. The heart of God is obvious. You can see it in the classic Bible stories of the Good Samaritan, Hosea, Joseph, and the father of the prodigal son, to name just a few. The Good Samaritan didn't have to go out of his way to help someone. Hosea didn't have to give his unfaithful wife another chance. Joseph was betrayed by his brothers, nearly killed, and sold into slavery; he didn't have to forgive or spare them when he became prince of Egypt. The father of the prodigal son wasn't obligated to welcome him back after he carelessly ran off and squandered his wealth. Yet all of them showed the heart of God's unconditional, selfless love. God helps people through people who are in the world but not of it.

If love didn't come, the guilty wouldn't have experienced freedom. If the Good Samaritan was too busy, if Hosea was enraged, if Joseph was resentful, if the prodigal son's father was bitter—if they all took things personally and said, "How could they do this to me?"—then no one won. The ~~perpetrators~~ troubled didn't get the help they need, and the offended didn't forgive when God does (which is ironic considering we all have sinned and fallen short of God's glory, so we're *equally* in need of His forgiveness).

It is love that helps us get back on our feet. It is love that remains faithful when we're unfaithful. Only love is strong enough to remove the heavy burdens of guilt and shame. Only love can forgive what the world deems unforgiveable. This love of God is the only chance anyone has at a better life, because it sets us free from the limitations of the world and ourselves.

We can find inspiration in these stories, but don't forget: His love isn't just for people from the past, but people in the present. People like *you*. In the world, we're served the VIP treatment. We're told we are very important people and we deserve to be happy, but we must do more for ourselves—we need more "me time." There are many different things we can do, and products we can buy, to help us achieve this elusive American Dream of self-sufficiency. Ironically, self-serving is the leading cause of life without God, lovelessness, and no hope beyond the grave.

Fortunately, love can connect you with God and set you free from yourself. It can enable you to make a positive impact by serving others. And it can give you hope for the future, if only you'd let it. Let's jump into discovering what the Bible tells us about our kingdom VIP status—our true value, identity, and purpose in Christ Jesus. There's no time like the present to start living like who we are: children of God, by faith in Christ.

Chapter 3:

Kingdom VIP

We were born into a fallen world and trained in self-serving, but the new you is emerging. The old has gone, the new has come. The world puts the weight on, but Jesus takes it off. We struggle under the weight of sin, but His love removes the heavy burdens we were never meant to carry. His love has made you a VIP—not only a very important person, a child of the King Himself, but a person with incredible **V**alue, awesome **I**dentity, and exciting **P**urpose. The prince of this world, the devil, tries to keep the truth hidden behind the curtains. But now is the time to let the Lord grab ahold of the veil and remove it.

Listening to the Wrong Voices

The wisdom of the world tries to tell us what we're worth, who we are, and what we're here for. There's the "positive" angle, but it's a language in which we're a god unto our self: "self-help." It says, "The sky is the limit. You can be anything you want to be. You're beautiful in every way. See how far you've come? Take a good look at everything you've accomplished. Put up and dust off that trophy case. Nobody does it like you do, and no one can stop you. You can do this. Pull yourself together. Shoulders back. Chin up. Don't back down. You can get that job. You can lose the weight. You can find the best partner and be the best catch."

It says, "Master yourself. Excel in every area. Be the best. Hang your certificates on the wall. Put your awards on display. Let your luxury car and your big house show that you've made it. That your hard work is paying off handsomely. The looks and praise you get will make you feel alive, and affirm you're on the right track. People gush over your successes, and some envy them; both are forms of flattery you can appreciate. But your competitors better watch out. You're determined to make your challengers shrink back in the face of your competitive edge and concede that you are the one on top. If they try to tell you that you can't do something, put them in their place. Let your hard-earned accomplishments do the talking. If you hit a wall, break through it. Run your own business. Be the boss. Leave a legacy. Motivate and inspire people to be the best, most successful person they can be. They're not like you, but you can bank on them wanting to be."

Then there's the less glamorous voice, and perhaps the one we're more familiar with. It says, "You're worthless. You never finish what you start. You don't have any real friends. You've wasted so much time. You'll always be the same old you. Why would your future be any different? People don't change. Your history is filled with failed relationships and unfinished business. You have a degree but no job in your field. You're just a lost cause. Other people seem to have it figured out. They seem happier and look healthier. You don't have a reason to feel better about yourself. Even if you lose the weight or build the muscle, you're still ugly inside and out. Remember the times you tried and gave up? You're a quitter. You said it wouldn't happen again and it did. Told you so. Does anyone look up to you? They hardly notice you. If there is a God, He's probably shaking His head in disappointment right now. Everyone wants to be happy and succeed. Some people have it, some people don't. It's not looking too good for you. You don't have much, and it doesn't look like that is about to change. Good luck with that."

These are some examples of many voices that don't come from God. If we listen to them, we'll be deceived and deprived of the best life we can have, which is only found in Jesus.

Lack of Growth from Lack of Knowledge

The devil doesn't want you to see yourself the way God sees you. Because if you did, you wouldn't adopt such loveless perspectives. You wouldn't be fooled into thinking your success saves your soul, and you wouldn't buy into the lie that you'll never amount to anything. Listening to the wisdom of the world—the way that seems right to a man—leads to certain death (Proverbs 14:12). This is what the Enemy wants. The enemies of God (Satan, fallen angels, and antichrists) are fighting to keep you stagnant and lifeless.

A mature tree with a solid, deeply rooted foundation isn't easily moved, but many of us just aren't there yet. Rather, we're a big, easy target with a loose foundation and dried-up roots. This is what happens when we're stuck in living with little to no revelation of God's life-changing love. We might know about the possibility of becoming a mature tree, but we don't know how to tap into it. So we cling to ourselves instead of clinging to God.

The tragedy of such a growthless life is due to a lack of knowledge. But the Word of God plants many seeds as creative, biblically based channels that amplify His voice. God speaks the language of love. Christians are learning how to become fluent in it. If you're new to this and don't yet understand the language of love, perhaps you can benefit from a translator. And if I can play a part in delivering the truth to you in some small, relatable fashion, great! It might even be enough to spark a revival in your heart.

Whatever the case, in sharing how love makes sense to me, I can only hope it will make sense to you too. I regularly ask God to write through me; this whole book is saturated with prayerfulness. So I trust He will accomplish what He seeks to accomplish through these words.

Here's what I'm getting at: If we will ever live life to the fullest, we *must* understand what the love of God says about us. His voice is the only voice worth listening too—the only one we can trust. We have given the ways of the world enough attention, but things will never end well without knowing the present promises of God and the future hope He's given us. So we must turn our ear to what He has to say about us, and find the faith to believe it.

<u>V</u>alue

Do you believe you're extremely valuable to God? If I told you, "You're worth the blood of Jesus," would you believe it? It's true! Despite your darkest of days (Romans 5:8), God proved His unconditional love by sending Jesus for you (John 3:16). His blood pleads mercy toward you. Therefore, you *are* worth the blood of Jesus to God the Father.

I didn't always believe this. At one point, I knew Jesus had to die for my sins, and I knew that I had redemption through His blood. I knew about the forgiveness of my sins. I knew He paid the price for me with His life. But I didn't know I was *worth it*.

As far as I was concerned, God got a bad deal. Trading righteous and powerful Jesus for sin-stained and weak me? Exchanging incorruptible for corruptible? Giving away a faithful lover in exchange for a loveless cheater? In the end, Jesus was resurrected, and I have the opportunity to have the same power of His resurrection within me for all eternity—all because Jesus came. He stopped at nothing to accomplish my redemption. He died, but death couldn't keep Him. He put death *to death* so I wouldn't have to face the eternal nonexistence of separation from God.

Why would God do that if He didn't see value in me? Why even bother sending Jesus? He could have said, "What's the use? Those bunch of selfish sinners will never change. They're hopeless. They don't give me the praise I deserve. To hell with them." Fortunately for us, God isn't selfish; God is love. Love seeks not its own life unto death—even death on a cross (1 Corinthians 13:5; Philippians 2:8). That is what love does. It lays down its life for others. Even death cannot stop it.

People will fail us, but love never fails (1 Corinthians 13:8). Jesus took the keys from death and overcame it (Revelation 1:18). The ways of this world collapse under His supreme reign. He splits curtains and shakes the earth's foundations loose (Matthew 27:51). He has the power to reconcile us to God by bridging the gap so we can be with Him where He is. In fact, it was His *pleasure* to do so (2 Corinthians 5:18; John 14:3; Hebrews 12:2).

The reason I never thought I was worth the blood of Jesus was because I couldn't make sense of this according to the world I knew. You just don't do "bad" people any favors. Even small ones. Especially not big ones. In the world, for example, if we hear about the grisly murder of an innocent child, the natural response is to say the murderer is a piece of garbage and deserves to die slowly and painfully. Not to take the death penalty upon myself so they can go free—that is madness! Yet that isn't far off from what Jesus did for us.

But He did it on an even grander scale. He gave His life for *everyone*, and buried *every* horrible atrocity to give each and every person a desperately needed second chance. And it's not only the criminals who need saving, but the upstanding citizens; we have *all* fallen short of God's glory (Romans 3:23). Perfection is an impossible standard to meet if you're not Jesus, which is why we need Him.

Even if I don't have a criminal record, I still need grace as much as anyone else. God gave us all an opportunity to walk free. He flung open our prison doors and held out His hand. We enter freedom when we decide to follow Jesus and be born again. Without Him, our sin gets us what we deserve—death (Romans 6:23). Big sins or smaller sins, the unrepentant sinner is facing major trouble on judgment day. Which is why we must know and appreciate how great the love of God is, and how valuable we are to Him and why.

I can't say it enough: We are worth the blood. God doesn't make mistakes. He creates people, in His image, with great potential to become love. He wants us to be in His story because we're precious to Him. He wants us to experience the healthiest and highest high available: living life with Him.

Evidently, He doesn't want a life without us, since we exist. God has a very large family, and He likes it that way, which is why He keeps creating people, blessing them with freedom and hope, and attempting to bring in the lost (Luke 15:1–17). It's wonderful to be in His family because love is at the heart of it. Better than a family that is fighting, gossiping, or distant.

Look at the prodigal son's reunion with his father: "While he was still a long way off, his father saw him and was filled with compassion for him; he ran to his son, threw his arms around him and kissed him" (Luke 15:20). Do you think his father valued him? I wonder if the son was happy to see and receive him, even after all the poor choices he made.

This, like many Bible stories, is a picture of God's unconditional love. It shows us how love values the lives of others and relinquishes its "rights" to withhold affection from them. In fact, love *enjoys* valuing life.

Do you still believe God doesn't value you? Maybe you think doing a better job living for Him will be enough to convince Him, or yourself, that you're valuable. But remember, there's nothing you can do that would make God love you more or less. Hard to grasp, but life-changing when understood.

You can be sure that God is *smiling* over you. God isn't mad at you. Jesus already took the wrath of God upon Himself because He hates the thought of losing you. You're precious to Him. He doesn't measure your value according to the mistakes you've made or even how well you're doing and how much success you've had. He just plain loves you. No matter what.

Still don't think He loves you? Look no further than the cross. He already said *I love you*, and He will forever do so. He can't help it because it's His unchangeable essence. He sees our value. He knows who we are—everything about us, good and bad—and He still sent Himself out of selfless love (Romans 5:8; John 3:16). This is a triune truth; since God is three-in-one, by sending Jesus He, in effect, sent Himself. Which makes sense since God is love and love lays down its life for others. Furthermore, His love doesn't stop at His essence, but also sees us for our potential in Him. He doesn't predict our failure on the basis of our faulty past. Even if we don't see the truth about us, He does. And the more we take a good look, the more we will see it too.

We better pay close attention to what He sees, or we'll settle for less and live loveless. If we're supposed to love others as we love ourselves, and we don't see what He sees, we don't stand a chance. Because if we don't know He loves us, we cannot properly love ourselves, and if we can't properly love ourselves, we can't properly love anyone else. Clearly, we are in need of a perspective shift.

Here's something to think about. When you look for a place to live, you try to find the best place you can. You want the right number of bedrooms and bathrooms. Enough square footage. A two-car garage. A safe neighborhood. And most importantly, something you can afford. Now, about God. He can live anywhere He wants to. Do you think He has a restricted budget, or are His options limitless? For many of us, when there's more money, we buy more place and higher quality. But God's ways are higher than our ways (Isaiah 55:8–9). When stuck in a fallen mindset, we tend to think we're not worth much, and we don't think others are worth much either.

But isn't it amazing that God chose to live inside you? Not to mention, your best life (Christ in you) cost Him His life. Out of all the places He could have lived, He pointed to you and said, *"That* is where I want to be!" He wants to make His home inside you. In fact, He paid the highest price to live there. The blood of Jesus proves our lives matter to God.

And get this. When He moves in, things change *because* He literally infuses us with a proper sense of ~~self-worth~~ "Son-worth" (our value according to what He says) and renovates our heart to think and choose differently, in correspondence with who we actually are in Christ. If He is in you, this is revealed in the work He does through you. Then, when people look at you, they're beholding God's masterpiece, and they say, "Wow!" Like how they do it on those shows when a couple's house gets renovated and they're in awe at the great reveal.

From a spiritual standpoint, the renewed life of a believer is showcasing the handiwork of God. Since we all have a need for work that only God can do, we have to invite Him to come and fix it all up. *God* is the ultimate Fixer-Upper! It's amazing the kind of potential some can see in a rundown, seemingly hopeless house. Next thing you know, the work is done and the house looks nothing like itself because it was made new, or "born again" (John 3).

God cares for you (1 Peter 5:7). He wants you to reach your fullest potential. He wants you to know your true worth. This beats falling for the lies of the world and turning away the Fixer-Upper because you think your home is a lost cause. Maybe you think it's irreparable. Too much damage is done, you say. So you tell Him He's better off finding somewhere else and you close the door.

Please don't talk yourself out of the best deal you can get!

A Valuable Conversation

I remember a time I spoke with my younger son on the phone. He seemed tired and sad; I could hear it in his voice. Monotone. Quiet. Crackly. After talking for a bit, we were about to get off the phone when I told him I had a question for him. He was mildly curious.

I asked, "Do you believe you are valuable to God?"

He paused. "Yeah."

"Good. Why do you believe that?"

"Huh?"

"Why do you believe you are valuable to God?" I asked.

"Because everyone is."

"Do you know why?"

"Not really."

"It's okay if you don't have the answer. But this is a good opportunity to think about it and discuss it, so we can understand why we're valuable to Him." I then proceeded to tell him about the blood of Jesus. That He didn't just die for our sins and that's all. He gave His life to reconcile us to God because we're worth the sacrifice. He wants us to be with Him. He removed our sins and revealed our potential in Him. If you wonder whether or not God loves you (or someone else), look no further than the cross.

My son didn't say anything.

I asked, "Does that make sense?"

"Yeah."

I was getting the impression this language wasn't accessible to him. It can be hard to relate to this stuff sometimes. Thankfully, the Holy Spirit turned on the light bulb and lit up the room.

I continued, "Think about it this way. God values people through His people. For example, right now God is in me. He's working through me to show you how He values you. You know I'm always excited to talk with you. I called you. I asked you how your day went. I think about you. I pray for you. I talk about important things with you because I want you to have your best shot at life. If you make a mistake, I don't give you a hard time for it. We work through it. I ask you questions. I listen to what you say. I love you, no matter what you do. Make sense?"

"Yeah."

It was a short reply, but as we wrapped up the conversation his tone became noticeably different. No longer did he sound tired and sad, but hopeful and happier. I could tell things clicked. The voice of God spoke through me—speaking the truth in love, turning on my son's light bulb, pulling him out of despondence and propelling him into joyfulness.

Unpacking the truth and listening to it reveals a treasure worth getting excited about: knowing God values us. I didn't know my son needed encouragement, but God knew. He meets us where we are, and often pursues us through His people. He speaks to us on our level and is relevant at every point.

There's no doubt about it: Your life matters.

Identity

What you do gives a hint about what you think. If I think I'm a good-for-nothing sinner, I will live like one. If I think I'm a righteous son of God, I will live like one. In other words, my lifestyle expresses what I believe about my identity. Since we're born selfish, we grow up in the way that seems right to a man, but in the end it leads to destruction (Proverbs 14:12). Naturally, we need to rethink who we are. It's time to grab ahold of who we are, why we're here, and what we ought to do about it, lest we follow a misguided course to the wrong destination.

So who am I anyway? I think it's fair to say that most of us define who we are by what we do (or don't do) and what we've been through. Of course, this is constantly changing throughout our lives because we don't always do the same things. Not to mention, we're about to go through things we've never gone through before.

Many biographies and memoirs are famous for showcasing the awful things people go through. Maybe *we* like to shock people with our unique set of troubles because it gets us attention. Talking about tough stuff isn't bad in itself, as long as it doesn't end there and God is properly exalted. But if He is mostly—if not entirely—kept out of the picture, what are we accomplishing?

Let's face it: It's more popular to present evidence of hell in our lives than heaven. Whether literature or film, hell sells. Why do you think pornography, brutality, and the majority of sin-infested feature films make absurd amounts of money? Clearly, there is an appetite for sin and an admiration of it. This is idolatry, and it proves we are drawing our identity from the wrong sources. Popular culture is begging to fashion us, and we often let it.

The world tells us it has what we need, but we didn't learn this from the Bible, which says, "For everything in the world—the lust of the flesh, the lust of the eyes, and the pride of life—comes not from the Father but from the world" (1 John 2:16). The Bible tells us the world isn't right about us. What we've been through doesn't determine who we are. Neither are we defined by the world; we are defined by the Word of God. We are not made for ourselves; we are made to love. We're not defined by what we did or didn't do, but what Jesus did and does.

Christians were never supposed to find their identity through anything but Christ. In Christ, we are not divorced, abused, or addicted; we are set free and made new. We are delivered, unified, healed, filled with hope, and busting at the seams with joy. This means people won't be able to tell if we've been through a lot.

After my coworkers have been around me for a while, they're often shocked to discover some things about my past. Probably because what they're hearing and seeing doesn't match up with what they know. It doesn't make sense that I would be this happy and peaceful—unless you believe God is real and can bring about real change in a person.

In the life of a Christian, everything revolves around Jesus—not me, not even others, but Jesus. How much are we talking about Him? Because Jesus changes *everything*. If we know Him, we will have testimonies of the many things He has conquered in our lives. The world tries to tell me I'm this and I'm that, but Jesus gave me a born-again, brand-new start. I am loved by God. Thanks to Him I have a promising future. In God's kingdom there are no dropouts, criminals, adulterers, or addicts.

Why? We are sons and daughters of the Most High! When we soak in His presence, He removes our worldly labels and scrubs off the stubborn sticky spots (you know, those labels that just don't want to come off). Just like that, we're made perfectly clean. Spotless. Shiny. The Enemy tries to distract us by stealing our focus, but when we see ourselves through God's eyes, we say "Look! Something shiny!" and the devil flees (James 4:7). We're submitting to God by acknowledging who we are because of what Jesus has accomplished.

Is this too good to be true? Or is God so good it is true? Why would we try to stick labels of sin on ourselves after Jesus removed them? Jesus rendered them unstickable. If He gave us a new name and we're trying to cover it up with an old one He didn't give us, aren't we then saying Jesus didn't do well enough? Furthermore, if we think we're not doing the Christian life well enough, then, by default, we don't think Jesus did well enough either. How so? Because if we're obsessed with our failures, there's no room to be impressed by His victories, which means we've made life about us instead of Him. Wouldn't it be tragic for us to ignore what Jesus did with our sins? We would do well to avoid underappreciating the results of this amazing grace.

Where are your sins? If you believe, they are nailed to the cross (Colossians 2:13–15), and you won't have to answer for them.

> Therefore, since we have been justified through faith, we have peace with God through our Lord Jesus Christ, through whom we have gained access by faith into this grace in which we now stand. And we boast in the hope of the glory of God. Not only so, but we also glory in our sufferings, because we know that suffering produces perseverance; perseverance, character; and character, hope. And hope does not put us to shame, because God's love has been poured out into our hearts through the Holy Spirit, who has been given to us. You see, at just the right time, when we were still powerless, Christ died for the ungodly. Very rarely will anyone die for a righteous person, though for a good person someone might possibly dare to die. But God demonstrates his own love for us in this: While we were still sinners, Christ died for us. Since we have now been justified by his blood, how much more shall we be saved from God's wrath through him! For if, while we were God's enemies, we were reconciled to him through the death of his Son, how much more, having been reconciled, shall we be saved through his life! Not only is this so, but we also boast in God through our Lord Jesus Christ, through whom we have now received reconciliation. (Romans 5:1–11)

A chapter later we're told to count ourselves dead to sin but alive to God in Christ (Romans 6:11). Rest (in in His love) assured, if you still do some things you aren't proud of, Jesus has got you covered—in a robe of righteousness! The reason you don't like such behavior is because God is purifying your heart. You're no longer a slave to sin, but a son or daughter clothed in righteousness.

Remember, Jesus doesn't take the robe away if you act like you're not righteous. That's right: Once you are a believer, any appearance of sin in your life is an act; it's no longer who you are. You are not a sinner—you're a daughter. You are not a sinner—you're a son. So let's stop acting like we are what we used to be just because a few weeds pop up for pulling.

> "But blessed is the one who trusts in the LORD,
> whose confidence is in him.
> They will be like a tree planted by the water
> that sends out its roots by the stream.
> It does not fear when heat comes;
> its leaves are always green.
> It has no worries in a year of drought
> and never fails to bear fruit."
> (Jeremiah 17:7–8)

It doesn't say "they will be like a weed by the water." God said we are better than that! The truth is, His love is unconditional and it sets us free from ourselves. His selfless sacrifice destroyed the works of the devil. The more we believe that and abide in Him, the less we will act like we're less than what He paid for.

Purpose

What's the point?

A lot of people are struggling to find meaning. This isn't a new thing, but neither is unbelief. Maybe they think their past has ruined their chances. Or they presently don't have the resources they need to do what they want. They see people on TV who have "made it," such as actors, athletes, TV personalities, and musicians. They don't believe success is on their future radar, so they live vicariously through books and movies. Or maybe they're desperately attempting to achieve their wildest dreams. To be the one that raises the bar. Determined not to lose. But try as they might, they're limited, and their future isn't looking good without God—especially beyond the grave. They need help just like the rest of us. They need meaning now and later.

Even the biggest stars, who have loads of validation (and criticism), look for a way out through drugs, spending, dating, state-of-the-art technologies, and the latest scientifically proven therapies. The thing is, people can start with nothing, get everything, and still not like themselves; internet trolls are famed for helping with that. This can easily destroy a self-sensitive person. I'm sure we've all heard those sad stories. People are unhappy. Just look around you. People need Jesus.

You can run but you can't hide—from yourself. If you start the race, you'll be there. If you cross the finish line, you'll be there. You have better luck catching your shadow than getting away from yourself. Even suicide isn't the end of a life, because we all will rise on judgment day, by the power of God, to give an account for how we lived. Our life is not our own (1 Corinthians 6:19–20). The sooner we figure that out, the better. Because you can't hide from God either (Psalm 139).

So what is our life? If we don't have meaning, we don't have purpose. If we don't see our meaning or purpose, we won't see value in ourselves or others. We may grasp for things, but we can't keep them. But that's okay because we aren't supposed to. Remember 1 John 2:17: "For all that is in the world—the lust of the flesh, the lust of the eyes, and the pride of life—is not of the Father but is of the world." The rest of the verse brings things full circle: "And the world is passing away, and the lust of it; but he who does the will of God abides forever" (NKJV).

What can we keep anyway?

Look at King Solomon. He had everything the world lusts after: superior intelligence (the wisest), inexhaustible wealth (the richest), one thousand women (literally), and great authority and exceptional skills (a master ruler and architect, governing many people and building a breathtaking temple and gardens). He was highly esteemed and sought after, but in Ecclesiastes, he says it's all meaningless:

Whatever my eyes desired I did not keep from them.
I did not withhold my heart from any pleasure,
For my heart rejoiced in all my labor;
And this was my reward from all my labor.
Then I looked on all the works that my hands had done
And on the labor in which I had toiled;
And indeed all was vanity and grasping for the wind.
There was no profit under the sun.
(Ecclesiastes 2:10–11 NKJV)

The book of Ecclesiastes is a short but profoundly sobering look at the meaninglessness of life lived in the pursuit of personal pleasures. King Solomon recognized it was all coming to nothing. In fact, he used the word *meaningless* about three dozen times! He was trying to get a point across. His main point came at the end: That a life lived in obedience to God is the only life worth living (Ecclesiastes 12:13).

Embracing the will of God is our purpose.

What Is the Will of God?

In *The Practice of the Presence of God,* a book of collected teachings by Father Joseph de Beaufort, he said this about Brother Lawrence (a.k.a. Nicholas Herman):

> That he had always been governed by love, without selfish views; and that having resolved to make the love of GOD the end of all his actions, he had found reasons to be well satisfied with his method. That he was pleased when he could take up a straw from the ground for the love of GOD, seeking Him only, and nothing else, not even His gifts. That in order to form a habit of conversing with GOD continually, and referring all we do to Him; we must at first apply to Him with some diligence: but that after a little care we should find His love inwardly excite us to it without any difficulty.[4]

Furthermore, we learn how his selfless journey began:

> In the deep of winter, Herman looked at a barren tree, stripped of leaves and fruit, waiting silently and patiently for the sure hope of summer abundance. Gazing at the tree, Herman grasped for the first time the extravagance of God's grace and the unfailing sovereignty of divine providence. Like the tree, he himself was seemingly dead, but God had life waiting for him, and the turn of seasons would bring fullness. At that moment, he said, that leafless tree "first flashed in upon my soul the fact of God," and a love for God that never after ceased to burn.[5]

This is an example of what happens when a person gains understanding about the love of God. They are changed! Naturally, after such a transformative moment of realization, Brother Lawrence began finding meaning not just in big things to do but the small things especially.

You could probably make a long list of things you do on any given day. Whether you do dishes, drive to work, change a diaper, or change a tire—whatever it is—you're most likely finding many things to do. These things don't sound very spiritual, so what is God's will for us concerning them?

Since Jesus doesn't tell you to change a diaper, does that mean you shouldn't do it? Some might like to think so, but what does love do? We don't have any trouble assigning top priority to some things while others seem menial, inconsequential, and even distracting from what we'd rather do. Then there are people like Brother Lawrence, who found meaning and contentment in the smallest things because he was aware of the greatest—God's presence. He said, "It is enough for me to pick up but a straw from the ground for the love of God."[6]

The trouble comes when we're used to doing *anything* without God. In his message "Including God in Everything," Todd White, of Lifestyle Christianity said, "I can't even pump gas without Jesus. People laugh at that, but I'm really not kidding you. He doesn't expect me to pump gas without Him. The problem is we can do most of what we do without Him, and we're used to it. And it's time we become unused to being without Him."[7]

What *are* we doing? More importantly, what—or whom—do we do it for, and why?

I'm sure we all mean well. We may participate in spiritual activities such as going to church and reading the Bible, which is great, but these are never the only things a person does in relationship to

God. It may be "hi and bye" with people, but never with God. Being with Him doesn't start when we enter the church doors, and end when we leave. It's never "I had fun during worship, God! See you next time." No. He says, "Surely I am with you always" (Matthew 28:20). This means if we treat Him like He's somewhere else, other than with us, we are in effect ignoring Him. Not cool! Let's not allow bad things—or good things—to direct our attention away from our personal, intimate, and prayerful connection with God.

Nobody's purpose is to be a pastor, write books, become a professional athlete, have a ministry, or whatever else. Maybe something like that is in our future, but it's not why we're here. Neither is our purpose to find a spouse, have kids, and retire young. Our purpose is not defined by our wishes; it is defined by our reason for being. According to the Word of God, there is only *one* reason for being: "For in him we live and move and have our being" (Acts 17:28).

Where is the purpose for our being found?

In Him.

You don't live to be a parent; it's not all about "your" kids. You don't live to be a pastor; it's not all about "your" congregation. You don't live to be an author; it's not all about "your" readers. You don't live to have a ministry; it's not all about "your" audience. You're here to know God. It's not about you or anyone else. You live to be in relationship with God and manifest His love everywhere you go, in everything you do. This will happen simply as a result of knowing Him intimately and learning to be aware of His presence at all times.

Jesus is the will of God, and He wants you to be with Him, know His love, and become His love; He wants your joy to be complete. That can't happen without Him. Together, being His and becoming love is your eternal purpose. They go hand in hand. Everything else is a bonus.

If you do what you love for a living, great. There's nothing wrong with that. Praise God! What you're doing might be your personal calling, but it's still not your purpose. Purpose isn't about doing what you love. As Christians, we don't just do what we love; we *are* love, therefore we *do* love. It's all about love.

We are called to "do everything in love" (1 Corinthians 16:14). It doesn't say, "Do some things in love," or "Only do what you love to do." No, it says do *everything* in love. You don't have to love or enjoy everything you do, but you will learn to do everything in love as long as you're abiding in Jesus (more on abiding in the next stage).

For instance, you don't have to love shopping, but you can love God and people *while* shopping. Likewise, you don't have to love your job, but you can love God and people *while* working. When you become love, your perspective on everything begins to change. Before love, you despised shopping and the people who got in your way. Before love, you thought you had a dead-end job and a bothersome boss (to put it nicely). But when love enters your heart, you see it all with a renewed sense of purpose. It's not just a building, an inconvenience, or a job anymore, but a chance to manifest the selfless love of God. Our purpose is to be with Him always, and our potential is to become like Him—now and later.

Considering our ways more than considering the will of God is an effective way of cutting ourselves off from our only source of hope. We need the truth, because only the truth can free us from selfishness. We would do well to take advantage of our kingdom VIP status, since we have tremendous potential, heavenly value, royal identity, and noble purpose in Christ.

When you receive truth like a tree receives air, water, and sunlight, you may start small but you'll grow tall in the strength of the Lord—rooted and built up in the unfailing love of Christ (Colossians 2:7).

Planting of the Lord

Remember, you're a tree of righteousness, "the planting of the LORD, that He may be glorified" (Isaiah 61:3 NKJV). Don't worry if you don't look fully mature at the moment. Instead, keep this in mind: A seed doesn't look like a tree yet, but it carries the *potential* of a tree (a tree is *in* the seed!). If you simply stay in the good soil, rest, and soak up all the nutrients, it won't be long until growth happens. So join Jesus and trust that His grace is sufficient for you (2 Corinthians 12:9).

We go in the ground like Him, and we come out of it like Him too (Romans 6:5). Not just on the day of Jesus' return, but starting when we're born again by putting our faith in Him (more about faith in the next stage). Then we'll break through the dirt with newfound strength and size, ever-lifting up to the ~~sun~~ Son as our redemption draws near (Luke 21:28). Of course, we can't accomplish this in our own strength, but when we abide, our fruit cannot hide.

> Thus says the Lord: "Cursed is the man who trusts in man and makes flesh his strength, whose heart departs from the Lord. For he shall be like a shrub in the desert, and shall not see when good comes, but shall inhabit the parched places in the wilderness, In a salt land which is not inhabited. Blessed is the man who trusts in the Lord, and whose hope is the Lord. For he shall be like a tree planted by the waters, which spreads out its roots by the river, and will not fear when heat comes; but its leaf will be green, and will not be anxious in the year of drought, nor will cease from yielding fruit." (Jeremiah 17:5–8 NKJV)

When you grow in knowing the Lord (gaining a deeper knowledge of Him and who we are in Him), love will become increasingly evident in your life. When you look at Him, you won't walk away looking the same. Of course, we don't always behave how we might like to, but our walk and our talk won't get any further out of line if we're truly walking with God. "If we say that we have fellowship with Him, and walk in darkness, we lie and do not practice the truth. But if we walk in the light as He is in the light, we have fellowship with one another, and the blood of Jesus Christ His Son cleanses us from all sin" (1 John 1:6–7 NKJV).

So how do we walk in the light as He is in the light and experience cleansing from sin? Like Jesus said, by holding onto, or abiding, in Him: "If you hold to my teaching, you are really my disciples. Then you will know the truth, and the truth will set you free" (John 8:31–32).

What Is Truth?

Truth is the overarching theme of stage one. After these first three chapters, I hope it's clear: Jesus *is* the truth. We can know Him and show Him. The truth isn't about having the right answer to a question, or stating a fact. Truth, in its highest form, is a person: Jesus. He said, "I am the way the truth and the life" (John 14:6). Therefore, if I say I know the truth, I'm saying I know Jesus. I can tell you what He's like, what He accomplished on the cross, where He is now, who you are because of Him, what His last recorded words in the Bible are, and what He said about His second coming.

I can tell you how He has changed everything about my life, circumstances, and feelings, and how He can change yours too. He is everything to those who believe. He is "the life" I live and "the way" I take. His way is love—supernatural, from-out-of-this-world, life-changing, selfless love on earth. It's the way citizens of heaven live here. He will revolutionize your life if you let Him.

Are you ready for this? It's time to explode out of the norm and venture into unexplored territory. Let's take a permanent vacation away from self, and make a move to the Promised Land of Love. It has been laid right before us. Things are about to get better than ever. It's time to step into what the Lord has for us. "The kingdom of heaven is like a treasure hidden in a field." Dig it up! The treasure hunt is over. It's time to joyfully "sell everything you own"—go all-in—because nothing compares to the magnificence of God's everlasting kingdom (Matthew 13:44). The *best* way to live is uncovered.

The joy of finding the kingdom treasure is the real deal. If what you're about to hear doesn't get you more encouraged and excited, then what you're hearing isn't the gospel. It's time to discover the incredible, matchless value of a life lived in unity with God, free from the limitations of self.

Lose yourself, and gain the only reward worth having—Jesus Himself (Matthew 10:39; 16:25). The world commands you to live for yourself. But what we find in the world are cheap treasures at a high cost. We were bought back by God at the highest price, but, sadly, we sell out cheap for the fleeting pleasures of this world. We grasp for more money, more pleasure, more power—but it's never enough.

First John 2:15–17 tells us, "Do not love the world or the things in the world. If anyone loves the world, the love of the Father is not in him. For all that *is* in the world—the lust of the flesh, the lust of the eyes, and the pride of life—is not of the Father but is of the world. And the world is passing away, and the lust of it; but he who does the will of God abides forever" (NKJV). Only love is enough. Jesus said, "Everyone who drinks this water will be thirsty again, but whoever drinks the water I give them will never thirst. Indeed, the water I give them will become in them a spring of water welling up to eternal life" (John 4:13–14).

Be encouraged! God is satisfying. Rest assured, God *is* growing you in love. Sometimes growth is imperceptible, especially if you're staring at yourself, but I'm confident you can move on toward something far greater than yourself. Simply seeing the truth about love is enough to break new ground and overpower what holds us down. "No one who is born of God will continue to sin, because God's seed remains in them; they cannot go on sinning, because they have been born of God" (1 John 3:9).

Regarding the physical, we can say a tree is in the seed because we know it has the potential to become a full-sized mature tree—under the right conditions. Now, think of the Holy Spirit as God's seed planted within you. Love is *in* the Holy Spirit, and the Holy Spirit has great potential to manifest mature, fruit-bearing Christlike love in your life—under the right conditions.

We can't become this kind of love unless we invite the Holy Spirit to take residence in us (see the appendix to find the best free gift ever). Receiving the Holy Spirit in this way is how we become one with Jesus and begin to experience the good life, as a good tree in the good soil producing good fruit. It's all good—with Jesus.

Stage One Summary

Planting a seed in good soil is essential to its proper death, which results in tremendous growth, going from a seed to a seedling, and eventually becoming a mature tree. However, sustained growth can only happen under the right conditions. The inevitable death of the seed is rendered useless if it remains apart from what it needs to reach its full potential. The weak seedling, if left to its own devices, doesn't receive the protection and power it needs to continue in growth. It's cut off and alone, with roots dried up below, branches withering above, and something coming to nothing (Job 18:16)—with no promise of help from itself or its surroundings.

In a spiritual sense, receiving the Holy Spirit allows our original seed of self to die and sprout promisingly once infused with this good seed from God. However, if we don't accept His Spirit, we can't grow in love. Oddly, we try to "save" ourselves from certain death by avoiding the only soil—the good soil of God—which produces greater life. But there's good news for believers: We don't have to try to grow the goods ourselves; God does the growing (1 Corinthians 3:6–7). All we must do is lose ourselves by joining Jesus (John 15:4).

Bottom line: God does the grafting and growing—not you, not me. Besides, our works are like filthy rags before the Lord (Isaiah 64:6). Don't brag about your rag; boast in the Lord! Do-it-yourself Christianity is self-sufficient based. It says, "I know best," "I can do it myself," "Look at what I've accomplished," or, "I'll never be good enough," and so on. Christians are accomplishing great things such as donating money to good causes and building churches, shelters, and orphanages. Even non-Christians are doing commendable things and making significant progress. But what's preventing our connection with God and inhibiting our progress with relational love?

Fortunately, becoming love is a possibility. It's the most important reality of all, yet we aren't connecting with God in a way that permits us to know Him intimately—on a level that births selfless love in us. Sadly, love is a rare reality, even in the church. But this shouldn't be!

So what can reverse this confusing trend within the twenty-first-century church? What hope is there for the down-and-out discouraged Christian and the self-sufficient super Christian? Gaining this knowledge of the problem of self is a good start. Better yet, when we gaze at Jesus, the truth lights up our mind's eye and renews our mind slowly but surely, as a dim light grows brighter and brighter to illuminate our path so we can move forward. "The path of the righteous is like the morning sun, shining ever brighter till the full light of day" (Proverbs 4:18).

This is how the renewing of our mind unfolds: if we can see clear, we will live clear. "The lamp of the body is the eye. If therefore your eye is good, your whole body will be full of light. But if your eye is bad, your whole body will be full of darkness. If therefore the light that is in you is darkness, how great is that darkness!" (Matthew 6:22–23 NKJV).

In baseball you keep your eye on the ball. In life, the key is to keep your eye on Jesus. I see the weak aspect of our growth as the transitionary period of moving from self-focus to Jesus-focus. This isn't a natural shift. It's supernatural. A born-again requirement. At first, a lot of energy and revelation goes into this exchange of self for Himself. There's a learning curve, although a simple one. Any rising complexities are most likely the result of things we must unlearn. After all, we're promised trouble in the world but encouraged to take heart because Jesus has overcome the world (John 16:33).

As children of the light, Christians are supposed to be the light of the world (Matthew 5:14–16). But *is* our light shining? Or does the love-limiting basket of self need to come off? Let's continue shedding these layers of selfishness with stark truth, our only hope of uncovering a love that shines eternally.

Jesus put it best: "Abide in Me, and I in you. As the branch cannot bear fruit of itself, unless it abides in the vine, neither can you, unless you abide in Me. I am the vine, you are the branches. He who abides in Me, and I in him, bears much fruit; for without Me you can do nothing" (John 15:4–5 NKJV). Now we must learn how to abide. It's time to reach a heightened level of connection with Jesus.

Let's uncover the secret growth agent: *faith*.

Stage Two:

Primary Growth

(T2: Thankfulness—Living by Faith)

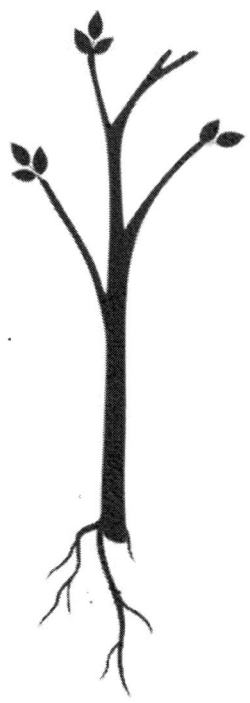

*"Primary growth is the second stage of tree growth and is the transitional period during which the plant **begins to mature** and the root system expands. During this stage, branches begin to **develop** and leaves start to **form**. While leaves vary in size depending on the tree, the bark on the tree is **still very immature.**"*[8]

Chapter 4:

How Faith Works

Stage one established a grounded perspective shift by which we can reasonably engage putting truth into practice. Stage two is when the roots expand and the branches begin lifting like hands to the sky. It explains how abiding in God happens and prepares the way for stage three, transformation. Living by faith is a critical component of this progression. But what is faith? And how does it work?

How Can I Live by Faith?

If we're going to capitalize on truth, we've got to have faith. Because truth invites faith, which invites grace, which we need for growth. Growth is great, but the point is knowing God. Spending time with Him. We can do this, but without faith we won't get very far. If your friend comes to pick you up in a car and you don't get in, how are you two going to get anywhere? It takes faith to move mountains, and it takes faith to get into God's presence.

It took me a long time to understand how faith works, let alone belief. Faith and belief used to be abstract concepts to me. Intangible realities.

When I was much younger, I remember thinking faith and belief pretty much equated to me saying I believe in God. If someone asked me if I believed in God, I'd answer yes—that meant I believe. If someone asked me where I'm going when I die, I'd answer heaven—that's faith. Or so I thought.

I did what a lot of Christians do: go to church, read the Bible (at church), go to youth group, and pray before meals and before bed. Other than that I didn't live much differently from anyone else, even non-Christians. In fact, I looked pretty bad compared to most of them. For starters, I had a child out of wedlock, barely graduated high school, and ended up getting divorced. Not the most glamorous start, but God sure used it as fuel for a glorious turnaround (I'm bragging about him, not me!).

I wasn't the most convincing case of a life touched by God, but I knew I had faith and believed the best way I knew how. Because if you couldn't tell already (since I was doing Christian stuff), all you had to do was ask me and I'd say I believe in God.

I'm not knocking church going, Bible reading, or prayer; those are good things, but they're not a shoo-in for transformation. I knew *about* a personal relationship with Jesus. I'd heard about how He changes lives. Yet my experiential knowledge didn't run very deep—not any deeper than my understanding of faith and belief.

I've learned a lot since then. Having a problem-free life wasn't the goal. Besides, it's an unrealistic expectation (John 16:33). Fortunately, God works with little faith. He has moved mountains in my life, and He can move them in yours.

The Bible says this about faith: "For in the gospel the righteousness of God is revealed—a righteousness that is by faith from first to last, just as it is written: 'The righteous will live by faith'" (Romans 1:17). Believers are "the righteous"; we have been made righteous through faith (Romans 5:1–2; James 2:23). Jesus made this possible: "This righteousness from God comes through faith in Jesus Christ to all who believe" (Romans 3:22).

Now, "the only thing that counts is faith expressing itself through love" (Galatians 5:6). In other words, love matters most, and love is the *evidence* of faith in God. This kind of *believing* creates evidence of our beliefs. If there's no evidence, there's no faith or belief. After all, "faith without works is dead" (James 2:20 NKJV).

Therefore, if I have faith, I'm doing *something*. But what exactly am I doing? *Believing.*

I used to think belief was just something you think or say, not *do*. Then several years ago, I heard my favorite definition of belief from Dallas Willard: "We believe something when we act as if it were true."[9] He used the example of a chair, saying we wouldn't sit on one if we didn't believe it would hold us up.

Fair enough. This means if I believe I have a job, I will suit up, drive to work, clock in, and start working. If I believe I'm thirsty, I'll pour a glass of water and drink it. Please note: I can't work before I drive there, and I can't drink my water before I pour it (this is important).

Simple enough. But what I believe and what I think are two different things that often get mixed up. It's essential we clarify these terms. For instance, if I say I believe exercising is good for me but I don't do it, then I don't actually *believe* it's good for me. I may *think* it's good, but I don't *believe* it is. Again, if I know exercise is good for me but I don't do it, it's because I don't *believe* in exercising. I think it is good for me, but I don't believe. Maybe I agree there are tremendous health benefits, but that doesn't mean I have to do it. We don't do things for many reasons. Sometimes we like other things better. Maybe we're too lazy or disinterested.

But my lack of belief can change if I find a new and inspiring way to think about exercise. Let's say I hear for the first time it is a great stress reliever. Or I see the positive changes it's made in the life of a friend or coworker. If there's a lot of stress in my life, the truth about exercise might appeal to me. If it sufficiently does, I'll choose it. Truth opens the door to faith.

Making that internal decision, or commitment, is how faith begins. So when I buy shoes, drive to the gym, and my feet hit that treadmill for the first time—you know I believe exercising is good for me. Even if I'm one day in with thirty pounds to lose, I'm living by faith, confident I will lose the weight in due time. This is evident because I'm doing something. Doing nothing is equivalent to giving up, which inhibits progress and exposes disbelief.

Do you see the spiritual parallels?

If I only *think* Jesus is the truth, I won't necessarily *do* anything. If I do nothing, it will be without Him (John 15:5), and my lack of belief will prevent me from knowing God and growing in His love. This scenario is what Jesus is referring to when He says, "You of little faith" (Matthew 8:26). The disciples didn't believe He could calm the storm; they were terrified. Likewise, we aren't showing any confidence in His power to make us righteous and loving if we doubt His ability. This little faith, or lack of belief, translates into Lukewarm Christian Central—where we *do* certain things, but not necessarily the things Jesus was talking about (more on that in a bit).

In the exercise analogy above, the noncommittal person (or lukewarm Christian) might buy running shoes but not *use* them. So it looks like they're taking things seriously, but are they? Maybe they got what they needed to hit the gym—shoes, athletic wear, and a gym membership—but do they make it to the treadmill? And if they do, do they last more than a week? If this is how their commitment to God looks, they're probably not seeing any change.

However, if I *believe* Jesus is the truth, I will have faith enough to do *something* (faith without works is dead). If I do this something right, I will experience a transformed life—because by faith, I believe. And when we live by faith, grace changes us.

We don't force our own change. We cooperate with how faith works. We can't make ourselves righteous; Jesus did that for us anyway. But God invites us to participate in our sanctification (Philippians 2:12–13).

"But what is my part?" you may be asking. "I want to do things the right way. What must I do?" *Be* is short for *believe*. *Do* is short for *done*, so do be thankful it is finished. *Doing* is the outcome of faith and belief. Therefore, if you believe in the truth as we've defined it (Jesus), there's only *one* outcome: love. *Love* is the doing Jesus promotes: "Do this and you will live!" (Luke 10:28). *This* = love.

The apostle Paul said, "And if I have a faith that can move mountains, but do not have love, I am nothing" (1 Corinthians 13:2). Faith may move mountains, but believing in Jesus will move your heart from selfish to selfless—a *mountainous* move.

Thinkers and Believers

If we don't take Jesus seriously, we won't bother attempting to do anything with Him. Therefore we can't become love since God is love, and if we don't know Him (believe in Him), His Spirit isn't living in us, and if His Spirit isn't living in us, where's our power to grow in a love that lives beyond death? Without Him we're left to the ways of the world, which are passing away quickly. Many people have tried everything this world has to offer, but they haven't "tried" Jesus.

So we either live by faith and believe, or have little faith and think we believe (or we have faith in nothing and don't believe at all). What's the difference between what the *thinkers* are doing and what the *believers* are doing?

Thinkers

In the lukewarm Christian example, I'm describing those of us doing Christian things like attending church, going to Bible study, wearing a Christian T-shirt, having a Christian bumper sticker, and even arguing for God's existence—all without knowing God personally, in what Dan Mohler describes as "God reality":

> God reality changes your life. If God becomes more real to you, your whole life changes just by knowing Him. ... God reality changes your life. ... You don't have to try not to sin. You don't have to try to think clean thoughts. When God is real, you're changed! You say, "Well, how does He become real?" Spending time with Him. Getting to know Him. Talk to Him when you're driving. Commune with Him when you're heading to work. Don't wonder if it's going to be a good day. Thank Him for the day! Thank Him He's in you. Don't complain about your boss and ask God to zip his lips today. You thank God that your life impacts your boss. Stop complaining about the things you need to change around you and you live changed![10]

We won't find our identity in doing Christian things, but only through *relationship* with Jesus. If we're not careful, we'll get stuck trying to do right *for* God instead of being right *with* Him.

What are believers doing?

Believers

Believers are doing the faith (that is, believing) and experiencing grace (God's miracle growth). Spending time with God—believing in Jesus—is the *doing* part of this equation. From here, love can grow. That's what we want!

But spending time with God means different things to different people. So how do we spend time with Him intimately, versus keeping Him at a distance?

Dan Mohler powerfully addresses this issue well in a sermon on going from self-centered to living by faith. He answers the question, "How do you let go of being so self-centered and make the transition from trying to have faith and actually live by faith?"

> The only way, the *only* way—'cause if there's any other way, it's your works, your strength, and your ability to do whatever you can do the best way you can do it, and it still won't be good enough. So let's just stop trying so hard. The *only way* is your communion and intimacy with God. You get alone with God, and you acknowledge from you heart that, "You know what, Lord, I wasn't created for me. I wasn't created to live self-centered. I wasn't created to be emotionally driven and live sensual, and moved by every whim and everything and live by how it seems. Father, I give myself to You. I am a man of faith. I thank you, Father. I surrender my life to You. I'm not here to live for myself. I'm here to live for you and your great name and the world around me, and I give myself to You. I thank you, Father, right now, that your grace is so abundantly upon me. You're the one that rules and reigns in my heart. You're the one that orchestrates my emotions and redeems me from the fall of man. I am not a hurt, I am not a despairing, I am not a disappointed fella. I am full of joy, full of life, and my eye agrees with you and I thank you that your love rules in my heart."

That's how you kill self and resurrect Christ. It's in your communion. All I'm doing is releasing my desire. 'Cause I can't make myself like God. But I can sure want to be like Him. And if you're so busy trying to be like Him in your flesh, you're going to be a discouraged, back-slidden Christian and say, "Did that, been there, done that, tried that, didn't work for me." And then you'll have a flesh excuse to be where you're at and it's all deception. Are you following me?[11]

Basically, if our growth is stunted, it's probably due to lack of faith and belief in God's sufficiency and competence to change us. Maybe we're too busy talking ourselves out of dramatic change even though it's possible. Consider Mark 9:23–24: "Jesus said to him, 'If you can believe, all things *are* possible to him who believes.' Immediately the father of the child cried out and said with tears, 'Lord, I believe; help my unbelief!'" (NKJV).

Maybe your heart's cry is "Help my unbelief!" I have no doubt we mean well, but meaning well doesn't usually turn out well. And I think we'd like things to turn out well. Hopefully we want it bad enough to try this believing business.

It's a good sign that most of us care enough to remedy our lack and open ourselves to biblical instruction. "The goal of our instruction is love from a pure heart and a good conscience and a sincere faith" (1 Timothy 1:5 NASB). So let's keep going and not look back (Philippians 3:13–14). Let's dig in deeper and discover what being with Him really looks like. Specifically.

If you want real change you have to get out of the dirt and into the cocoon!

Chapter 5:

The Cocoon of Communion

What is the secret sauce of transformed Christians? You know, the ones who are "to God the pleasing aroma of Christ among those who are being saved and those who are perishing" (2 Corinthians 2:15). Not all of us have had the privilege of meeting such people. If you haven't met one yet, why not become one?

Sounds great, right? But how do we get there? More importantly, how do we get there without becoming legalistic?

Well, we're already off to a good start: gaining an understanding of truth, and beginning to learn about living by faith. Now, arriving at this point is where things get more practical and quite exciting! Before we jump into the particulars of what we can do, the following verses will keep legalism at bay by reminding us it's God who does our good works: "For by grace you have been saved through faith, and that not of yourselves; it is the gift of God, not of works, lest anyone should boast. For we are His workmanship, created in Christ Jesus for good works, which God prepared beforehand that we should walk in them" (Ephesians 2:8–10 NKJV). And "Continue to work out your salvation with fear and trembling, for it is God who works in you to will and to act in order to fulfill his good purpose" (Philippians 2:12–13).

Continue to work out … for it is God who works in …

In other words, we show up to work and He does the heavy lifting.

As for the fear and trembling part, here's my paraphrase of the verse: "Continue to be amazed that the spirit of God is making you love inside and out because you are simply with Him." Furthermore, God sanctifies you—not you. He is faithful; He will do it (1 Thessalonians 5:23–24). So what's our job?

Here's the good news: it isn't complicated for Him to do good works in us. There's one way, and it's seriously fun. I'm not making this up. We have the privilege of working with God. It's pleasurable to work with Him. It's light. Fun. Productive. Easy.

We have one job—the best job *ever*. All we have to do is *show up* to work. Just show up. What do I mean by show up to work? Look no further than the caterpillar.

What Is the Cocoon of Communion?

Butterflies are incredible. Especially considering what they were: caterpillars. Don't get me wrong, caterpillars are amazing little creatures. But how one becomes a butterfly is nothing short of a miraculous transformation. I wrapped up the last chapter saying, "If you want real change, you have to get out of the dirt and into the cocoon." Why? What happens in the cocoon?

The cocoon is where the caterpillar loses itself only to find itself a new creature without its previous limitations. Likewise, we can say *communion* is the Christian equivalent of the caterpillar's cocoon. "Therefore, if anyone is in Christ, he is a new creation; old things have passed away; behold, all things have become new" (2 Corinthians 5:17 NKJV).

Being *in* Christ means we're in communion with Him. If we're in communion, we're *with* Him. If we're with Him, we're *abiding*. If we're abiding, we're *spending time together*. When we spend time with someone, we get to *know* them. That's what we're after: *knowing* God. Remember, God reality.

All the caterpillar has to do is show up—get into the cocoon—and God does the work (metamorphosis). Eventually, it emerges and no longer resembles what it once was, simply because God changed it within the cocoon. The caterpillar didn't have to do anything but *be* there. Now it flies about, glorifying God just by *revealing* what He has already done.

When a Christian walks away changed, they're revealing the character of Christ; this is their witness of His finished work.

In the cocoon of communion is where it all goes down. When you're fully submitted and surrendered to His good will, God can do His best work. Simply *being* in His presence, by faith, and trusting He is doing a good work in you will change your life. The caterpillar doesn't become a butterfly before it enters the cocoon, but after.

Have you experienced life with Christ beyond the cocoon? Or is it time to venture into unknown territory? Maybe it's time for you to see what He's capable of doing through you. For the caterpillar, the cocoon is essential for change to happen. For the believer destined for Christlikeness, communing with God is where it's at.

Communion isn't stale crackers and non-alcoholic juice. Communion is more like a cocoon than a cracker. One is a symbolic ceremony remembering the sacrifice of Christ and awaiting His future return, and the other is a metaphor about the present: becoming one with Him now.

Since we know where the good stuff happens, let's get into the cocoon and see what's going on inside.

Getting Alone with God

Where is this cocoon of communion?

Scripture gives us a hint: "When you pray, go into your room, and when you have shut your door, pray to your Father who is in the secret place; and your Father who sees in secret will reward you openly" (Matthew 6:6 NKJV). I like to think of my entering my room as going through the gates to His room (Psalm 100:4).

How do I rest in God's love within this place? *Worship* is the key! Psalm 100 puts it perfectly:

Shout for joy to the Lord, all the earth.
Worship the Lord with gladness;
come before him with joyful songs.
Know that the Lord is God.
It is he who made us, and we are his;
we are his people, the sheep of his pasture.
Enter his gates with thanksgiving
and his courts with praise;
give thanks to him and praise his name.
For the Lord is good and his love endures forever;
his faithfulness continues through all generations.

There's nothing bland, misguided, or depressing about that! It's not about our sins or our failures, trying to do what we can't do and making a case for what a miserable sinner we are and how we need help (as if the help He's already given us isn't enough).

Connecting with God isn't supposed to be a selfish, sad, or scary experience. Neither should it be tiresome, dry, and boring. Worship is the ultimate expression of our love for God.

A woman leading worship once said she heard someone say that singing worship songs is loving God with all our heart, soul, mind, and strength. Our entire body is engaged in doing so with a hungry heart, a passionate soul, a Word-focused mind, and physical strength to sing words and move (swaying, clapping, dancing, tapping a foot, or whatever else). Such wholesome worship can only spring out of faith based on God's grace, and understanding His first love for us (1 John 4:19). My relationship with God is not all about loving Him, but first and foremost knowing He loves me. Worship affords us a beautiful exchange between the two.

But what exactly is this "springing up," and how does it happen? What is the hallmark of worship? Thankfulness.

Look at Psalm 100 again, and see how lively and God-centered worship is. There's *shouting* for joy. When was the last time you literally gave a shout for joy to the Lord? There's *happiness*. When was the last time you were *excited* to pray, or even smiling and laughing while doing so? There's *singing*. When was the last time you were alone with God, and you sang Him a song, with passion, when no one was looking or listening? There's *appreciation*. Have you told God the many specific ways you recognize His work in your life, and told Him how satisfied you are with His presents and presence?

There's *admiration*. Have you experienced tremendous pleasure in simply contemplating Him, perhaps in awe of how far He has brought you? There's *energy*. Have you ever broken a sweat while worshiping? Or suddenly found the electrifying strength to "turn it on" when you felt too weak to try? There's *focus*—no distractions, with all attention aimed at how great and good God is. When was the last time you were *alone* with God (and wanted to be!), without distractions?

Are such expressions of thankfulness the trademark of your worship experience? Or does something else steal the show? We tell God we're thankful, but does our countenance agree? Maybe the lifeless sound of our voice betrays the supposed joy in our hearts. Or, when we secretly meet alone with God, do we well up with pure cheer, harmonious inflection, and a happy face? What does your face say about your heart?

King Solomon said, "A merry heart makes a cheerful countenance, but by sorrow of the heart the spirit is broken" (Proverbs 15:13 NKJV). The definition of *sorrow* is "a feeling of deep distress caused by loss, disappointment, or other misfortune suffered by oneself or others."[12] Its synonyms include sadness, unhappiness, misery, despondency, regret, depression, despair, desolation, dejection, wretchedness, gloom, dolefulness, melancholy, woe, heartache, grief, etc.

Merry, on the other hand, means "cheerful and lively" and "characterized by festivity and rejoicing."[13] Its synonyms include cheerful, cheery, in high spirits, high-spirited, bright, sunny, smiling, lighthearted, buoyant, lively, carefree, without a care in the world, joyful, joyous, jolly, convivial, festive, mirthful, gleeful, happy, glad, laughing, etc.

That said, loss happens, and sorrow isn't a crime. But don't stay there too long (people don't need help feeling down). Instead, let them serve as a springboard to the Lord, as King David did. The book of Psalms is jam-packed with joyful worship. Look at all the times David says, "Praise the Lord!" The words *praise*, *thanks*, and *worship* were used hundreds of times, especially *praise*. A definition of Christian praise is "the joyful thanking and adoring of God, the celebration of His goodness and grace."[14]

Since God called David a man after His heart, we would do well to recognize that the heart of David was worship (praise and thanksgiving) and ours should be too. Maybe it sounds silly, but I find such energetic joy in telling my voice, eyes, feet, legs, hands, fingers, and so on to, "Praise God! Praise God! Praise God!" I tell the trees, animals, and sun—all creation—to praise God. Praise is the heart of Psalms, which is the heart of the Bible—literally located in the middle, page wise. Not to mention, it's the longest book in the Bible. Many of David's psalms are merry-filled, and the ones that begin with sorrow almost always end with rejoicing—a shift takes place, from the weakness of himself to the strength of God. David continuously holds God in higher regard than himself. Under the new covenant we especially have much to, specifically, thank God for—namely, Jesus!

However, if our hearts are deeply stricken by sorrow, we run the risk of traveling nowhere near giving thanks. We're most likely focused on our sins or the sins of others and despairing over how hurt we are. This is sad business. Don't get me wrong, there's a time and a place for confession and concern, but God's forgiveness is once and for all, as demonstrated on the cross of Christ: "Father, forgive them, for they know not what they do" (Luke 23:34 NKJV) and "It is finished" (John 19:30 NKJV). Maybe we ought to admit we're redeemed by the blood of Christ and that nobody owes us anything. We would do well to remember we're victorious in Christ, and thank Jesus for His sacrifice.

A broken spirit says, "I'm a mess. Look at what they've done to me." A bright countenance says, "I'm clean. Look at what He has done to me!"

It's worth mentioning that thanks to God is different from thanks in the world. In the world, we thank people for a gift or act of kindness. We might practice gratitude and make a list of things we're thankful for, like our job, our children, or ice cream. We hear that being grateful is good for us; it helps us feel better about ourselves and gets us the good "karma" we want and need to succeed. Furthermore, we obviously don't thank people for insulting us. If someone holds you at knifepoint and demands your wallet, you don't thank the thief for doing that. But you might feel paralyzed with fear. You might seethe with anger. You might wish ill will upon the thief or even throw a few punches, endangering your life and his. You're certainly not thanking anybody.

Thanks to God, however, places everything in reference to Christ. This means we're not only thankful people, counting our blessings and showing respect toward others; we're the kind of people who are so thankful, it's radical. In the case of the thief, we see a person whom God loves. We don't fear for our life (because we know our fate is secure); we fear for theirs, because if they're doing such a thing, they must not know who they are in Christ. They're the one in trouble.

The Christian can thank God for that person's life because they recognize they're worth the blood of Jesus to God the Father. So we show them kindness and go the extra mile. Maybe before they leave with our wallet, we remember we have some cash in our pocket and say, "Wait, I have some more in my pocket. Here. I know times are tough, but I'll pray for you. God loves you, man." Probably not the kind of response a thief is used to hearing or seeing. But it just might be enough love to disarm the robber, who then puts down the knife and invites you to minister to their heart. There are real stories like this.

I'm not saying that's exactly how *you* should handle such a situation if you were in it. God will guide you in that. What I'm saying is that love—not fear or anger—is the heart of the believer, and it looks absolutely radical in action. Out of this world.

Jesus said we will face trouble in this world (John 16:33). "But thanks be to God! He gives us the victory through our Lord Jesus Christ" (1 Corinthians 15:57).

So how does all of this translate into prayer?

We have righteousness, peace, and joy in the Holy Spirit (Romans 14:17), and living by faith with thankfulness encapsulates them all. Yes, faith has us in the room, and we need to be in the room, but thankfulness is the language of confidence in God (also known as belief, based on truth of course), which we need in order to receive the transforming power of His grace. In prayer, it goes something like this:

> Thank you, Lord, for depositing your Holy Spirit within me and making me righteous by your blood. I'm not destroyed by how I missed the mark. I am saved because you hit the mark on my behalf. Thank you

Jesus, for reconciling me to God. You are my peace with God. If the world tells me my circumstances are turmoil, I will not despair because you have overcome the world. Thank you, Holy Spirit, for overflowing me with your joy. I'm not made for discouragement. Rather, I am encouraged, for you are with me and you're renewing my spirit. You bring a smile to my face and healing to my bones. Your comfort frees my heart with laughter.

These are a few simple examples of how thankfulness is the heart of worship. A heart overflowing with thanksgiving is at rest in God's love. When I'm truly resting in His love, I'm no longer trying to be accepted by good behavior; rather, I thank God for accepting me in spite of my worst behavior. I'm not trying to save myself through my good deeds; I thank God for saving me through His works and doing a good work in me through the power of His Holy Spirit. I don't beg God to forgive me; I thank Him I am forgiven!

When we're alone with God in our room, thankfulness based on truth equals life-changing. In this context of communion, thankfulness *is* worship. Thankfulness *is* prayer. Thankfulness *is* abiding. Thankfulness *is* belief. Thankfulness encapsulates them all. Not to mention, this kind of thankfulness is selfless because it prizes the sufficiency of God.

The apostle Paul said, "Continue to live your lives in him, rooted and built up in him, strengthened in the faith as you were taught, and overflowing with thankfulness" (Colossians 2:6–7). Jesus said He is the vine and we are the branches, and we must remain in Him to bear fruit because without Him we cannot. If we remain in His love we will love each other as He loves us (John 15:4–11).

Consider Philippians 4:4–8:

Rejoice in the Lord always. I will say it again: Rejoice! Let your gentleness be evident to all. The Lord is near. Do not be anxious about anything, but in every situation, by prayer and petition, with thanksgiving, present your requests to God. And the peace of God, which transcends all understanding, will guard your hearts and your minds in Christ Jesus. Finally, brothers and sisters, whatever is true, whatever is noble, whatever is right, whatever is pure, whatever is lovely, whatever is admirable—if anything is excellent or praiseworthy—think about such things.

And 1 Thessalonians 5:16–18: "Rejoice always, pray continually, give thanks in all circumstances; for this is God's will for you in Christ Jesus."

Now, a question: How can you give thanks always *and* pray without ceasing if they're not the same thing?

Thankfulness *is* the heart of prayer. Giving thanks to God is a positive acknowledgment in which you're actively putting your faith in Him. Proverbs 3:5–6 tells us, "Trust in the Lord with all your heart, and do not lean on your own understanding. In all your ways acknowledge Him, and He will make your paths straight" (NASB). In other words, thankfulness *is* acknowledging God.

For example, if I'm about to lose my job, my own understanding tells me to be afraid. It anxiously asks, "How am I going to pay the bills? What if I can't find work? God, I've been going to church and trying to do the right thing, so why would you do this to me? Did I do something wrong?"

But if I'm giving thanks in every circumstance—including losing my job—I say, "Thank you, Lord, for watching over me. Thank you for the time I had at this job. I don't know why it's coming to a close, but you know. You are my good Father, and I know you'll provide for me, as you always have. I will not be afraid because you haven't given me a spirit of fear. Your hands are big enough to meet my needs. Thanks for loving me, Lord. I trust your timing and have confidence in your care. You will make a way to get the bills paid. I don't have to worry because you are my God. Your grace is sufficient for me."

Thankfulness *is* trusting in the Lord; it's based on the truth of His Word. God is faithful, generous, and good—all the time. What better way to respond then by giving thanks?

What Happens Inside the Cocoon?

Thankfulness, in the privacy of our room, is the best way to spend quality time with God. Thankfulness, in the cocoon of communion, is where the making of a butterfly begins.

Of course, being with Him isn't limited to your bedroom, as if He isn't in any other place. But you have to start somewhere, and this is the best place to start because it's removed from distractions (Jesus often slipped away to pray by Himself). Otherwise, the demands of the day will overcrowd your schedule, and next thing you know, you haven't spent intimate time with the Lord for days, weeks, months, years …

This reminds me of a time I got together with a friend I hadn't seen in a while. We only had a few hours to hang out, and for some reason we thought going to a movie would be a good idea. After the movie, we had to part ways. In the end, we both realized we'd hardly looked at each other, let alone conversed. It was like we weren't even together—because we were distracted by the big screen.

I think we do this with God too. I know I have. Often it happens in a corporate worship gathering. There are so many sights and sounds triggering sensory stimulation overload. It's an inviting environment for people-watching and mindless singing, if we're not careful. Suddenly, we may be struck by the irony of realizing God is there, and we are there to worship *Him*. In my experience, it's easier to worship Him with focus in church when I have a background of worshiping Him in private.

Starting with training wheels helps prevent unnecessary accidents. You can't stop them all, but stopping them isn't the point. The idea is to get the right "mechanics" down. Then when you leave the safe place, you take your new skills with you. We need to learn to be with Him elsewhere too, but this is the starting point.

Being alone with God is where we begin to shed our self-consciousness. It's also where we become less preoccupied with how other people look and act. Maybe I was too shy to sing at church, but now I do because I began singing outside church—inside my room. Or maybe I thought someone was wearing a silly outfit. Now I don't even see it, but I *do* see a person that God loves. Maybe I felt hypocritical, feeling downcast and assuming others could perceive I was a phony Christian, but now I hold my head up high because I understand I'm righteous in Christ, therefore I can no longer be condemned—by myself or anyone else.

Aside from church, perhaps I was bothered by how mad everyone seems in public. But now I can't help but be happy in the face of it all because I've been with God in the quiet place and I've experienced His joy firsthand. Instead of trying to *conceal* how I really feel, now I can cease the opportunity to *reveal* God's love is real.

These examples are just a glimpse of what God can do through our communion with Him. Much more to come on that later. For now, we must concern ourselves with how to pray in a life-altering way.

How to Pray

"Close your eyes, fold your hands, bow your head, and sound sad. You must do it for about fifteen to ninety seconds each time you eat and before bed; if you don't, you'll probably feel convicted about it, and you should. But don't worry, you can tell God you're sorry and ask Him for forgiveness. Ask Him for help because everyone knows you need it. You're weak, lowly, unworthy, and unqualified. Approach God without happiness, for it is a fearful matter to be a sinner in His presence. Don't expect Him to be happy to see you. What do you have to be proud of anyway? What have you done that can hold up under scrutiny in the presence of God? So keep your emotions in check; this is a serious matter. Also, don't pray in tongues; it's weird, maybe even demonic. Rather, ask God for help—always ask Him for help. Although it will never look like you actually get help because you keep on asking as though you don't. And pray to one God—not three (even though He is three-in-one) …"

That's how I used to treat prayer. Now I break all the rules.

My eyes are closed *and* open. My hands are folded *and* lifted high. My head was bowed but now it is lifted up. I used to sound sad, but now I'm happy. I would pray for a short period of time and feel relieved when I was done because I did my duty, but now I enjoy praying for ten times as long, not wanting it to end. There's no remorse for not praying, only eagerness to do so. I don't ask Him for help so much as I thank Him for helping me, because I know He's always doing so. I no longer feel weak, lowly, unworthy, and unqualified because He has made me strong, lifted me high, proved my tremendous worth, and qualified me for His eternal kingdom all by the blood of Jesus (Colossians 1:12–14).

I run to Him with excitement like a small child rushing into the arms of their father or mother. I'm not afraid to jump up and down with great cheer as I approach my heavenly Father with confidence, because I know He said I can, and I understand He's happy to see me every single time. Even if I mess something up, He receives me joyfully just as the father of the prodigal son did.

I have nothing to be afraid of when I'm with God. I'm not a sinner in His presence, but a son. I know He's proud of me and empowering me through the Holy Spirit. Sometimes He leads me into calm and quiet. Other times I'm made loud, electrified, and amped up, even with the hairs on my arms standing. His Spirit moves me positively with passion, whether this means inflection in my speech, praising in my posture, joy on my face, or quickness in my feet. Praying is no longer a drag and a duty but a privilege and a pleasure. Connecting with God through prayer is seriously fun and supremely meaningful.

I engage in dynamic prayer with the Father, Son, and Holy Spirit. There's never a dull moment. This divine connection has many resultant gifts or personal expressions through the Spirit, which includes the speaking of heavenly tongues. Have you ever had a hard time putting things into words in prayer? Speaking in tongues is a manner of praying that releases the things we cannot put into words. We can find great encouragement, and tangible presence, through opening such gifts.

Whether you pray in tongues or not, I simply wish to illustrate (and clarify) the power of joyful prayer. The ways my prayer life has changed is evidence that God is helping me and strengthening me in my mind, body, and spirit. After all, if we believe the gospel is good news, there will be great joy in our lives and prayers (Luke 2:10–11). Thankfulness and joy are the heart of prayer; they go hand in hand. The best place to begin "training" (1 Timothy 4:7–8) is in your room.

When you learn to lose yourself in the presence of God, privately, it becomes surprisingly easy to function freely from yourself and others publicly. The Holy Spirit will guide you into freedom from yourself—trying to look right, sound right, and do right, and getting upset if you aren't done right and don't get what you want or perhaps think you deserve.

The Spirit of God will also teach you how to find freedom from others, and preoccupations with how they look at you, talk to you, do you wrong, and bother you. But we can't make selflessness real in public unless it's first real in private. Let's take a deeper dive into some of these key components of intimately connecting with God's love in the secret place.

Father, Son, and Holy Spirit

I think the first foundational aspect of prayer concerns exactly who we're praying to. Obviously, we're praying to God, but God is three-in-one, so which one are we praying to?

For many years, I didn't make the distinction, in my prayers, between God the Father, the Son, and the Holy Spirit. Sometimes I would address "Lord Jesus" or "God" but never the Holy Spirit. Ironically, understanding how they're separate helps me understand how they are one—better yet, how *we* are one—and this has greatly improved my prayerful connection with God.

Here's the easiest way I can explain this.

God the Father isn't a Person you can literally put your finger on (that's Jesus). Rather, "God is Spirit, and those who worship Him must worship in spirit and truth" (John 4:24 NKJV). This means He's invisible (Colossians 1:15; 1 Timothy 1:17). Therefore, since He's not limited to a body, He can be all places at once (omnipresent—everywhere). He can hear you, see you, and perceive your thoughts (omniscient—all-knowing). He is the uncreated power and order of all living things in the universe from which all life derives its form and purpose (omnipotent—all-powerful). The sun, moons, stars, earth, animals, babies, food, trees, you, and so on are all evidence of the Source from which life is birthed and ordered (Genesis 1; Job 38). All creation is a cooperative effort managed by both God the Father and God the Son (John 1; Colossians 1:16).

Jesus is the Son of God. He is God in a body (Colossians 2:9). He came to earth as a human (John 1:1). "God with us," as it were. His disciples touched Him before His death and after His resurrection. He's the tangible, relatable image of God that walked among us in the flesh with glory subdued enough to preserve our lives; if we saw Him in the fullness of His glory, we wouldn't live.

As long as we're in a corruptible, mortal body, we can't bear the weight of the fullness of His glory until we're raised imperishable at His second coming. Then we'll we see His unrestricted glory and receive the strength benefit from it completely without being destroyed (1 Corinthians 15). The disciples saw Jesus ascend into heaven in His glorified body, where He now sits at the right hand of God, praying for us (Mark 16:19; Romans 8:34). Jesus is praying for you! He embodies the truth, and the Holy Spirit is the "Spirit of truth" (John 14:17), which God graciously sends and deposits within believers as a seal for the day of redemption (Ephesians 4:30).

God the Holy Spirit is the Spirit of Christ Jesus *inside* your body (Colossians 1:27; 1 Corinthians 6:19–20). Your physical body is the residence of His Holy Spirit, which is the same powerful spirit inhabiting the body of Jesus. Once you confessed Jesus is Lord, His Spirit made His home in you. Now you have Him as your Helper, Teacher, Comforter, and Counselor (John 14:16–17, 26). He prays for us, and teaches us to pray (Romans 8:26–27). The Spirit can't be seen—much like the wind—but its effects are noticeable, also like the wind. We've all seen how the wind moves things. Likewise, the Holy Spirit moves things in our lives. The way it moves is a visible manifestation (through your body) of an invisible, internal reality of righteousness, peace, and joy (Romans 14:17), and power, love, and a sound mind—not fear (2 Timothy 1:7). Things inside and outside you become beautifully affected by this (this is explored more in "T3: Transformation").

So what does the Trinity have to do with me?

Basically, I can't live without God. I don't have hope without Jesus, and I can't become love without the Holy Spirit. How does all of this translate into prayer, or "living by faith" with thankfulness?

Since true worshipers worship in spirit according to truth (John 4:23–24), I get alone with God the Father and thank Him for making me. I also thank Jesus for reconciling me to God. And I thank the Holy Spirit for sanctifying me. Of course, it doesn't stop there. Let's continue with some others basic essentials. Such as the following manner of asking, thanking, confessing, and forgiving.

When love clicked with me, truth changed the *manner* in which I was praying. I used to ask God to forgive me. Now I say, "Thank you for forgiving me." I used to confess my sins. Now I confess, "I'm made righteous by the blood of Jesus." And if I do something wrong, I thank Him for purifying my heart, not giving up on me where I have failed, but staying with me and seeing me for my potential to outgrow such things. I thank Him for giving me the assistance I need; it is a kind gift.

Also, I used to plead with God to save me, time and time again, lacking assurance of my salvation and often "rededicating" my life to Christ. Now I say, "Thank you for saving me. I believe I'm saved." I used to try and love God and get frustrated with my frequent mistakes. Now I say, "Thank you for loving me. I believe you love me. There's nothing I can do to make you love me less, and there's nothing I can do to make you love me more." In this way I find freedom from the weakness of myself by putting my confidence in His strength.

Why continue talking about my sins when I've been made righteous? Shouldn't I be thanking God for justifying me (just as if I'd never sinned) by the perfect sacrifice of Jesus Christ my Lord and Savior? Why continue asking for forgiveness when I'm already forgiven? Shouldn't I thank God because He *has* forgiven me? And if the heart of a Christian is love, and love is forgiving, and we're to forgive as we've been forgiven, how could I possibly withhold mercy from anyone in my life unless I don't have a life-transforming knowledge of God?

Don't get me wrong, confessing sin, asking forgiveness, and inviting the Holy Spirit to inhabit us is necessary—for *becoming a Christian*. But thanking God for the reality that we're *now* clean, forgiven and eternally one—this is necessary for *becoming love*. Living by faith according to truth is an open door to God's transforming grace, and thankfulness moves through it. This is worshiping in the Spirit.

In other words, if I keep talking and thinking about my sins when Jesus paid the price to set me free from sin, who am I glorifying? Me and my ability to fail, or Jesus and His ability to reconcile me to God and purify my heart through the power of His Holy Spirit? Furthermore, if I keep asking God to forgive me, I'm *not* living by faith. Rather, I'm denying the fact that I'm already forgiven!

It's true. If you believe in Jesus, you are forgiven. No matter how bad you've been, the blood of Jesus acquits you of everything you've ever done. Everything—past, present, future. So long as you abide in Him. This means you're always giving thanks to God for the biblical reality of your innocence by His blood.

But don't forget this also means we must forgive others as God forgave us (Matthew 6:12; Ephesians 4:32). We will do this if we've properly understood and embraced forgiveness. Which isn't merely something to receive, but especially something to be given, if in fact you have received it. After all, only lovers know God. Only lovers are truly forgiven (Luke 7:47).

Love is not only forgiving but *for giving*.

Therefore, in prayer we actively and freely give forgiveness to all others, regardless of what they did to us and whether or not they're accepting of our forgiveness or apologetic about what they did. Some of us have been through a lot, and I'm sorry for that, but please remember Jesus has been through more than all of us. The difference is, He has the power to overcome suffering with joy because He is love. Love lays down its life, relinquishes its rights, and seeks not its own but the good of others. No record of wrongs is kept.

God sees all, and He experiences what we go through because He's in us. He joins us in our suffering. He knows what it's like, how much life can hurt, and why we easily spiral into depression, anger, lust, and so on. But if we join Him in *His* suffering, we can overcome *our* suffering—with joy! Giving thanks to God in *all* circumstances is how this happens.

This doesn't happen solely with our words, but with our bodies too. After all, your body is an instrument of righteousness (Romans 6:13). "Play" it in prayer. Use it for His glory. Honor God in your body; it was designed for this.

What Does Heavenly Body Language Look Like?

Hands Up!

Growing up I remember only a few people who regularly lifted a hand during worship at church. I was just a kid, but I remember thinking they were strange because the majority of people weren't doing it. I wondered what might be wrong with these special few.

Looking back now, I'm saddened that such an expression of praise was a rare event, and I'm sorry I thought it was weird. Not until much later did I begin to appreciate a more expressive form of worship. How could it not be expressive? Eventually, I did the unthinkable: I raised my hands in worship. I did so alone, at a worship concert, and at several church services thereafter. Currently, I mostly do it in the privacy of my room. The point isn't where and how often you do it but, quite simply, to do it. The Holy Spirit will guide you in matters of when and where.

When you put your entire body into glorifying God, it's an exhilarating experience, especially the first time. For instance, take something as simple as lifting your hands in praise. This may come as a surprise to some, but many Christians have never done that in public, let alone in private. I may be prone to doing it more in private than public, but not doing it at all is what concerns me. It's hard to believe I went so many years without doing this, even judging people who were, as though it was somehow wrong of them to worship God expressively and right of me to judge silently. Then again, given the way I was accustomed to praying, I can see why I didn't think I had a reason to lift my hands. Prayer was not treated as a special occasion for joyful worship.

What looks more like praise: arms folded across the chest or hands lifted high? What looks more thankful: pursed lips and a furrowed brow or a smile with raised eyebrows? Yes, even eyebrows can lift up in praise! God is helping us up in so many ways—some obvious, some subtle. Our bodies call for and cry out to Him. When I'm filled with joy, I can't help but pace and jump around. We're being conditioned for the day we're caught up in the air with the Lord (1 Thessalonians 4:17).

Worship Workout

King David shows us the purpose of music is to worship God. He did this with instruments, singing, shouting, and dancing. He wrote songs and poems. The book of Psalms makes it clear God was always on David's mind. Twice God considers David a man after His own heart (1 Samuel 13:14; Acts 13:22). If God values such things, why would we judge anyone doing them to His glory?

If anyone knew how to get a good workout in, it was David. Just look at his worship workout in 2 Samuel 6:14, 16: "David was dancing before the LORD with all his might ... leaping and dancing" or, as the NKJV puts it, "whirling" before the Lord. Again, he did this with *all* his might. That's intense. I don't know about you, but anytime I do anything with all my might, my heart is racing and I'm sweating.

Have you ever broken a sweat worshiping? You have to take praising God seriously in order to do that. I think we all know what it's like to run and break a sweat, but are we breaking a sweat running the race Paul refers to in Hebrews 12:1? You may have tried various workout regimens, but maybe it's time to commit to David's workout. I'm not saying it isn't worship if you're not sweating. But I am saying it's normal for a Christian to take worship seriously—sweat or no sweat.

David reminds us it's important to be still (Psalm 46:10) and not sweat, but it's just as important that we move (as many psalms indicate). Of course, moving doesn't always mean sweating, but on a good day we will sweat.

Basically, once I embraced movement in my most intimate prayers, I quickly realized how compatible movement is with joy. When you feel great pleasure, it's difficult to stay still and speak monotone. If your prayer life seems dead, praying passionately in the ways we've discussed will revolutionize what you know about prayer. Let the Holy Spirit move your body gracefully and powerfully with great energy and enthusiasm. Lift your hands, jump, dance, clap, sing, and shout victoriously—shedding all idleness and self-consciousness.

"Oh, clap your hands, all you peoples! Shout to God with the voice of triumph! For the LORD Most High is awesome; He is a great King over all the earth" (Psalm 47:1–2 NKJV). If this is how you pray, you know there are delightful physical and spiritual health benefits that come with the territory. But maybe you don't worship this way because you think it's hype. Perhaps you don't feel like doing it because you're tired. Maybe it just isn't you, or so you say.

Yet anything that holds back the fullness of your engagement in worship is a good indicator you need to dive in and get soaked. I'm not quick to tell someone what they need, but I can confidently assert we are heavily dependent upon God. Therefore, we must connect with Him through worship as demonstrated by the poster boy of worship, King David. I think we're built to worship this way. Therefore, if we're used to something else, we're behaving contrary to our design. Try as we might to connect, we're actively weakening our connection strength with God.

Balance

Maybe you think such charisma is fitting for extroverts but not introverts. But what are extroverts and introverts in the kingdom? I know this level of output won't feel natural at first, especially if you have introverted tendencies, but at least give this a dedicated go. I know what it's like. I have long been soft-spoken, and the history of my prayers doesn't lend itself to much expression. But keep in mind, not everything is a walk in the park for those with extroverted tendencies. It can be very difficult to simply get alone in a room with God because we enjoy being around people so much. Each trait will face its own challenges. That said, don't overthink this; the Holy Spirit will help you strike the proper balance.

The important thing isn't whether or not you're this or that, but that our prayers are well-rounded. This means those of us with introverted tendencies must learn to break out of the shell, and those with extroverted inclinations take a mini-vacation from social situations.

Furthermore, if you're used to talking quietly, get loud. If you normally sound monotone, flat, and passionless, practice inflection. Some quietness is good, but some is based on fear. If you feel afraid or weak, choose to speak loudly with authority, boldness (Hebrews 4:16), and great passion. Scared people sound like small people; they're being snuffed out by fear. But there is no fear in love (1 John 4:18), so we confidently approach the throne (Hebrews 4:6).

If you're used to being motionless, run around, jump up and down, and make animated gestures with your hands. By all means return to your "default" position, just don't hang out there all the time. If you're a loud and fast talker, speak softly and slowly. If you feel like you need to move constantly and see and hear everything going on around you, get in a silent room with no people, don't move, close your eyes, and listen carefully for the "still small voice" (1 Kings 19:12).

I like how the following passage juxtaposes power and gentleness: Then He said, "Go out, and stand on the mountain before the LORD." And behold, the LORD passed by, and a great and strong wind tore into the mountains and broke the rocks in pieces before the LORD, but the LORD was not in the wind; and after the wind an earthquake, but the LORD was not in the earthquake; and after the earthquake a fire, but the LORD was not in the fire; and after the fire a still small voice. So it was, when Elijah heard it, that he wrapped his face in his mantle and went out and stood in the entrance of the cave. Suddenly a voice came to him, and said, "What are you doing here, Elijah?" (1 Kings 19:11–13 NKJV)

In God's revelation to Elijah, He made a powerful entrance but a gentle appearance. The NKJV also describes the still small voice as "a delicate whispering voice."

Relaxed, Calm, Quiet, and Gentle

Prayer is sometimes loud and fast, but other times it's soft and slow. I might be bouncing off the walls one moment and still as a statue the next. Think of this as the cool-down period of the workout, though you may stop and start several times, alternating between the two. This is okay because passion often looks energetic, but not always.

Sometimes passion is what moves you into motionlessness. I feel peace in such a place. The calm after the storm, so to speak. The storm was never the problem; lack of faith is. God is with you through it all, and He will calm your soul just as Jesus calmed the storm for His disciples (Mark 4:35–41; Matthew 8:23–27). He has the power to quiet a troubled and busy soul with a feeling of peace that is pleasantly sobering and honest. This has you feeling patient, unmoved, and gentle. Next thing you know, you're stepping out into the world with authority to overcome storms by His power. Even in the face of wrath, a gentle spirit will prevail (Proverbs 15:1) because a gentle tongue has great power (Proverbs 25:15).

Praying Aloud

In worship there's a time to be still, silent, and listening, but there's also a time to make some noise—with words. Jesus used words to calm the storm. Saying words has an effect. Hearing words has an effect too. Simply stated, words make a difference.

If you don't believe me, say something to someone. Even if you say something aloud and no one else hears it, you'll be impacted by what you said. So if what you're praying or speaking sounds like worries and complaints, you'll make a negative difference (in yourself and potentially others). However, if you speak of His power, love, and faithfulness, you'll make a positive difference. If this is your first time adopting such an approach, speaking selfless instead of selfish, I'm excited for you because I know what wisely chosen words are capable of. Simply hearing yourself say things you've never said before will release life-changing power.

Please, Thank You, I Appreciate

When spoken with a sincere and gentle tone, these three phrases are simple yet powerful. Unfortunately, due to rising lovelessness, these basic kindnesses have been thrown out the window along with other forms of common courtesy.

If we struggle with negativity, these are some of the best phrases we can practice. Prayer is the best place to begin our training. That said, I think it's important to say we're not trying to be courteous but

Christlike. After all, if we are Christlike, we will be courteous. The reason I'm making a distinction is because we're not just trying to have better manners. Anyone can do that. Rather, we first and foremost are aiming at seeking to know the heart of God. Then all else will properly fall into place.

As we've discussed thus far, living by faith by giving thanks is what prayer is all about. If that's what we're doing, saying these three phrases in prayer ought to be commonplace. Beyond that, how we talk in prayer will spill over into how we talk with people. However, if these phrases are absent in our daily exchanges with people, they're probably absent from our prayers too. Maybe we pray, "God, give me strength," or "Be with me," which not only denies the fact that He *is* strengthening us and He *is* with us, but it also isn't asking or thanking but directing and demanding (as if God follows our orders).

Symptoms of a loveless heart are often pride, distance, and disrespect. Pride doesn't want to give thanks but get it, only giving it on a conditional basis insofar as it serves itself. Distance says, "I'll do it myself," and disrespect says, "I can do better than that." But saying *please*, *thank you*, and *I appreciate* do a good job driving loveless symptoms away.

In the same vein, a simple hug might be the tangible equivalent of something small that makes a rather large difference.

Hug Yourself Sometimes

Why? Because it's the closest you can get to hugging the Holy Spirit. Not to mention, the Holy Spirit wants to give *you* a hug. So wrap your arms around yourself and feel His embrace. This won't seem silly if you know where the Holy Spirit lives, and if you believe He has the power to literally move you.

Hold Your Arms Out As If on a Cross

Jesus spread His arms out on the cross to show you He loves you more than Himself. He did this with joy because He knew this incredible act would reconcile us to God. Tell the Lord Jesus you appreciate His selfless sacrifice. Hold out your arms. Tell Him you lay down your life for Him in return, and that you'll deny yourself and follow Him daily, loving others the way He loves you. Thank Him for all He accomplished by enduring the cross. *That* is praying Scripture. The truth, as portrayed in the Holy Bible, is the guiding principle of our prayers.

Crying and Laughing

These can happen independently or simultaneously. Some of my most meaningful experiences were filled with one or the other, or both. I wasn't looking for an emotional experience, but it sure is sobering and fun when it happens. The Holy Spirit guides us in our emotions. We should welcome them when they come.

One day I was home alone doing the dishes and listening to "How He Loves Us" (written by Mark McMillan, sang by Kim Walker-Smith) when suddenly the Spirit of God overwhelmed me with love. I had to stop doing the dishes. I had goosebumps, all my hairs were standing, and I felt a buzzing peace in my chest and the warmth of His love wrapping around me like a soft blanket. Joy began bubbling up into happy, healing tears and easy victorious laughter. I wasn't hunting for an encounter with God, but I got one.

I have several stories like this. They all have one thing in common: worship. I had an attitude of worship in an atmosphere of worship. An emotional event can happen at church, with people, at home, or alone, wherever and whenever because God is everywhere. These are special moments that happen without force. I praise God for these gifts.

In a context of worship, crying is a taste of healing and laughing is a sound of victory. Maybe you haven't cried or laughed during worship in weeks, months, or years. Perhaps you've never had such an experience. Maybe you cry a lot. Whatever the case, don't be discouraged and don't be proud. We are here to worship God, not get a feeling.

Get Alone, But Remember ...

Get alone, but remember that the bedroom isn't the only place we pray. I'm simply emphasizing its importance as "home base." It's the headquarters from which we carry out the love we've received. We're the portable home of the Holy Spirit, so anywhere we go, God is with us. The special feature of a bedroom is the intimacy factor. It's the easiest place to get away from distractions, bare all, and focus on who you're with. (In T3: Transformation, we'll go deeper and talk about how we can be with Him while we're with others.)

Daily Like Daniel

People were plotting against Daniel and his faith in God, yet "in his upper room, with his windows open toward Jerusalem, he knelt down on his knees three times that day, and prayed and gave thanks before his God, as was his custom since early days" (Daniel 6:10 NKJV). I hope the words *room* and *thanks* jumped out at you. Daniel was a noble and honorable man of God, so it's a privilege to have this sneak peek into how he prayed—alone, three times a day, with thanks.

His is a great example to emulate, but how does praying without ceasing fit into this?

I like to use the analogy of eating three times a day. When you eat, you're not grazing all day; you take a break between meals. Why? It's not realistic to do nothing but eat. We have places to go, people to see, jobs to do. As you go about your business, your body is making use of the food in your stomach by converting it into energy. In other words, what you eat in the morning will have lasting effects, carrying you through the day for hours until your next meal when your stomach has emptied and your body needs nourishment again (because your body is dependent on food).

Food becomes energy to live. Prayer becomes power to give.

Spiritually, when we pray in our room with thanks, we will walk into the world with a fresh touch of power from on high. Power to love in all places, love all people, love at any job—because we have been alone with God. It becomes easy to understand praying without ceasing when we think about what it means to do the opposite: ceasing to pray. When you cease to pray, you don't pray. On the flipside, when you pray without ceasing, you pray regularly.

If you sow sparingly, you reap sparingly, but if you sow generously you reap much (2 Corinthians 9:6). In other words, if I only pray once in a great while, I'm most likely spiritually malnourished. If I don't pray at all, I'm on the brink of starving. If I'm a fruitless Christian, lack of prayer is probably the cause. Fortunately, this is easily remedied. A valuable lesson can be learned by observing Daniel's healthy habit of prayer.

Daniel prayed *daily*.

We must keep feeding in order to grow. Inconsistent growth comes from inconsistent prayer!

Consistency is the point. Interestingly, the more you do it, the more you realize you're carrying on a conversation with God everywhere you go. It's like you never stop, unless you stop. Pray today!

For Others

In prayer, you're not only talking about God and yourself but other people too. Praying for people prepares you to love them when you face them. When you talk with them, you learn to do so prayerfully. The heart of God thinks about and looks after others. Love wishes people well and does what it can to help. In the quiet place, God teaches us how to love a person the way He does. To see them through His eyes, think about them with His mind, feel for them with His heart, and reach out to them through His Spirit. Gaining this knowledge prepares us to step into public armed with grace and ready to face anyone. Loving people is the evidence of a person that prays properly.

Selfishness keeps people to themselves. They don't notice you. But love notices people. It's hard to have your mind on yourself when it's on others. Get used to it, because your old self is quickly coming to nothing.

Meltdown of Self

When you're in the cocoon, what happens to the old you? What happens to all the fear, frustration, doubt, contention, disappointment, anger, depression, worry, anxiety, and discouragement?

Caterpillars go through a "biological meltdown" inside the cocoon, according to NPR's John Nielsen.[15] They look entirely different when they become butterflies, but they still remember some things from their caterpillar days. We too remember parts of our past but no longer live in those memories. *"That* isn't me anymore," we rightly say. Metamorphosis happened in the cocoon, when no one was looking.

Similarly, by looking at us now, people shouldn't be able to tell we were once stuck in the dirt unless we're acting like something we're not, clipping our wings and crawling again. Wouldn't that be a tragedy! Why act old when we're brand new—born again, "forgetting those things which are behind and reaching forward to those things which are ahead" (Philippians 3:13 NKJV). Life-transforming love happens inside the cocoon of communion by God's grace as a result of our free choice to be there faithfully and thankfully.

When no one is looking, are we spending time with our Father? Or are we going it alone, doing it our way, and wondering why nothing has changed? Still struggling, trying to carry burdens we're not meant to carry. Tired. Exhausted. Thankless. On the verge of giving up.
Want to watch all of your bad habits gradually melt away under the intense heat of God's purifying fire? You can find the secret in the sauce. Hint: If faith is the sauce, thankfulness is the secret. It's the unique ingredient that makes rest work. It's the language of acknowledging what *God* did, does, and will do. When you thank Him, you thank Him for something *He* did—not you. As such, it's not your work you are acknowledging, but His.

It's time to live by faith with thankfulness. If you're no stranger to spending one-on-one time with God, you can attest to the joy He gives. This is you the way you were designed to be—joyfully with Him. If you haven't experienced this, you can. Give thanks continually. Make a habit out of it. And remember, faith works through thanks. So increasing thanks equals increasing faith. If you have little faith and want more, this will matter to you. The days of playing in the dirt are over; you're being made new.

Isn't it terrible to see a butterfly living beneath its potential, injured and wriggling on the ground, or with its life tragically ended upon the grill of a car? It's also tragic when Christians live beneath their potential by giving sin more attention than Jesus, "letting life speak louder than truth,"[16] looking lifeless and living loveless. We must understand Jesus brings victory—not defeat. Joy—not depression. Thankfulness—not complaining. After all, you're a child of the King of Heaven.

Of course, the Enemy fights to muddy our perception with lies, and the old self clamors for attention on its way to total destruction. We must guard our hearts against opposing forces by reveling in our victory in Christ. Otherwise defeat will choke out our joy. Fortunately, light easily overcomes darkness.

So let's get into it—the light, that is. It's time to explore additional important aspects of prayer and how we can respond to negative feelings and impressions that threaten to steal, kill, and destroy our joy. Fortunately, this is an easy battle, even though it feels like it isn't.

Chapter 6:

Yeah, But What If …

As exciting as this new growth is, "the bark on the tree is still very immature,"[17] which means we're still vulnerable to damaging attacks if we're not careful. Many twisted perspectives threaten to steal our lunch. They can sneak up on us if they haven't successfully done so already. Once this happens, it isn't long before bad habits of thought, word, and deed are cemented.

But this isn't a hopeless situation. In fact, we can choose to use any temptation or torment as a springboard into relationship with God. Remember, there are always cracks in the concrete, and many plants will make it through them. A flower in the concrete is quite a sight.

But what if we're stuck? How can we break out of captivity?

The Holy Spirit is the power that moves us. He does an inside job with outward effects, beginning with infiltrating corrupted belief systems. He arrests the things that plot against us and liberates us from destabilizing forces.

Some of the strongest opposition comes in the form of, "Yeah, but …" It's obsessed with "What if …" and "I feel …" It isn't wrong to say things like "*Yeah, but* I need to go to the grocery store first," or "*What if* I take my vacation in September instead of October?" or "*I feel* cold." So these phrases aren't always bad, but they can be sneaky little devils. Just look at how the devil slipped Scripture into the conversation when he was tempting Jesus in the wilderness.

But don't worry. The problematic versions of these phrases are rather simple to detect. Fortunately, truth easily exposes lies, and the best part comes when we learn to use what comes against us as fuel for stoking the fire of God within us.

Defining "Yeah, But ..." and "What If ..."

The heart of these statements is doubt and disagreement. *Doubt* is about uncertainty or unbelief, lack of conviction, suspicion, and confusion. It says, "I don't know about that." *Disagreement* is contentiousness. It is argumentative, disputing claims and causing conflicts. It says, "You're wrong. Here's why."

Again, some level of doubt and disagreement is okay. For instance, if I doubt winter will last all year, where's the harm in that? As well, if someone tells me it's fine to run a red light when late for work, I will politely disagree and encourage them to follow the law for their own good and the safety of others. Even in a spiritual context, some doubt and disagreement are okay. Naturally, truth doesn't believe in lies. It doubts the wisdom of the world and disagrees with "the way that seems right to a man" (Proverbs 14:12).

The problem comes when we hear the truth and respond to it with "Yeah, but ..." and "What if ..." Let's use the simplest example of truth: God loves you. The following are problematic responses to that truth:

- "Yeah, but why is there pain and suffering in the world if He is so loving?" (Disagreement) (Truth: God is good and God is love, therefore He does no evil.)
- "What if I screw up and God punishes me?" (Doubt) (Truth: There is nothing you can do to make Him love you less.)
- "What if I don't feel like God loves me?" (Disagreement) (Truth: "For God so loved the world ...")

Speaking of feelings ...

Defining "I Feel ..."

Like with other things, feelings are not inherently bad. You just don't want to base your life on them. Why? Because they're unpredictable. A frivolous pursuit. Like chasing the wind (Ecclesiastes 1:14) or predicting the weather. You might do so with some success, but inevitably, the unexpected will happen and disappointment will soon follow.

Feelings change. They go up and down and all around. One moment is pleasure, the next is pain. Just watch a good show interrupted by commercials. It's okay to feel, but danger will come when we live according feelings instead of faith. We're helpless at the mercy of feelings because feelings make a poor leader. They're not trustworthy. They'll get us into trouble and make us and others pay handsomely.

Once you commit to following your feelings, everything becomes self-serving. "I feel better when I eat this," "I look better when I wear that," "I impress people when I do this," "I will get this if I give that." Try as we might, we aim for validation and mastery. We grasp for control, as if grasping for the wind, but never manage to catch it.

Feelings are unpredictable, not trustworthy, and out of control. God, however, remains the same and is trustworthy and in control. We would do well to put our faith in Him. That is the truth. But the truth isn't good enough for our feelings, because faith denies them the center of attention, and feelings don't like being denied. Feelings come at us like a fastball, but faith doesn't get hit by deception; it knocks it out of the park!

Let's take a snapshot of the interplay between feelings versus faith.

Feelings say, "I feel afraid," but faith says, "I am not afraid for you are with me and you have not given me a spirit of fear but of power" (Isaiah 41:10; 2 Timothy 1:7).

- Feelings say, "I can't forgive them," but faith says, "Father, forgive them" (Luke 23:34).
- Feelings say, "I can't be Christlike," but faith says, "It can happen" (John 13:34–35).
- Feelings say, "I can't do it," but faith says, "God can" (Matthew 19:26).
- Feelings say, "You owe me," but faith says, "You owe me nothing."
- Feelings say, "Don't break my heart," but faith says, "My heart is unbreakable."
- Feelings can't stop talking about themselves, but faith can't stop talking about God.
- Feelings can't get enough, but faith is satisfied.
- Feelings look for better, but faith has found the best.
- Feelings tend to themselves, but faith looks after others.
- Feelings might happen in prayer, but faith isn't fishing for them.
- Feelings get awards and lose them, but faith has found an eternal reward: Jesus, God's best effort at redeeming us.

We could say more, but I think you get the idea.

The aforementioned intruders ("Yeah, but," "What if," and "I feel") have an agenda of usurping truth from the heart and establishing red flags of deception. They make waves of unbelief (doubts, disagreements, and flighty feelings). Next thing you know, we're questioning God's ability to move in our lives even after taking steps toward Him.

Like the desperate father who brought his sick boy to Jesus in hope of healing: The man pleaded with Jesus and said, "'If You can do anything, have compassion on us and help us.' Jesus said to him, 'If you can believe, all things *are* possible to him who believes.' Immediately the father of the child cried out and said with tears, 'Lord, I believe; help my unbelief!'" (Mark 9:22–24 NKJV).

If You Can ...

Feelings say, "If you can," but faith literally says, "I believe," which *does* help us with our unbelief. Fortunately, the man's son was healed because God compassionately gives us the help we need: the gift of faith in Him.

If we live by faith, there is no more room for unbelief.

The heart of faith speaks truth and gives thanks to God in every single circumstance. Especially the challenging ones. The effective Christian sees such as opportunities—not inconveniences.

How to Use a Springboard (Further Examples of Faith over Feelings)

Trouble will come, but Jesus has overcome.

What does that mean for Christians? We are conquerors in Christ (Romans 8:37). A Christian lets troubles propel them into the presence of God. "We demolish arguments and every pretension that sets itself up against the knowledge of God, and we take captive every thought to make it obedient to Christ" (2 Corinthians 10:5).

However, we may have adopted some mindsets that are holding us back. It's much easier to avoid falling into a hole if we can see clearly, as in the daytime. Thankfully, if we follow the Lord, His light will safely guide our way, at which point it becomes pretty obvious where the traps lie and how we can avoid them. Let's address some common perspectives that work against us and how we can flip them for God's glory.

Concerning the Hard Life and the Goodness of God

I understand bad things happen, but God is greater than our circumstances. We have the opportunity to live with joy despite our trials. If we don't get a grip on this, we'll continue to put what we've been through above Him, what He has done, and who we are because of Him. That is idolatry. But isn't experiencing this level of victory easier said than done?

Scripture paints a clear picture:

Our present sufferings are not worth comparing with the glory that will be revealed in us. ... And we know that in all things God works for the good of those who love him. ... Christ Jesus who died—more than that, who was raised to life—is at the right hand of God and is also interceding for us. Who shall separate us from the love of Christ? Shall trouble or hardship or persecution or famine or nakedness or danger or sword? As it is written: "For your sake we face death all day long; we are considered as sheep to be slaughtered." No, in all these things we are more than conquerors through him who loved us. For I am convinced that neither death nor life, neither angels nor demons, neither the present nor the future, nor any powers, neither height nor depth, nor anything else in all creation, will be able to separate us from the love of God that is in Christ Jesus our Lord." (Romans 8:18, 28, 34–39).

In other words, there is no worst-case scenario for a child of God. Paul certainly didn't think so (1 Corinthians 4), and he urged us to imitate him (v. 16). In addition, Jesus demonstrated the kingdom of God by healing the sick (like the father's boy in Mark 9) and raising the dead (Lazarus, Jesus, and all believers when Jesus returns to earth). There is no fear in love, and love never fails. If we're not living a life of love, we will be afraid and suffer many failures. Love wins. "If God is for us, who can be against us?" (Romans 8:31).

Here comes the "Yeah, but ..."

"Yeah, but what if I feel like my circumstances are telling me God isn't in my corner? I feel like He's punishing me. If He is for me, then why did _____ happen? I know I don't always do the right thing, but I certainly try (apparently not hard enough). What if He gave Satan permission to torment me for crossing Him?"

Jesus came to destroy the works of the devil (1 John 3:8). Why would He team up with His enemy and torment you? And just because something bad happened doesn't mean it was God's will for you. How can a good God do evil? Instead, He redeems what has been lost by making all things new. He doesn't inflict you with a paddleboard when you've been bad. We were bad, but not bad enough to keep love off a cross; rather, we were justified freely (Romans 3:23–24).

Often, but not always, pain and troubles are self-imposed. For instance, you can't blame God for lung cancer if you chose to smoke your entire life. Other conditions have less obvious causes, but sickness and disease are not gifts of God; Jesus came to heal the sick, not give the healthy sickness. Also, you can't blame God for your broken marriage if you chose to have an affair. You also can't blame God if you were cheated on while remaining faithful. Again, He does no evil. In fact, He is so good that the world sees His goodness as nothing less than preposterous since His love teaches us that we can't even blame others (a business the world thrives on).

What *does* God do? While we might blame Him or this person or that person, God is busy curing cancer and providing wisdom for preventing it. If you have cancer, He provides power to shine through it and prove that cancer doesn't have to keep you from living for His glory, connecting with Him and loving others. He gives comfort, assurance, and trust in the fact that this too shall pass (2 Corinthians

4:17–18) when we are changed in the twinkling of an eye (1 Corinthians 15:52). Things always get better with God at the center.

Furthermore, He pours love into our hearts so our marriages have the best chance of success. Love *prevents* affairs; it isn't the reason for them (selfish lust is). Love also forgives and reconciles, but sometimes it sadly watches people disconnect from what is good. God has been cheated on far more than anyone; in fact, more than everyone put together throughout all history. His creation has long denied Him. Yet in His overwhelming love, He became a man who *denied Himself* in attempt to give us the best life possible.

If the goodness of God grips our hearts, our confidence in His trustworthiness will leave no room for questioning Him in undesirable circumstances. It is evil that wreaks havoc and causes chaos. Circumstances change. People change. Feelings change. But God never changes. God is good—all the time. He brings order, power to love, the blessed hope of His return, and the promise of a brighter eternal future where pain and suffering no longer exist.

"Yeah, but why does it exist now?"

It must need to. For reasons that will not presently satisfy a contentious viewpoint. Not unless we recognize God's sovereignty and put our faith in His goodness and holiness. Justice will be served (Deuteronomy 32:35; Romans 12:17–19). Answers will be given when they can be understood. Jesus said, "I have much more to say to you, more than you can now bear" (John 16:12).

Isn't it possible there are some things we don't know and *can't* know? Even the best experts haven't exhausted their respective fields of research. Suppose I want to become a doctor. It will take several years of intense study to learn what I need to know. Is the process of understanding evil in the world any less complicated? And we spend how much time trying to sort that out? Perhaps childlike faith will get us by. After all, we can know God is good *now*.

Think of it this way. There are some things we can't tell our children when they're toddlers because they're not prepared to understand it. Sometimes all we say is no, and they don't like it. They protest, not peacefully either. But if they remain with a good father, things will make sense soon enough. Until then, it's possible they will no longer feel the need to know a deeper answer because they're content with knowing their loving father has their best interests in mind. So they follow his lead.

I'm not asking you to be happy because of bad things. Be happy because you know Jesus. He is the only successful Way through it all.

Concerning Feeling God

Many people tell stories about their dramatic encounters with God. We might even witness such a thing. But what if we don't? People say God is real and His presence is overwhelming, but have we tasted that for ourselves? I have felt God, but I don't *need* to. I've had a handful of such experiences, which usually occurred in the most difficult of circumstances.

"Yeah, but doesn't God want me to feel Him? I feel like I would believe in Him more if He did, so why shouldn't He?"

Don't worry. God knows what you need and when you need it. Remember, everything He does is for your benefit. This includes both feeling Him and not feeling Him.

"Yeah, but most people I know have felt Him in some way. What am I doing wrong?"

Again, you'll feel Him if you need to, but He decides when that is—not you. And please don't envy someone else's encounter. Be happy for them. You can tell God it would be fun to experience that but you're okay without it because you live by faith, not feelings. If you're convinced you *must* have a sensory experience of God, you assign yourself to the same company as doubting Thomas. Despite his doubts, Jesus graciously allowed Him to not only see but feel His tangible presence—for the benefit of Thomas (conceivably, more so those of us who learn from the story). Once he felt the resurrected body of Jesus, Thomas believed. But Jesus was not impressed: "Then Jesus told him, "Because you have seen me, you have believed; blessed are those who have not seen and yet have believed" (John 20:29).

Some of us think there's something wrong with us because we haven't "encountered" God. If that's you, remember this: whether you feel God or not, you're blessed if you believe. If we believe, we have faith. "The just shall live by faith" (Romans 1:17 NKJV). It doesn't say the righteous shall live by *feelings*. When we live by *faith,* we are giving thanks regardless of how we feel.

We ought to aim for His presence, not getting presents. Prayer was never meant to be self-centered but Christ-centered, delighting in God—regarding ourselves insofar as it glorifies Him and affords us the opportunity to boast about Him. It is about intimacy, not to be confused with feelings. That said, I'm confident you'll feel Him at some point. When it happens, be grateful. When it doesn't, remain thankful. Don't get upset or depressed. Faith is stronger than that.

Concerning Ups and Downs

I told my amazing counselor, the late Loren Synstelien, how frustrated I was with my spiritual inconsistency. One day I would feel great, in touch with the Holy Spirit and walking straight. The next day I would feel tired and depressed, like it wasn't possible for me to have a more stable experience.

Many times both would happen in the same day, alternating between feeling negative and feeling positive (depending on the ever-changing circumstances, not on my never-changing God). I would normally get off to a good start, but it wasn't long before someone derailed me by doing something I didn't like.

If I had a really good day, I was patient enough to overlook the first few infractions. But any more than that and I would break. I would get upset, and then be upset that I was upset because I was trying to do the right thing. When I felt good, it was easier to do good things. When I felt bad, it was easier to mess up. It was hard to snap out of feeling bad, but easy to stop feeling good. Maybe you can relate to this.

As you know, feelings change. If you let them lead you, you'll change with them. As for me, I was living sensually (according to my feelings). No doubt I meant well, but I wasn't *doing* well because I was believing a lie that life could somehow work by living for myself instead of denying myself and becoming love. I was trying to live for God and myself at the same time; this is a conflicted recipe that will always end in disaster. You don't use gun powder as a flour substitute.

James said a double-minded man is unstable in all his ways (James 1:8). And Jesus said, "No one can serve two masters" (Matthew 6:24). I was on an exhausting, emotional roller-coaster ride that would never stop unless this thing got powered down somehow. Fortunately, a wise and mature man of God came to my rescue.

I told Loren I was thinking too much. He gently replied, "Is thinking too much the problem, or what you're thinking about?" Then he pulled out a piece of paper, drew the following diagram, and explained.

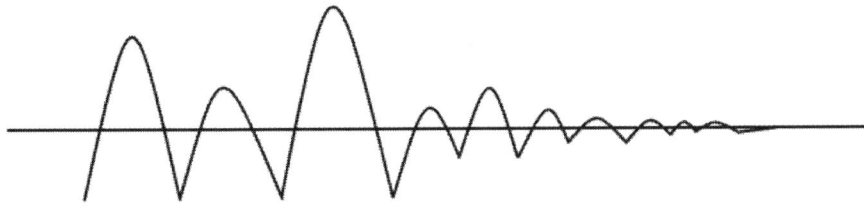

The straight line represents unchanging truth. The ups and downs are reflective of erratic thoughts and feelings. Above the line is positive and below is negative. Your feelings will not function optimally unless you fixate on the truth consistently. Over time, these fluctuations will stabilize. Thoughts and feelings will then be subservient to the truth. Truth is what we follow by faith. Truth is the Way that frees us from serving ourselves, expecting of others, and depending on our circumstances. Therefore, anytime we are at the top of a peak or the bottom of a valley, we use that point as a springboard back to the straight line of truth.

Yeah, but ups and downs are a part of life. There's no getting away from that.

That might be impatience talking. I'm far more stable now than I've ever been, but I'll admit that took time. I didn't want it to take time, but it did. What I learned is this: The best thing you can do is avoid getting bothered by not doing better, and rest assured that God is growing you. Everything else will take care of itself. When you feel up or especially down, don't sweat it. Remember, you're growing so long as you abide in truth the way we've discussed it. Getting frustrated with our failures and manic about our successes will only increase the distance between us and the truth. Relax and enjoy your communion with God.

Concerning Lack of Spiritual Maturity and Comparing to Others

There are four stages of tree growth. Do you know which one maturity is? The *last* one. Because maturity takes time. Whether we're talking about trees, humans, or fruit, they all go through a growth process. It's no different with a fruitful Christian. It takes time to bear fruit, but not time alone.

You won't bear fruit unless you have the right conditions along the way. If we're concerned about our lack of spiritual maturity, it might be because we haven't given things enough time. Or maybe we just aren't very good at noticing the changes (though others may very well have noticed improvement). Yet I'm convinced the most famous culprit is lack of communion with God. Because when you're with Him in the ways we've discussed thus far, He can make *huge* changes in you quickly. So if changes aren't happening, that's the first place to look.

Think about how fast trees and children grow in the early stages. It's incredible. Over time, the growth becomes less noticeable since prominent features are well established, such as height. Trees and children eventually reach their highest height (in what seems like no time), but other features are constantly taking shape, whether it's the fruit cycle on a tree or gray hair on an adult.

"Yeah, but I'm not so sure I'm growing at all. I still have the same old problems. But I've been a Christian for a long time. Shouldn't I have reached maturity by now? What if Jesus is cursing me like He cursed the fig tree that didn't bear fruit?"

First, why would Jesus curse you? "Christ has redeemed us from the curse of the law, having become a curse for us (for it is written, 'Cursed *is* everyone who hangs on a tree'), that the blessing of Abraham might come upon the Gentiles in Christ Jesus, that we might receive the promise of the Spirit through faith" (Galatians 3:13–14 NKJV).

Second, don't worry if you can't feel or see a discernible difference in your spiritual growth. Think about it this way: If you plant a small tree and stare at it for several hours, you won't see it grow. Sometimes we can't even tell if our children have grown until the measuring tape tells us so. Here's another example: grass. You can see it, but you can't see it getting longer unless you look away for a while. When you look a week later, you'll notice the difference. Then you can look back and say it was growing all along. Ironically, the longer you stare at it, the harder it is to see it.

What's the spiritual implication? We don't keep our eyes on our growth; we turn our eyes upon Jesus, the originator and perfecter of our faith (Hebrews 12:2). Next thing you know, we look nothing like our old self because He has made us new. Trees grow at an imperceptible rate, and some species grow faster than others and serve different purposes. But rest assured, you *are* growing if you are attached to the vine. "I am the vine; you are the branches" (John 15:5); the whole chapter describes this at length.

So don't worry about the growing. Just stick to abiding in Jesus. Which comes first, growing or knowing? Knowing. Why? Because you can't grow unless you know. It's about knowing God. Then He grows the fruit—not you. "So neither the one who plants nor the one who waters is anything, but only God, who makes things grow" (1 Corinthians 3:7). Our only role is committing to connecting with God. Our job is learning to be with Him at all times, thereby getting to know Him, and reveling in His power and thanking Him, by faith, for His grace of growth. Whether you see fruit or not, you trust it's developing. Besides, it's not about the fruit; it's about the vine (John 15). Remember, we're branches. What do branches do? Nothing but abide. *Then* they bear good fruit, but as they remain connected to the True Vine—Jesus.

When I was reading a book about investing, I learned low-index funds have good returns over time. Between the initial investment and the day you reap the reward, there's little you have to do. But some people don't make it that far because they're emotional investors. Their short-term view sees a rapidly fluctuating market. So they panic and make poor investment choices. As a result, they compromise what could have been a better future. All they had to do was wait out the storms and trust the best was yet to come. Because when you step back and take a look, you don't see the ups and downs so much as you see a consistent upward trajectory.

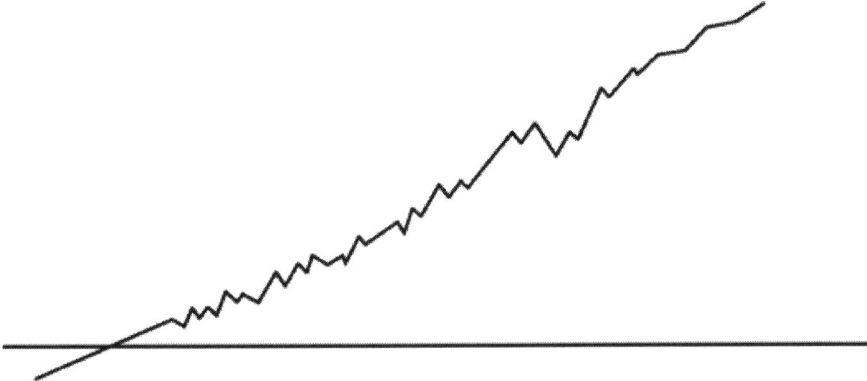

Do you see the spiritual parallels? We invest our time in prayer and watch God grow us every *stage* of the way as we rest in His life-changing love.

Concerning Comparing Yourself to Others

Some people do a pretty awesome job at being a Christian. Many have inspirational stories that can leave you feeling encouraged or discouraged, depending on the quality of your filter. You might find yourself motivated to keep on or laid out by your self-perceived lack (maybe a combination of both). We're told to be the best version of ourselves.

"Yeah, but my best version is way behind! I feel like it's time for an update. What if I want to be more like *that* person? You know, that pastor … that missionary … that worship leader? They're on another level. But I can't seem to compete. They're just plain better than me. I might as well accept my inferiority. If only I could download their anointing."

Comparing yourself to others is a good way to get discouraged, or even proud. If you measure yourself by your deeds, you'll measure others by theirs too. This means you'll either envy or pity them. If you see them above you or below you or even at the same level, you're emphasizing what you see, and missing the tree.

That's the other thing comparing does: it distracts your attention from what deserves your utmost attention—God. Envying others is like taking a saw to your own branch, which will eventually lead to self-initiated separation from the True Vine. Don't get distracted by other branches. Besides, maybe they aren't as clean as they look. Even if that's the case, it's not our job to look for the dirt, nor is it our job to say they have none. It would be a shame to uncover a dirty secret and derive comfort from confirming that other people make mistakes too. It's too complicated a matter to sort out the heart and mind of man; only God can do that (Psalm 44:21).

Anytime you're jealous of others or get obsessed with your own fruitfulness, or lack of it, you run the risk of becoming a fruitless branch. Hence, we must cling to Jesus, not "super-Christian" ideals. Jesus is the One we admire. The One with no dark secrets. He makes believers righteous, even if our lives don't seem up to par. This means we see others for their potential and victory in Christ, not their failures. We see them standing righteous by the power of the blood. We don't deserve grace, but we get it. God deserves our attention, so let's give it.

Give thanks for His fruit in others and pray for their increase. Thank God you don't need to compete anymore because you're satisfied with His presence and the work He's doing in you. You're no longer here to be impatient. Tell Him you trust His perfect timing. Remember, you don't have to *feel* like you believe what you're saying. Just say it and eventually your feelings will line up with your faith and you'll know on all levels (including feelings) that you believe.

Furthermore, even if you don't see it, thank God for growing His fruit in your life. Declare that you abide in Him by faith, and thank Him that you don't have to perform up to your own standards in order to get His attention. The cross proves you don't need to perform religion better. The cross of Christ draws us into relationship with God. Thank Him for loving you and producing His love in you. Expect more fruit.

Concerning Ineffective Prayer

James 5:16 tells us, "The prayer of a righteous person is powerful and effective."

"Yeah, but what if I *have* prayed and nothing has happened? I've tried many times, but my prayers don't work. I feel like someone else needs to pray for me, someone with an anointing. Maybe at church or a conference. Maybe I should call my pastor. This faith thing isn't working. I'm not seeing results in the real world. I feel phony when I pray this way. I'm still the same old hypocrite. A poser."

Consider James 1:4–8: "Let perseverance finish its work so that you may be mature and complete, not lacking anything. If any of you lacks wisdom, you should ask God, who gives generously to all without finding fault, and it will be given to you. But when you ask, you must believe and not doubt, because the one who doubts is like a wave of the sea, blown and tossed by the wind. That person should not expect to receive anything from the Lord. Such a person is double-minded and unstable in all they do."

On our way to maturity, there will be roadblocks. But if we persevere by regularly praying the way we've discussed, we'll smooth-sail over them. Feelings become a cue to live by faith. The wicked whisper of negativity gives rise to a bold and crushing thankfulness. Doubts become a springboard launching us toward confidence in Christ. The anointing of others is no longer something we try to obtain, but something we already have—the Holy Spirit. The same Spirit who rose Jesus from the dead is living in you (Romans 8:11).

What more anointing is there?

If we want our prayers answered (whether the answer is yes, no, or maybe), believing we're righteous is a great place to start. Why? Because the prayer of a righteous person is powerful and effective (James 5:16). All you need to do is go into your room, lift your hands as high as you can, and thank God for making you righteous by the blood of Jesus. Say it like you mean it. "Thank you, Jesus, for clothing me in a robe of righteousness." We say this by faith—regardless of how we feel in that moment, and our faith is credited to us as righteousness (Genesis 15:6; Romans 4:22; James 2:23).

That's it.

"Yeah, but it seems too simple. I don't feel like it's true. What if—"

No. Don't let anything talk you out of this. Rather, commit to doing it again and again. Do it until it feels normal—until you actually begin to believe what you're confessing with your mouth. Don't give up! This is the kind of faith and perseverance that leads to maturity over time. Answered prayers burst forth from such communion with God. We would do well to put our confidence in what He has done and is doing, not take the bench and sulk about how things aren't working out.

Communion isn't about telling God where you've fallen short or asking Him to help you overcome problems. It's not about venting worries. Communion isn't a study session or confession time; nothing about it is narcissistic or pessimistic. Rather, it's all about praising His name and thanking Him for His blood, gifts, mercies, hope, victories, and power beyond your character and circumstances. It's all about Him. In other words, the reason I struggled in and out of relationship with God my whole life is because anytime I sought Him, I was only seeking Him for myself. And if you live to serve yourself and only go to Him when you need a favor, you can't possibly seek Him consistently well. Instead, I must die to myself by praising, declaring, claiming, and proclaiming Him. Choosing Him consistently—daily—is the idea.

In this way, praying over time has profound effects just like other things we do over time. You'll get better at anything you practice repetitively. Repetition translates into greater and easier effectiveness. For example, my kids got me into bottle flipping. It took me some time to get it down, but eventually I took out this newly acquired skill set in front of my coworkers and wowed them all with a successful first flip. (I know, yay for me.)

Here's the point: When you practice faith in prayer with thanksgiving, hence believing you're righteous, your prayers will become effective. However, if you don't do this, or if you do it irregularly, there's valid reason to believe your prayers will remain ineffective.

No one can make you pray this way. *You* decide whether or not you'll flip the bottle, and *you* decide whether you'll give up or persevere. God is moving. Are you? Effectiveness awaits.

Concerning our Hurts, Forgiveness, and Pride

No one is more or less deserving of God's grace than we are. We all equally fell short, therefore we're all equally in need of a Savior.

"Yeah, but I don't feel like forgiving them. They're not remorseful or repentant. I'm not about to overlook the terrible things some people did to me that have scarred me for life. I still have flashbacks, and some of that stuff was over twenty years ago. I was victimized and left with problems while the perpetrators run free. It's not right. I believe God forgave me, but how could He forgive them? How could I? They don't even try. Some act clean now, but I'm not fooled. I know what they did."

But God forgave them. And maybe underneath that front, there's a person who won't forgive themselves. In which case, they haven't properly received the forgiveness of God (a resistance to give forgiveness is a strong indicator of this). There's never a shortage of self-centered reasons to withhold forgiveness.

"What if I reach out in an effort to make peace and they humiliate me with rejection? I won't make a fool of myself. They can come to me when they're ready. Besides, why should I? They don't deserve it."

Was Jesus rejected? He came to His own and they didn't receive Him. He was innocent and loving yet rejected to the point of death. He wasn't worried about looking like a fool because He knew who the fools were and that they needed His love. They needed help, not hell.

Going through divorce is a hellish experience for most. No one is blameless, yet it's dangerously easy to hold someone in contempt for suffered wrongs. But if we live by the Spirit, love takes no account of a suffered wrong. "It does not dishonor others, it is not self-seeking, it is not easily angered, it keeps no record of wrongs" (1 Corinthians 13:5). How often do we see this manner of communication between former spouses?

Divorce is a fitting example to look at because it's incredibly painful on many levels, and it becomes dangerously easy to blame the other person for the fallout. If we're not careful, grudges and resentment will form a hard layer around our hearts. If we don't humble ourselves, don't admit and apologize for the wrong we did, and hold onto resentments, it's a reflection of our lack of intimacy with God.

Many years ago, saying I forgave my ex-spouse for the first time, in prayer, was a huge step of growth for me. It was important for me to *hear* myself say that (praying aloud is a big deal). This step of faith empowered me to lay down my pride, confess my imperfections, and pick up my cross and follow the loving way of Jesus. It hurt to say it the first several times, but I kept at it and eventually became convinced I had in fact forgiven her.

What's more, this step of faith armed me with the strength of humility to admit *my* faults and apologize for *my* role. My new agenda became giving respect, not demanding it. This respectfulness hasn't always been perfectly evident in my interactions, but it undoubtedly remains my heart's desire to make peace, and my resolve has only gotten stronger.

In addition to forgiving her, I also received God's forgiveness toward *myself*—because I needed it just as much as she did (*all* have fallen short). When we're preoccupied with the faults of others, our faults get buried in the process, which gives us the illusion they're not even there (deception). Fortunately, the Holy Spirit is an amazing Housekeeper. Pulling back the rug and uncovering my part of the problem was a blow to my pride. But that's good because pride must get knocked out of a Christian's life.

We all have dirt in our lives, but God doesn't sweep it under the rug; we do. God throws it out of the house. Then it doesn't just look clean; it *is* clean. Over time, once I let God do the cleaning, I went from resentment and pride to being humbled and feeling great compassion toward my former spouse on many occasions. Now I frequently pray for her success with God, and I ask the Lord to bless her. As a Christian, I should want good things for her and her household.

Forgiveness sets us up for the best future. When I got remarried, it wasn't remarried in God's eyes; God sees my present wife as my *first* wife. Because He redeems us of our past and clears the record. He gives us a fresh start as a new creation. If we understand this, we can live free from the old order of things and the way we used to be. Now that all things are new in Christ, why would I spend any more time fretting over what I once was, or what anyone else was? Now that love is in our hearts, we ought to see people for their potential and who they are in Christ.

God's selfless love forgives *everyone*. It goes a step further and thanks God for the people we once resented, and asks the heavenly Power for showers of blessings upon them and their family (relationally, spiritually, emotionally, physically, financially, and so on). Why wouldn't I show good will toward people if the Spirit of God lives inside me?

The only reason I wouldn't be conformed to the likeness of Christ is if I'm living by deception, not faith. In which case, it's time to reconnect with God and reach out to others in love. I must give up my flesh-felt "rights" (derived from a fallen nature) to be hurt and resentful. By laying down my self-centeredness, pride is laid down and my cross is picked up. This is spirit-laden humility derived from heavenly country, where Christians have their citizenship. Embracing truth allows us to see clear enough to look to the interests of others, but we must sign off on the removal of our judgmental pride if we will ever taste freedom (Matthew 7:3–5).

Concerning Unexpected Troubles Robbing Us of our Peace

Peace cannot be found in circumstances, but in a Person: Jesus. "For He himself is our peace" (Ephesians 2:14). That is to say "we have peace with God through our Lord Jesus Christ" (Romans 5:1).

"Yeah, but I'm going through some stuff right now and I'm not feeling very peaceful ..."

The peace of God is different from "peace" according to the world, which strives toward material ideals such as a nice house, a high-paying job, a car that works, a spouse that adores us, kids that obey, a warm coat in the winter, and on and on. To some extent we expect such things—to at least *have* a house or *have* a coat. These things are fine, but if you think you need them, you won't be content without them.

In fact, this might be all it takes to push our fickle faith over the edge. If you lose your home, your job, or your health, how would you respond? I hope we would all respond in faith. I don't deny life happens and things get tough, but our faith should never be compromised or crushed under the pressure of undesirable circumstances and feelings.

Look at Job, who was blameless and upright, had everything anyone could ever want, and wound up losing *everything*. When he learned of the tragedies, how did he respond? Job "arose, tore his robe, and shaved his head; and he fell to the ground and worshiped" and said, "Blessed be the name of the Lord" (Job 1:20–21 NKJV).

Obviously, he was overcome with emotion and grief. Thankfulness doesn't mean you have to smile or feel happy when something terrible happens. That would be weird. But we should acknowledge God with praise as Job did. We're not supposed to surrender to the merciless forces of misery and hopelessness; we surrender to our merciful God. He is like the good parent who takes away something a child shouldn't be playing with. If the one with authority asks for it, you would do well to hand it over. Job handed it over by praising God, not blaming Him (v. 21–22).

In the end, the Lord restored Job's fortunes, giving him back twice as much as he had before. There's no indication he expected such a return. He simply surrendered to the will of God, who wants to bless us (Job 42:2–6).

If you've lost things, bouncing back and checking all the items off your list isn't the key to peace and happiness. Nothing you get is ever enough (Proverbs 27:20) unless you put your confidence in God alone (John 4:14). Peace gets easily confused with preferable circumstances and material comforts. Whereas the peace that God brings will rise above any situation.

Jesus made peace *with* God for us (Colossians 1:19–20), but what is the peace of God *in* us?

Peace is the third listed fruit of the Spirit, out of nine (Galatians 5:22). It's interesting to note that it comes after (1) love and (2) joy, which I like to think of as truth (T1) and thankfulness (T2). Remember, God is Spirit and His fruit is Spirit, therefore the peace of God is not based on material things or better circumstances, but knowing Him. Peace is in the Holy Spirit, and the Holy Spirit is in us.

Since spiritual fruit is produced by faith, we aren't trying to be peaceful; we *are* peaceful—when we pray. By giving thanks (a.k.a. living by faith), we're experiencing and demonstrating a spiritual reality much larger than our troubles.

The peace of God transcends our stress and self-focus and preserves God's will in our lives through thankfulness in prayer:

> *Rejoice* in the Lord always. I will say it again: *Rejoice!* Let your gentleness be evident to all. The Lord is near. Do not be anxious about anything, but in every situation, *by prayer* and petition, *with thanksgiving*, present your requests to God. And the *peace* of God, which transcends all understanding, will guard your hearts and your minds in Christ Jesus. Finally, brothers and sisters, whatever is true, whatever is noble, whatever is right, whatever is pure, whatever is lovely, whatever is admirable—if anything is excellent or praiseworthy—think about such things. Whatever you have learned or received or heard from me, or seen in me—put it into *practice*. And the God of *peace* will be with you. (Philippians 4:4–9)

As you can see, peace comes *after* rejoicing and praying with thanksgiving. You will experience this every time you put faith and thankfulness into *practice.*

Paul continues, "I have learned to be *content whatever the circumstances*. I know what it is to be in need, and I know what it is to have plenty. I have learned the *secret* of being content *in any and every situation*, whether well fed or hungry, whether living in plenty or in want. I can do all this through him who gives me strength" (v. 11–13).

What is Paul's secret sauce? The same one described in the last chapter: thankfulness. That is how you put your faith in God and *receive* the strength of His peace, which overcomes all understanding. Faith is the only "*receiving*" word."[18] (Of course, I think there are others, such as "I believe," "I trust," "I know," "I will," and "I am.")

Basically, Paul is "content whatever the circumstances" because He is always living by faith "in any and every situation." That leaves nothing out, and he knew hardships better than most: "To this very hour we go hungry and thirsty, we are in rags, we are brutally treated, we are homeless. We work hard with our own hands. When we are cursed, we bless; when we are persecuted, we endure it; when we are slandered, we answer kindly. We have become the scum of the earth, the garbage of the world—right up to this moment" (1 Corinthians 4:11–13).

If that isn't enough, He says, "I urge you to imitate me" (v. 16). And he sends Timothy to remind the Corinthians of his "way of life in Christ Jesus" (v. 17).

Does that mean we're supposed to look for a beating or dress in rags? No, but we are capitalizing on every opportunity to love like Jesus did—despite difficult people and circumstances. Love doesn't take offense, and thankfulness doesn't complain.

"Yeah, but I'm having car troubles …"

How does Job and Paul make my car troubles look? Pretty insignificant. Taking God personally is significant.

Recently, my car needed a headlight bulb and fuel line replaced. Car issues are never convenient. The car was at the shop for two days while I drove the company's courtesy car, which was a dirty, old, stinky van. I didn't enjoy driving it. It was a relief to get my car back, but it sure was hard to watch several hundred hard-earned dollars go toward car repairs when I could think of so many other things I'd rather do with the money. What an opportunity to complain.

But in God's kingdom, there is no complaining (Philippians 2:14). There is righteousness, peace, and joy in the Holy Spirit; that's the kingdom of God (Romans 14:17). So I seized the opportunity to shine with thanksgiving.

There was so much to be positive about. The auto shop replaced the bulb and did our diagnostic ($99 value) for free. The manager refused to take advantage of me when he easily could have. I thanked God for a trustworthy repair shop and this man's kindness; I asked for showers of blessing upon him. Furthermore, while it still cost hundreds of dollars, at least I could afford the repair. I was supposed to go on a road trip, but this was caught and fixed beforehand. Better than having things go wrong hundreds of miles away from home. Finally, about that lovely courtesy car: at least they had a car for me. Otherwise, using a taxi for a few days would have ran the bill up.

I can breakdown and spout off about the inconvenience, or I can take it all to God and flip it with faith.

Concerning How to Not Stink at Life

Life is good with God because God *is* good.

"Yeah, but I can't seem to do anything right. I overcome one thing and something else pops up. There are other stubborn things I've been struggling with for a while. It's just my luck. My spiritual life stinks."

We all know what helps remedy the stink factor—a shower. Trust me, I know from experience. If you stink, you take a shower. Right? As a result, you smell good, but only for a while. Eventually, you stink again. Time for another shower. Sure, there are things you can do to stay fresh throughout the day—but nothing compares to a full shower. Putting on deodorant and body spray might get you through the day but not the week.

Likewise, if I don't spend time with God, my life will wreak of sin. A church service and devotions might get me through the week, but my opinions, frustrations, and disappointments are fighting to overtake me like body odor.

"Yeah, but isn't it normal to stink? Everybody stinks sometime."

Sure, but if I stink, it's a good indicator I need a shower. Like now. Before stink overtakes me and the noses around me. (Of course, you can't make every nose happy. I like to wear peppermint essential oil, but I discovered not everyone likes that smell.) Things can improve if you do what is necessary. In this case, a shower. And the sooner you understand that, the quicker you will ~~see~~ smell positive results.

"So you're saying a shower will make me clean?"

Yes, if you use soap. Just like God keeps you squeaky clean when you remain in His purifying presence. Taking a spiritual shower is essential to our spiritual hygiene. "For we are to God the pleasing aroma of Christ among those who are being saved and those who are perishing" (2 Corinthians 2:15).

Concerning Spiritual Burnout, Busyness, and the Possibility of Becoming Love

We *can* become like Jesus. We can learn to love selflessly. If that wasn't possible, Jesus wouldn't have told us it is, Paul wouldn't have spent so much time telling us the same, and the disciples in the early church wouldn't have demonstrated this so powerfully (Acts).

Wouldn't it be cruel to ask something of someone when you know they can't possibly fulfill it? What if your boss said you could keep your job if you drive your car to the moon and bring him back a moon rock? Not going to happen. Jesus wouldn't do such a thing either. If He says you should love like Him (John 13:34), you can.

"Yeah, but I'm so tired of trying and seeing no results. I feel physically exhausted and spiritually drained. I'm no Paul. The worst of it is I don't even have the desire or energy for this because I've experienced so many disappointments. A lot of people I know feel the same way. I know it sounds terrible, but I've been at this for so long; I feel like I've tried everything. I can't run on a dead battery."

Love is growing colder as we get deeper into the dark and frigid last days. In fact, love is near death in the lives of many self-proclaimed Christians. Some hearts are on the verge of total collapse. Their power to love is almost depleted. But Jesus offers us a simple solution: Plug in (John 15:4)!

Concerning Plugging In

The first time I shared the following analogy was with a co-worker, and she told me, months later, how much she loves it and has shared it with others. If it helped her, it may help you too, which is why I thought I should include it here.

If the battery on your phone is running low, what do you do?

Plug it in. Soon enough, you'll have a full charge. Before you set out the next day, you plug it in again. This way you are equipped to access all of its features at all times. You do this again and again, day in and day out.

But what happens if you *don't* plug in your phone?

The battery dies. The phone goes dark, and great is the darkness. A dead phone is of no use because it can no longer do what it was intricately designed to do. The light won't come on and you won't have access to its features until it gets charged by a power source outside itself.

In other words, if the phone is the Holy Spirit, the charger is Jesus (bridging the gap), the outlet is God (our power source), and the dead battery is us, we need to plug in to the power source of life (the all-powerful Trinity) if we'll ever live with a full charge.

Faith is the hand that makes the connection work. Thankfulness is the process of a full charge.

I know this isn't a perfect analogy, but hopefully it serves to make this point: If we don't plug in, is it any surprise we're low on energy and output? But if we *do* plug in, is it any wonder we look like Jesus?

This book is an in-depth attempt to explain how exactly we can plug in, or connect with God on a personal love-empowered level. A strong surge of truth will wake you up!

"Yeah, but I'm too tired. It's so hard to wake up from a deep sleep. I know you talk about worship-workout stuff, but I just can't get into it. I feel like I can turn it on once in a while, but it doesn't last very long."

The first month is the worst part of working out. You feel sore and tired a lot because your body is adjusting to new workloads, breaking down and repairing tissues, and juggling hormonal changes. But if you stick with it and persevere despite these uncomfortable challenges, you'll reach the best part of working out: enjoying it.

The enjoyment may arrive sooner than one month in. Next thing you know, you're feeling strong, energized, and positive. It's often hard to start an exercise session, but once you get going it feels great and sometimes you don't want to stop. Eventually, you do it long enough that it becomes a habit and you can't imagine doing life without it.

If you stop, however, you can expect to lose out on your progress and have a difficult time getting back into it. That's why consistency is so important. This is no different from establishing a habit of spending time with God alone in prayer.

There's nothing wrong with putting effort into being with God. This is where the role of habits come into play with our new-nature formation. The ability to form habits is a God-given gift, which makes taking off the old and putting on the new a realistic process thanks to His graceful design. All we need to do is be with Him.

Trust me, you can "turn it on." All it takes is a decision to do it. It starts with going into your room. Then thank Him for living in you and helping you become love. Tell Him you believe He loves you and thank Him for all the people who bother you and pray blessings upon them. The Spirit will lead you from there. But there's nowhere to go if you decide not to move. Just like there's no weight to lose or muscle to gain if you won't move.

The less you do it, the less you will want to do it. It's hard at first because it's new for you. The good news is the more you do it, the more you'll want to do it. Make the effort. Take a leap of faith. Put everything you've got into God. His energy can empower you more than you might realize. Spiritual feeding will open doors to greater revelation. I once heard it said that in the physical we eat to get full, while in the spiritual we eat to get hungry.

If you eat, you'll taste the goodness of God and grow as a result.

"Yeah, but I'm so busy that it's hard to find time to pray."

If this is important to you, you'll make it happen. People are good at making room for what matters to them. But isn't it interesting how eager we are to put time and energy into anything but prayer? We accept that it takes work to get paid, studying to graduate, and practice to gain skill, but do we pray to become love and fulfill our Christian privilege and duty? After all, if we don't work we won't get paid, if we don't study we won't graduate, and if we don't practice we won't acquire skill, and if we don't pray we won't become love.

Maybe we stray away from prayer because it feels unproductive, especially when there are other things we "need" to do. We're used to getting things done at work, around the house, at school, and on the golf course (maybe). Ironically, not getting something done is a big part of prayer—resting in His love is where the good stuff is at. It's about spending quality time with God and praising Him for what He's done, is doing, and will do. Even if you actively pray and break a sweat, you're still resting in His love. You're no longer trying to be self-sufficient since you've learned there's no sense in attempting to accomplish a transformation of love independent of abiding in Jesus.

If God is truly first in our lives, won't we put the same, if not more, amount of effort and resources into our faith as we do into our hobbies, education, and profession? We can learn to be with God in those things, but nothing replaces one-on-three-in-one time with Him. If you commit to daily prayer, you'll see many powerful changes in and around you.

"Yeah, but we all make mistakes. A former coworker once told me, 'People don't change.' Even Paul wrestled with stuff like we do; just look at Romans 7:15–20."

People do change! We're always evolving for better or worse. Paul changed so much that his name changed with him—from Saul to Paul. He went from persecuting Christians to being a persecuted Christian. He learned to do the things Jesus taught (Matthew 5–7; 1 Corinthians 4:12–13). In Romans 7:15–20, Paul admits a battle was waging between the law and the Spirit, just as Jesus did, saying He came not to abolish the law but to fulfill it (Matthew 5:17). Which is why Paul rejoices in verse 25, if only we would read that far: "Thanks be to God, who delivers me through Jesus Christ our Lord!"

He said this immediately after admitting his wretchedness and desperation for help. It gets even better in the next chapter of Romans, where Paul rightly hones in on Jesus as opposed to his own problems (no wonder he grew so much!). He gushes about the change Jesus brings now that we're no longer condemned but righteous and able to live according to the Spirit. We are sons and daughters, with a Spirit that helps us in our weaknesses and a God that does us good and glorifies us actively. We are victorious in Christ, and *nothing* can separate us from His love. That is chapter 8. In chapter 6, before the chapter 7 struggle passage, Paul was going off about how dead we are to sin and how alive we are in Christ, encouraging us to live up to our secured identity in Him.

There's more. Preceding chapter 6, Paul said this:

Therefore, since we have been justified through faith, we have peace with God through our Lord Jesus Christ, through whom we have gained access by faith into this grace in which we now stand. And we boast in the hope of the glory of God. Not only so, but we also glory in our sufferings, because we know that suffering produces perseverance; perseverance, character; and character, hope. And hope does not put us to shame, because God's love has been poured out into our hearts through the Holy Spirit, who has been given to us. (Romans 5:1–5)

As you can see, the small struggle passage pales in comparison to the context. It's when you isolate that passage that you run into interpretational struggle. Can you see how small he considered his own problems in light of all else he said surrounding them? He was obsessed with—or rather, *possessed by*—the Spirit of God as revealed and dispersed by Jesus. How could Paul *not* grow in strength with such a solid perspective built on boasting in the Lord?

If we look at Romans 5:3–5 compared to the struggles Paul briefly mentioned later (Romans 7:15–20), it becomes even more obvious that he didn't see his weaknesses as a roadblock but a *springboard*. When we put your faith in Jesus, we glory in suffering and grow stronger through it all because of the Holy Spirit.

Then the Holy Spirit can renew our mind, train our tongue for blessing, and pour out His love into our hearts and through our actions. It is His love that has the power to break old sinful habits and establish a new nature grounded in good habits.

We can do this. We just need to get our eyes off of ourselves and onto our good-natured Father.

Concerning Overcoming without Getting into Legalism

If I say I disciplined myself and worked hard at overcoming certain areas, then I can boast in what I've done by my own will power and spiritualize it by saying it was the Holy Spirit (when I know full well I was a big part of the victory). Then I acquire the "right" to be disappointed if I don't get a better reward than people who didn't work as hard as I did, therefore I'm "entitled" to a greater reward. But that isn't boasting in the cross of Christ; it's boasting in self-sufficiency, which Paul warned about on several occasions.

"Yeah, but I can't deny I have a part to play in my sanctification. I have to do something."

It's true we have to do something. But this includes nothing more than resting in God's love. Yes, I know it's ironic, but we must put effort into resting. Otherwise, we'll strive and struggle to produce fruit apart from intimacy with God, which will only lead to pride or guilt. Whereas faith rests in relationship and enjoys victorious living.

So how do you overcome sin and become love without getting into legalism and the pride of your works?

You separate it from your identity by declaring the truth about who you are in Christ.

Concerning Hypocrisy and a License to Sin

"Yeah, but that doesn't mean I have a license to sin. What if I do something sinful? Are you saying that's okay? I feel like it is hypocritical to say I'm clean when I'm dirty."

Hypocrisy is most commonly understood as acting like you're clean when you're not, or acting like you're better than you are. However, when you're born again, a different kind of hypocrisy threatens you. Hypocrisy, for the born-again Christian, is acting like you're not clean when you are. A Christian hypocrite wears a mask of sinful habits to disguise the righteousness underneath.

In other words, you *are* clean, but *acting* dirty.

Maybe you feel like you're sincerely messing up—not acting. But if the Word of God says you're justified and dead to sin, which it does (for the believer), then you're clean, and your sinful habits are nearing an end as you fast approach the day you're raised incorruptible and completely changed (1 Corinthians 15:52 KJV).

Remember, in the life of a believer, sinful manifestations are quickly reducing and coming nothing. This physical analogy helps me put this into perspective: "Following the first few seconds of death, the remaining oxygen in the body makes for an escape while 'brain activity surges' as neurons, which need oxygen to survive, go wild. The body then may sporadically twitch as the remaining energy, stored as adenosine triphosphate (ATP) in the corpse, needs to escape somehow."[19]

It goes on to say some areas twitch while other areas don't. That's what science says about the human body. How does this apply to the spiritual? We struggle with some things but not others. Think of a sin as a twitch, occurring after the death of your old nature. Maybe you've been a Christian for many years, so how come you're still "twitching" sometimes? Why do our sporadic sins last more than a few seconds after conversion? Well, how does our time here compare to eternity? If the average life expectancy is seventy-two years compared to infinity, we're looking at *less* than a few seconds.

For now, we don't like when we do improper things because our hearts are pure, but instead of getting discouraged and deceived into thinking we're a bad tree, we must remain in the good tree if we will ever see better fruit.

Of course, being clean doesn't mean we care less about holiness; if we have faith enough to believe we are clean, we will care *more*. Likewise, being justified doesn't mean we reach for the all-you-can-sin buffet. Rather, our righteousness reveals we have reached for the only One who can make us full: Jesus. Sin is never enough, but Jesus is. Sin doesn't satisfy, but Jesus does. When you're with Him, sin is out of business. The more you think of Him, the less you think of sin. When you focus on Jesus, you're looking at sin less, thereby living sinless.

You won't stay on the road for long if your eyes aren't on it. But if you're living by faith, fixing your eyes on Jesus, you'll go from glory to glory, not sin to sin. By faith we are no longer slaves to sin but slaves to righteousness (Romans 6:15–23). Yes, we are helplessly righteous! Jesus issued our license to righteousness.

When you're filled with the Holy Spirit, you begin to lose your appetite for sin.

Sin isn't the problem anymore; hypocrisy is. The problem of hypocrisy comes for the Christian when we say we believe God loves us but don't spend time with Him. When we say we know Him but don't spend time with Him. We may not behave perfectly at all times, but that's okay because there's only one thing we need to do perfectly that we can do—spend time with God daily. Abiding. Resting. Worship is the key.

Otherwise, we don't really know Him personally, and there may come a day when He speaks these dreadful words: "I never knew you" (Matthew 7:23). If we're not careful, we will emphasize what we've done over what Jesus has done. We will mistake our good deeds for intimacy, and all the things we're busy doing will take the place of getting to know Him in the secret place (Matthew 7:21–23).

It isn't about behaving like a saint but *being* a son or daughter. We are children of God! Talk with Him. Listen to Him. Think about Him. Dance, sing, and laugh with Him. Do everything with Him. Read the Word of God. Enjoy Him. Be inspired by Him. Love like He does. Aspire to be like Him: "I want to be just like Dad when I grow up." Run into His arms. Be glad to see Him. Seek Him. Then He will say, "I know you." Just be with Him.

We could sift through more challenges that attempt to keep us away from our Lord, but that won't be necessary since, in principle, our biblical directive remains the same: live by faith according to truth with thankfulness. That is what Jesus meant when He said, "If you hold to my teaching, you are really my disciples. Then you will know the truth, and the truth will set you free" (John 8:31–32).

Something New on the Horizon

There is freedom, lightness, strength, and lift-off in Christ.

Matthew 11:28–30 tells us, "Come to me, all you who are weary and burdened, and I will give you rest. Take my yoke upon you and learn from me, for I am gentle and humble in heart, and you will find rest for your souls. For my yoke is easy and my burden is light."

And Isaiah 40:31 says, "Those who hope in the Lord will renew their strength. They will soar on wings like eagles; they will run and not grow weary, they will walk and not be faint."

Consistently getting alone with God demonstrates we are actively following Jesus. Specifically, thankfulness in the secret place begins the breakdown of self and leads to the emergence and lift-off of our new self in Christ Jesus, made to love. We must take what we learned in T1 (Truth) into the bedroom so we can get to know Truth Himself, and He will set us free from ourselves in visibly dramatic fashion, just as He does for the caterpillar that finds rest in the cocoon and comes out a beautiful butterfly. All we need to do is live by faith—resting in God's love with thanksgiving.

It's time to realize the truth about who you are in Christ and what He has accomplished and is continuing to accomplish for you. Prepare to emerge, fly high, and enjoy the best view. Gaining understanding and living by faith will usher in a radical, life-changing perspective shift. So many exciting discoveries are about to unfold if only you would commit to seeking His truth with thankfulness in the quiet place.

God will reveal new and awesome things to you while He takes you from glory to glory. This is how sanctification works. As we remain in Jesus, we are on the up and up, growing constantly. God is unlimited in creativity, energy, and power. It's a simple task for Him to grow you. Just plug in regularly. Get connected and you will stay charged. The more you are with Him, the better you will get to know Him, and the easier it will become to show His love.

You depend on Him now, not yourself. It's time to become, like Jesus, the visible proof of a human body possessed by the supernatural power of the Holy Spirit and reaching out to others with selfless love.

Stage Two Summary

In this stage of tree growth, our roots have expanded in preparation for much growth. We are quickly reaching up to the sky and growing in our vertical relationship (with God). As tree branches begin reaching out and lifting up to the sky, we too assume a praising posture by lifting our hands up in worship. Then we really begin to look like what we are: a planting of the Lord (Isaiah 61:3).

He fashions His love within us in private so He can begin to reveal His real and relevant love through us, in public. The private, vertical connection we share with God is where we really get to know Him well. Then a horizontal connection is established, and we develop an increasing strength to love people. Once we step into public, we carry God's work of love in us, with us.

Don't be discouraged by lack of love and spiritual maturity. Even if your love doesn't explode right out of the gate, persevere in thankfulness, patiently and joyfully with everything you've got. Pour all your energy into living by faith. Do your best to rest. Be assured, the fruit of transformation is coming. But don't worry about the fruit. Just talk with Jesus. Abide. Enjoy the relationship each step of the way. Growth is a process. Trust God's timing. Celebrate your relationship with Him. Rest in the cocoon of communion, and prepare to emerge transformed on a whole new level: loving people with the same love as Christ Jesus.

Now join me in T3 (Transformation), and we'll explore the finer details of how love changes everything—personally and relationally.

Stage Three:

Secondary Growth

(T3: Transformation—Walking in Love)

*"Secondary growth is the third stage of tree growth and results in the **increase** of trunk diameter. The branches **become** longer and stronger, and the tree **fills out** with twigs and leaves. In the ground, the roots begin to **spread out** to provide the tree with a more firm and solid base. This is the final stage before a tree reaches full maturity."*[20]

Chapter 7:

The New You

"To deflect suspicion that he is Superman, Clark Kent adopted a largely passive and introverted personality with conservative mannerisms, a higher-pitched voice, and a slight slouch. This personality is typically described as 'mild-mannered.' ... These traits extended into Clark's wardrobe, which typically consists of a bland-colored business suit, a red necktie, black-rimmed glasses, combed-back hair, and occasionally a fedora."[21]

When Clark Kent rushes into a phone booth what happens while he's in there? He changes. What happens when he comes out? A superhero is revealed.

Apparently, it's hard to get dressed in a phone booth, because his super-tighties were put on the *outside* of his pants. But we won't hold that against him (we've all put things in wrong places). Besides, that's not the point. Rather, no one thinks it's Clark anymore because he doesn't look like Clark or act like him. He trades his bland business suit for eye-popping colorful spandex, loses the glasses, and stands tall with his hands on his hips. Strength and confidence are on full display. He's no longer wearing a disguise. Even his *name* changed. People wouldn't say, "Look! It's a bird ... It's a plane ... It's Clark Kent!" No, they would say, "It's Superman!"

Clark had all the same powers as his alter-ego, but he put the full range of his superhuman powers to use only when he put on a compatible suit. Then he embraced his superhuman vision, hearing, strength, speed, and so on. The world needed Superman more than it needed Clark.

So why am I talking about a fictional superhero? To set the stage for a real Superhero, Jesus, and His sidekick, *you*.

Jesus is the original Superhero—our Savior—and he calls us into a duo with Him. His powers are vested in us for the joy of becoming like Him. He is the Teacher, we are the students. He is the Father, we are the children. As God's children, we're like "little Christs" or little superheroes. He trains us unto godliness. He gives us weapons of love and the armor of the Spirit. We're given a righteous robe to wear, but we must choose to wear it by taking off the old, sin-stained clothes and putting on the new, unblemished robe. We do this by engaging with Him in the prayerful solitude of praise-filled communion, beginning alone in our room.

Baptism is also a symbol of our new life in Christ. It served as a symbol for the beginning of Jesus's ministry. There's no record of Him proclaiming the good news of the kingdom and healing the sick prior to His baptism. He was a private man most of His earthly life, then the time came to go public, walking in love by the power of the Holy Spirit.

Many times God has changed a name. Saul's defining moment came dramatically, and his name was changed to Paul (Acts 9). Jesus renamed Simon Peter (John 1:42). Your name doesn't literally have to change, but there's utility in these examples because they're suggestive of new life—a new beginning.

A seed is destined to become a tree. The caterpillar is meant to emerge as a butterfly. Clark Kent comes out of the phone booth as Superman. We come out of our prayer closet as a selfless lover.

Now it's our time to begin revealing our change in Christ by becoming love in the privacy of communion and carrying it into public, revealing the appeal of selfless love in a self-centered world. The world needs your love more than it needs you to hide it.

The tree had to shed the shell of its seed. The butterfly had to shed its cocoon. Superman had to shed his disguise. Now we must shed the old self and stop hiding our robe of righteousness under the disguise of unsuitable things we have no business wearing as Christians; it is time to put on what we've been given (Colossians 3). This is what transformation is all about: knowing God, shedding selfishness, and walking in love—not the ways your used to "in the life you once lived" (v. 7).

Truth and thankfulness set a solid foundation for us to build on, but if we overlook them and try skipping straight into transformation, we'll slip into the loveless bondage of legalism. We won't successfully move toward maturity unless we start at the beginning of the growth process and subject ourselves to the right conditions.

It's time to explore the increase of love in our lives as we personally fill out and publicly spread out in selfless, Jesus-driven, Holy-Spirit-empowered love.

Super-Powered

What do we do with our new powers in Christ?

Use them! Put them to work. A caterpillar doesn't have power to fly, but when it's transformed into a butterfly, it can do what it couldn't do before. A butterfly doesn't have wings for staying grounded but to fly.

Things are different for us now too. We were all paralyzed before, unable to move in love until Jesus came. But now you can love God and all people because your faith has made you well enough to walk in the power of love: "You were taught, with regard to your former way of life, to put off your old self, which is being corrupted by its deceitful desires; to be made new in the attitude of your minds; and to put on the new self, created to be like God in true righteousness and holiness" (Ephesians 4:22–24).

SELFLESS-SUFFICIENT

Selfless-sufficient love is a lifestyle of freedom and transformation, independent of the old self and others with a new dependence solely on God.

"Therefore, if anyone is in Christ, he is a new creation; old things have passed away; behold, all things have become new" (2 Corinthians 5:17 NKJV). Remaining in Christ accomplishes our training unto godliness (1 Timothy 4:7). We can fight the good fight of the faith (1 Timothy 6:12) if we start where Jesus finished and run the race with perseverance (Hebrews 12:1). But you have to walk (in love) before you can run.

If we will see the victory of God in every area of our lives, we must put on the armor of God, stay alert, keep on praying, encourage others, and declare the gospel of peace and love fearlessly (Ephesians 6:10–20). When we don't move, our circulation is poor and we become colder. If your love has grown cold, it's time to put your on robe of righteousness and holiness and *move*—walk in love.

Fortunately, walking is easy. It makes sense, then, that Jesus would say it's easy to follow Him (Matthew 11:28–30). Imagine if He said, "Follow me," but He was a really fast runner. Pardon the pun, but He would probably be running short on disciples; I know I wouldn't be able to catch Him.

This reminds me of how stressful and exhausting it was for me to go on bike rides with a childhood friend because he was always far ahead of me. I didn't have the strength to keep up. Sometimes I would yell for him to stop before he was out of sight. Thankfully, the Holy Spirit is a faithful and close friend; He's so close you don't even need a two-seater. If you stop, He stops. If you go, He goes. Sometimes He does the pedaling and sometimes you do. Either way, His power is always present and His strength is made perfect in your weaknesses (2 Corinthians 12:9–10).

The Holy Spirit provides us with supernatural power to love with everything He's got through everything God gave us.

Coming Out Changed

The purpose of our endeavors is not to simply go in the cocoon of communion and *stay* in the cocoon. No, the purpose is *transformation*. Metamorphosis. *Change*. To become a *new* creation and *reveal* our transformation. We are changed inside so we can bring change outside. Being the change you want to see will help others become the change they want to see.

The goals of a Christian are to know God and become selfless love. This heaven-born love is expressed through us in ways common to others but also creatively since we're made uniquely individual and different from others. We're designed to fly from glory to glory in the strength that so gloriously supports us.

Here comes my favorite part of the butterfly analogy: The making of a butterfly happens when the caterpillar is wrapped in a warm blanket of cocoon, but we cannot fully appreciate or recognize what it has become until it emerges from the chrysalis, spreads its wings, and soars above where it once crawled. What used to be a caterpillar has now emerged as a beautiful butterfly—a new creation—no longer bearing its previous limitations or living below its full potential.

Likewise, a person is transformed through prayer in the closet of communion with God and remade into a born-again, selfless Christian. As a new creation in Christ, they no longer resemble their previous self, nor do they carry the heavy-spirited burden of potentially paralyzing selfishness.

So it is, we have discussed what happens to us *inside* the cocoon, but what happens when we get *out*?

God shows us new things inside there, like who we are because of Him and how He is faithful through the fires. But He also shows us new things *outside* of there, like how we can manifest love and help others. As we abide, we learn to be with Him in private *and* public. For instance, maybe I don't crack an inappropriate joke at work when I otherwise would have, simply because I've been alone with God. In the privacy of my bedroom, perhaps He caused me to realize such a joke isn't compatible with love that edifies, so why speak that way with others when I am in His presence? After all, He's not just with us in our room; He is with us wherever we go (Joshua 1:9).

Glowing

My wife can tell when I've been praying. I love that because it tells me this: Prayer doesn't just renew *your* mind; it changes things from *other* people's perspectives too. When you soak in the presence of God, you'll come out looking soaked. Have you ever seen someone come into a building drenched? Clearly, they were caught in the rain. Likewise for Christians, it should be obvious to others that we got soaked under the floodgates of heaven. If you come out looking dry, were you looking on high?

My favorite compliment I ever received came from my wife (she's the most appreciative person I know). It didn't come immediately after prayer either, but it doesn't have to, because when you get soaked, you stay wet for a while. Similarly, we talked about food earlier and how eating provides energy until the next meal. Ironically, this particular instance occurred when I got out of the shower.

So, having been literally soaked, I dried off the best I could (my hair still stubbornly wet), got dressed, and emerged from the bathroom. At once I noticed my wife sitting on the couch, casting an affectionate look toward me. She said, "I see God in you, a lot."

Whoa. I received that deep into my heart. For as long as I can remember, I've maintained hope that it's possible to live like Jesus, but I never had anyone tell me this was a noticeable reality in *my* life. It just melted me. What an honor. What an affirmation. I wasn't fishing for this. She cast the net! God caught me and encouraged me through her. The best part is she has said things like this and "I see Jesus in you" many times.

Worshiping God literally changes your countenance (Moses and Jesus being the most dramatic examples). King Solomon said, "A merry heart makes a cheerful countenance" (Proverbs 15:13 NKJV). This is true in my experience. My wife has told me on several occasions that I come out of the prayer closet glowing. On one particular occasion, I came out of our room beaming and she said, "Wow. You got into the good stuff." She always sees it on me.

I can feel it too. It changes the way I look and act. I gave her a sincere look of compassion and a heartfelt embrace, and told her I love her very much. Then she beamed. All of this without trying to do a better job. Best of all, I came out merry and loving simply because I had been spending quality time with my heavenly Father. He nourished my spirit. Clothed me with strength. Goosebumps ran up and down my body like electricity as I felt God's presence resting upon me in worship.

David was right, worship is the key. Not the key to getting more blessings but the key to forgetting everything other than just being with Him. Being His—that's what it's all about—thanking, praising, and worshiping Him. It is not about "spiritual disciplines," increased head knowledge, and polishing performance pride. Prayer is not a discipline. If love was about religion, we could call it that, but it's not, and it was never meant to be.

Love-producing prayer is communion. *Communion.*

You'll come out showing Christlikeness too, if you simply spend time with Him. That sure beats a long face, a tired heart, and checking the box. There was a time when I came out of prayer with fear at the thought of losing my peace in the chaos of the world. I felt like I was leaving a safe place and exposing my vulnerability to attack. Fortunately, my manner of prayer and perspective was overhauled with love—not fear. Now I'm *on the attack.*

Love freaks fear out—literally! Fear has nowhere to go but out when love is in the house. But we'll never enjoy this freedom if we don't get to know Jesus *first* by inviting Him into the privacy of our hearts (Revelation 3:20).

I remember my late dear friend and counselor, Loren, telling me, "You are who you hang around." Jesus said, "For where your treasure is, there your heart will be also" (Matthew 6:21). Therefore, it's essential we spend as much time alone with God as we can. The more you know Him, the more you'll glow like Him. Just change your clothes; spend quality time with God and you'll be "clothed with power from on high" (Luke 24:49). Then you can step out in this *transfiguration*, dazzling in your robe of righteousness.

We need to know, on an individual basis, that it is possible to know God and live like Jesus by the *real-life* power of the Holy Spirit. Others need to know this possibility exists too. We have the opportunity to walk in love (T3) and help connect them with Christ (T4). People benefit from the example of others. Paul knew this and often mentioned it (1 Corinthians 4:16; 1 Corinthians 11:1; Philippians 3:17; Hebrews 13:7). Basically, people can come to know and learn to show God's love for others simply by witnessing His love at work in your life.

Do you know *you* can become love like Jesus?

Getting that glow can happen. If you're regularly with Him in quiet places, surely you will glow in public spaces.

How Love Changes Everything

Remember, the key to communion that unlocks the most meaningful and abundant life is this: resting in God's love. It's about *enjoying* His presence. *Celebrating* who He is and what your identity and inheritance is through Him. *Accepting* His unconditional love for you and *receiving* His hope-filled, joy-inducing promise of His return and eternal togetherness. His love will change all the details of your life.

Ironically, not needing to do anything is what makes me want to do something. For instance, I don't have to read the Bible to get favor; I already have favor with God, so it's His first love that compels me to read the Bible and get refreshed by it, whereas I used to find it boring, intimidating, and confusing. Love inspires me to sing spiritual songs and meditate on the Lord. It's love that motivates me to commit to and enjoy prayer more than entertainment. Not to mention, I used to strongly dislike and make fun of Christian music; now love causes me to prefer worship music only. After all, worship is the purpose of music, which King David demonstrated. You don't have to like all of it, but what matters most is that God is glorified in music. We have the privilege of participating in worship by singing spiritual songs, which the apostle Paul encouraged us to do.

I also used to dread going to church, but love gets me in there and makes me leave looking more like Jesus. Love causes me to reflect wisely and learn something from any sermon. Love both increases and satisfies my hunger for fellowship with God and His people through personal communion, corporate worship, one-on-one conversations, and small-group studies.

Gaining an understanding of the truth about love gives rise to rest, faith, and life-changing love. Discovering kingdom treasure is incomparably awesome, and once you truly find it, you'll be filled with so much joy you'll see the value in selling all that you own, so to speak. Leaving it all behind, you'll pay the highest price you can in order to gain the most valuable treasure of all: the kingdom of heaven in Christ Jesus (Matthew 13:44).

It's our turn to love. If only we would release our "rights" to ourselves and love our Maker and His creation more than our own life. After all, He did lay down His to lift up ours—for our benefit. The least and most we can do is give Him praise and love His children.

Once we commit to going all-in on being with God and following Jesus, a shift takes place and our heart's dearest affections lead to transformation of the way we look, think, and act. The Holy Spirit pours out His love into our hearts (Romans 5:5). His love spills over and transforms our five senses: sight, sound, taste, smell, and touch. Love affects what we look at, how we see it, and what we're looking for (sight); what we hear, how we interpret it, what we're listening for, and how we speak (sound—words, tone, and inflection); what we eat and why (taste and smell); and how we move our bodies and use our hands (as the primary vehicle of touch). For the believer, these natural senses become supernaturally enhanced instruments of God's love.

His love causes us to think and act differently than we used to, in *every* situation, whether driving, eating, or watching a movie (yes, even the so-called "mundane" things). Remember, *all* things are new (2 Corinthians 5:17). Sometimes the smallest details reveal where our greatest affections lie. Such specific love might seem inconceivable, unnecessary, or even impossible, but if we're a new creation, we live in a body that can do everything in love (1 Corinthians 16:14; Colossians 3:17). We grow *up* in Christ. Not down, and certainly not stagnant. Growth is about progressing to maturity, not instant perfection in holy living. When you plant a seed, a fully grown tree doesn't shoot out as soon as you pack the dirt over it.

Comprehensive love isn't about religious perfection or keeping a checklist. It's not an obsession with works but a relational passion, a spiritual essence, and an increasingly loving nature. Learning to love isn't a duty or drudgery so much as it's a privilege and pleasure. It isn't forced but natural; our new nature becomes our second nature. We may do abnormal things from the world's perspective, but living a life of selfless love should be normal for a Christian.

We aren't trying to get love. We do unforced things as the Spirit leads us because we *are* loved. We don't *have* to become love; we *get* to. It's about being in love with God above all else and doing everything we possibly can for His glory. We don't force love; we submit to it. If life in Christ feels light, free, even easy and enjoyable—then you're on the right track.

Stephen had the face of an angel moments before his death, and he asked God to forgive the men stoning him (Acts 6–7). If life feels stressful, or like your circumstances change your countenance more than God does, it's time to step back and revisit the beginning (T1) or dive into passionate prayer (T2). Love does many things, but the point isn't doing the *same* things everyone else does, but to follow the Holy Spirit's counsel for *you*. If you care enough to pray, you'll discover the answer.

The Hallmark of a Christian

From a personal standpoint, I can say without hesitation that once I began to think and pray the selfless-sufficient way, love got a grip on me and I began to care—really care—about becoming love. I started caring about stuff I didn't use to care about. The sooner you understand the basics of love (as described in T1 & T2), the quicker you'll grow in showing love. It took me many years to catch on since I was lacking a clear perspective, and that's one reason I wrote this book, in the hope that others can learn sooner rather than later. Being a Christian for years without caring about many things (including people) is a strong indicator something needs to change.

Love is the hallmark of a true Christian; therefore we should be known for being the most caring people. *Care* is a good word for describing biblical love because it concerns itself with the protection of someone or something; we know from 1 Corinthians 13:7 that love "always protects."

In addition, it pays attention and uses caution. It attaches importance to things and seeks to preserve what is good and healthy and improve what is lacking. It keeps watch and looks out for others. It takes interest in things deserving notice: things that impact people and the planet. It does no harm but responsibly looks after and tends to the needs of oneself and others. Sounds a lot like biblical love, doesn't it? (Matthew 5:13; Philippians 2:4; Matthew 25:13; Matthew 26:41; Acts 20:28; Romans 13:10).

What looks more like love than caring for someone?

The short of it is Christians *care* about glorifying God in *everything.*

If we know the truth but don't choose to engage with it, our lack of care is made obvious; we don't care to change. This is scary and tragic. It's the mindset of the lukewarm, ineffective, loveless Christian, and it doesn't end well. The world chews these types up and spits them out. God Himself says, "So, because you are lukewarm—neither hot nor cold—I am about to spit you out of my mouth" (Revelation 3:16). I don't know about you, but I don't want this to happen to me. I was lukewarm long enough.

But don't worry. If you're currently lukewarm and reading this, it's not too late to start caring. This far into the book, perhaps you feel a surging care already, especially if you've begun praying in the manner previously discussed. Here's an additional tip for your prayers concerning this particular issue. Ironically, when I didn't care about certain things I knew I should care about, I started with a blunt confession: "I don't care, but I want to care." Then take it to the next level. Add some icing on the cake by saying, "Thank you, Holy Spirit, for teaching me to care about what you care about," and trust it will happen. Tell Him, "I believe you're teaching me now. Thank you." That is faith. We need to have faith in God if we'll ever care about what's good.

Starting here and throughout the next chapter, I'll illustrate love with personal examples and stories. I think this is a critical component of "getting it"; I know it was for me. I learn best through analogies, examples, and stories. The Bible is full of such things for good reason. So let's take what we've learned so far and think about it in more practical terms and high-definition detail. HD love enhances our perspective, which may be all we need to see clearly enough to take the next step and emerge from communion as a selfless Christian.

Seeing love in another person can help you become it. We don't need to see them in person or on video when we can see them in our mind's eye through story.

Love Illustrated: Personally

Spiritual and Mental Health

There's a mental health crisis in America because there was a spiritual crisis first (paradise lost). Some professionals say everyone has a mental illness. According to mentalhealth.gov, "Mental health includes our emotional, psychological, and social well-being. It affects how we think, feel, and act. It also helps determine how we handle stress, relate to others, and make choices. Mental health is important at every stage of life, from childhood and adolescence through adulthood."[22]

We could say the same about our spiritual health. How our faith affects our well-being, thoughts, feelings, and actions. How truth determines the way we handle stress, relate to others, and make choices. How abiding in Christ is important at every stage of life, from seedling to maturity. But the article doesn't use spiritual language.

The article provides the following list of early warning signs related to mental health problems:

- Eating or sleeping too much or too little
- Pulling away from people and usual activities
- Having low or no energy
- Feeling numb or like nothing matters
- Having unexplained aches and pains
- Feeling helpless or hopeless
- Smoking, drinking, or using drugs more than usual
- Feeling unusually confused, forgetful, on edge, angry, upset, worried, or scared
- Yelling or fighting with family and friends
- Experiencing severe mood swings that cause problems in relationships
- Having persistent thoughts and memories you can't get out of your head
- Hearing voices or believing things that are not true
- Thinking of harming yourself or others
- Inability to perform daily tasks like taking care of your kids or getting to work or school

If we're honest we can relate to some of these, if not many or all. We're no stranger to such symptoms and habits because we inherited them through Adam after the fall of man.

The article continues by saying positive mental health allows people to:
- Realize their full potential
- Cope with the stresses of life
- Work productively
- Make meaningful contributions to their communities

It ends with ways to maintain positive mental health including:
- Getting professional help if you need it
- Connecting with others
- Staying positive
- Getting physically active
- Helping others
- Getting enough sleep
- Developing coping skills

We can probably relate to the benefit in some or all of these. In addition, we may realize our faith in Christ accomplishes them through His Holy Spirit in us and our fellow believers.

I used to struggle with several of the listed problems, but I can attest to the power that sufficiently overcame them in my life: the love of the Holy Spirit. The presence of God crushes *all* of the previously mentioned mental health problems. This doesn't mean you won't have problems, but you do have the best solution available, and you have the promise that things will get better over time, if you remain in Christ.

In which case, the love of God makes your sleep *sweeter*. Love compels you to *reach out* to people and achieve *excellence* in your usual activities with unusual strength and creativity. Love *increases* your energy. Love feels *alive* and is the most *meaningful* and *satisfying* pursuit. Love crowds out stress and puts your body at ease. Love promotes better feelings and the highest hope. Love *overpowers* smoking, drinking, and using drugs. Love creates clarity and calm.

Love apologizes, forgives, turns away wrath with gentleness, and *makes peace* with family and friends. Love stops the mood swings and causes great success in relationships. Love *looks at the eyes* and sees a person as valuable and created in the image of God with the potential to know Him and show Him. Love destroys intrusive thoughts and negative obsessions with *positive, persistent thoughts* of truth and memories of God's faithfulness. Love tells you the truth and causes your beliefs to reflect *supernatural* reality. Love doesn't worry about intrusive thoughts of harm because it's busy seeking God and helping everyone, thereby *doing no harm.* Love empowers you to carry out your tasks to *completion.* Love is enough. Jesus's self-sacrificial love is the cause and effect of all things good!

Positive mental health comes naturally as we connect with the love of God (Isaiah 26:3–4), which brings out our full potential. Love doesn't cope with stress, it destroys it! Love inspires us to work productively and contribute prosperity to the community.

Also, love maintains what is good, such as positive mental health. If we will have our best shot at life, we need attention—the right kind of attention. The Holy Spirit gives the best professional help, guaranteed to work and free of charge with unlimited sessions and time allotments.

Humble yourself and invite Him to help you. He connects you with the right people at the right time and teaches you to live a life of love. Love creates a positive momentum of confidence, optimism, and proactivity. The heart of the problem is selfishness, but the love of God frees you from yourself and restores your image to what it was created to be: like Him. It's the Holy Spirit who moves us to help people and showcase God's glory and power. In various ways, He gives us rest and strength, enough to overcome common problems in a fallen world.

New Creations Can Use Some Help

God helps us through His Spirit through His people. New creations benefit greatly from the help of mature believers, just as a child benefits from the care of a parent. Of course, God is whom we depend on. Yet one of the ways He nurtures us is through other believers.

A big part of my spiritual and mental health success was seeing the love of Jesus in the godliest man I knew, my former counselor, Loren. He was filled with the Holy Spirit and instrumental in rekindling my faith, helping me wisely navigate my way through divorce and out of defeat. He embodied the fruit of the Spirit and nourished my starving soul with it.

He taught me how to connect with the right people, think wisely, and carefully consider the impact of my choices. He helped me have hope and take initiative to overcome the darkness with light. He's the one who overwhelmed me with valuable insights, such as this helpful sequence of questions: "What does the devil say? What does God say? What do I say?" Lies, truth, and choice. Asking yourself these questions will help you cultivate an ear for the Spirit and determine how you may glorify God in any situation.

Loren was so gentle, patient, kind, and in control. Just by the sincerity of his facial expressions, his calm manner, the patience of his cadence, and the warmness of his vocal tone, I knew he was caring and trustworthy. It was easy to tell he had many years of experience with people and prayer. He generously gave me countless counseling sessions free of charge because I couldn't afford it. I told him I wanted to repay him, but he thought I would find a way that wasn't monetary.

His spiritual maturity encouraged me to grow in the Lord. His words were always so timely and rich. He often quoted Proverbs. I learned he spent two hours a day reading Proverbs for more than twenty years! That is commitment. No wonder he easily passed as the wisest man I've ever known. When I read Proverbs 2–4, I don't have a hard time imagining the words coming from Loren.

Proverbs 4:5 says, "Get wisdom, get understanding." Not only did he help me find healing, wisdom, and understanding, but he also helped me learn how to pass it on. He's the one who said, "You are who you hang around." Even though he's temporarily gone, his mark is still on me and I'll continue to mark others with his wisdom.

I highly recommend finding a mentor beyond your years and wisdom to encourage you in the faith. It's not only of benefit to you but more so for them. Jesus Himself said, "It is more blessed to give than to receive" (Acts 20:35). Mentoring is a win-win situation—not just about receiving, but giving. Occasionally, I would give Loren a random call just to say I appreciate him.

Sometimes we simply happen to meet the right people at the right time (as was the case for me with Loren), but sometimes we must do the reaching out. The Holy Spirit will prompt you if the time has come.

Jon is another example of a spiritual father, or mentor, in my life. We met in a Sunday school class he was teaching because I introduced myself. A studious man with a caring heart, Jon gladly welcomed my offer for coffee. My heart was burning to reach out to him because I saw a sincerity, authenticity, and passion about him that I needed to get closer to.

More than anything else, Jon showed me availability and accessibility. He was a busy man between working full time, managing several children, and devoutly studying the Word of God. Yet he somehow remained accessible to me. We met dozens of times. We would talk about God for hours; sometimes we were at the restaurant for up to three or four hours at a time.

He always listened and never hurried. He always paid for my order. He offered me a place to stay when I was homeless. He prayed for me and my family. He gave me books and unique insight. We don't live in the same city anymore, so I haven't seen him in a while, and different people come to us in different seasons, but Jon will forever be a dear friend to me. Looking back, what I remember most is his having the heart of the Father (which makes sense because the Holy Spirit is in him). During the darkest of my days, he was there for me.

Last, I must mention Dan Mohler. I've quoted him at length already. I think of him as a sort of virtual mentor, but I've spoken with him on the phone, met him in person, and watched many hours of his messages on YouTube. I quickly realized he was an important building block on my foundation. I don't know of a better teacher or follower of Christ. Love is absolutely exploding out of him. He delivers the good news so clearly and powerfully, and he taught me loads about love. The least I can do is mention him and hope that you experience these revelations for yourself and tell others about him. He's not after notoriety, but the way he delivers the message is resonating with thousands of people and the numbers are rising quickly.

When I spoke with him on the phone, I asked permission to quote him and he said I could quote him word for word for all he cares; he just wants the truth to get out there freely. There's something special about Dan. I see him as a pioneer in bringing the church back to its roots. We need people like this in our lives to spur us on in love. Thank God for the wonderful ways He works through believers.

Many things in my life, including this book, would not have been possible without such men of God as John Kilde, Loren, Jon, and Pastor Dan. I thank God for them. God's grace alone is sufficient for us, but that doesn't mean we don't need Him through other people.

Expect Victory

My spiritual and mental health is by far the best it has ever been. There's so much God has overcome in my life. He's guided me through the fires of mental illness, loneliness, foster care, jealousy, premarital sex, guilt, depression, anxiety, panic attacks, teenage parenting, porn and masturbation, low self-esteem, near-death events, divorce, faith crisis, intrusive thoughts, unwanted dreams, alcohol abuse, thousands of dollars in financial debt, homelessness, long-distance relationships, job insecurity, immigration woes, and physical health issues. Each area could fill its own book, but the point isn't what I've been through, but how we can overcome such things by the power and victory of God in our lives through Christ Jesus our Lord. My joy has never been greater!

Do you know what's especially awesome about being a Christian in the fire? God safely guides us through and everything remains miraculously intact—our hair and clothing are not singed, there's no smell of fire, and everyone who witnesses our lives gives praise to our God instead of theirs because they see God's life-changing power at work in real life (Daniel 3:16–28). In other words, God works through our example to help others enter His marvelous kingdom.

Perhaps the best evidence of God's victory in my life is currently seen in my smile, heard in my easy laughter, and demonstrated in my calm disposition and care for others. I've had coworkers think I was a "good Christian boy" who hit the ground running in life, safely dodging all adversity, only to discover the opposite (to their surprise). Another coworker said I'm one of the nicest guys she knows, but she doesn't know about a lot of the not-so-nice things I've done. Fortunately, those things don't matter when you become a new creation in Christ, because all is made new! His love permeates every fiber, affecting the smallest details, sometimes down to your posture and the way you walk.

Just today, I was told I have a "happy walk." I think that's a good compliment. Having powerful, worship-filled days at home and at church makes a lifestyle of love flow effortlessly. This kind of positive kingdom engagement also promotes better posture, which I have also been recognized for (even after several years at a desk job). People may not know what's happening behind the scenes, but they can see the effects of it. I normally feel relaxed, jovial, quiet at times, but bold when necessary. This is a fun place to minister from because people respond well to positivity.

What makes a Christian different? And what makes a non-Christian want what Christians have? *Overcoming.* People need someone who has made it through something they're stuck in. They need hope. Someone who can help them out of a hole, not remain stuck in it with them. So if I'm a Christian but I'm stressed out all the time, do you think my anxious non-believer friend will ask me what the secret is? No.

Victory-based, love-infused living is not the automatic result of simply going through tough times, but abiding with God along the way long enough to see His triumphant hand work a miracle. People can't see troubles from the past on me because they're not supposed to—not because I'm hiding them, but because I've been changed. *That* isn't me anymore. New creations learn to travel light, without baggage.

Sure, we hold on to some bags longer than others, but don't be discouraged if you're still unloading. I used to unload semi-trailers full of packages—thousands of them stacked up to eight feet high. The task looked daunting at first, but wasn't so bad once I got going. Next thing I knew, the trailers were empty. But that wouldn't have happened if I held onto one package the whole time. Gripping one thing with both hands prevents you from grabbing anything else unless you drop what you're holding onto first.

In other words, holding onto Jesus is a great idea, but holding onto anything other than Him will keep the baggage trailers full. Therefore, if we'll pick up our cross and follow Jesus, we must let go of everything else. He wants to help you unload, and He's brought His friends (believers). "Many hands make light work," as the saying goes. After all, His burden is light. Pretty soon you're not even thinking about the baggage because you're enjoying good company and the process of accomplishment. So please be encouraged about the good work the Lord is doing in your life. Rejoice and rest in His love. Thrive in the energy of His joy. The best is yet to come!

Remember, the butterfly doesn't look like a caterpillar anymore. Sure, it takes time to change—but change it will. Neither does the tree look like the seedling because it has transformed over time into something much larger than what it once was. Likewise, my life doesn't look like *that life* anymore because I died to myself in conformance to the image of Christ by the power of the Holy Spirit, who has rooted and built me up in Him, over time, and will *continue* this good work until it is completed (Colossians 2:7; Philippians 1:6).

What matters most is that you go all-in on pursuing God and not giving up. If you wander, just come back. His arms are open. Don't stop seeking Him. A revelation of love wasn't received overnight for me, but I persevered from this sermon to that sermon, this book to that book, one mistake to more mistakes, this counseling session to that one, this relationship to that relationship, through all the peaks and valleys of life and so on.

Whatever happens, love doesn't quit!

Be encouraged. Things *are* getting better (Romans 8:28). Genesis 50:20 reminds us, "You intended to harm me, but God intended it for good to accomplish what is now being done, the saving of many lives." The Holy Spirit gives you everything you need to walk this thing out. He is strengthening you with great power for good purposes.

A Renewed Mind and Body

Our mind and body, or mental health and physical health, are on Team Love. They are intertwined, each assisting and depending on the other. It's important to think about how you live from your body because love looks like *something*. Love in action happens both invisibly (in your mind) and visibly (through your body). In particular, if we wish to grow in Christlikeness, we would do well to consider, or be aware of, not only how love thinks but how love transforms the use of our five physical senses (sight, sound, touch, taste, and smell).

Romans 12:1–2 says, "Therefore, I urge you, brothers and sisters, in view of God's mercy, to *offer your bodies as a living sacrifice*, holy and pleasing to God—this is your true and proper worship. Do not conform to the pattern of this world, but *be transformed by the renewing of your mind.*" Even Paul speaks of our bodies and minds as separate but connected. Though he speaks of the body first, one doesn't necessarily come before the other. He proceeds to speak of how our bodies have different parts for different purposes (vv. 3–8). Interestingly, he moves into describing love in action when the mind and body work together to glorify God.

The remaining verses (vv. 9–21) are worth quoting:

Let love be without hypocrisy. Abhor what is evil. Cling to what is good. Be kindly affectionate to one another with brotherly love, in honor giving preference to one another; not lagging in diligence, fervent in spirit, serving the Lord; rejoicing in hope, patient in tribulation, continuing steadfastly in prayer; distributing to the needs of the saints, given to hospitality. Bless those who persecute you; bless and do not curse. Rejoice with those who rejoice, and weep with those who weep. Be of the same mind toward one another. Do not

> set your mind on high things, but associate with the humble. Do not be wise in your own opinion. Repay no one evil for evil. Have regard for good things in the sight of all men. If it is possible, as much as depends on you, live peaceably with all men. Beloved, do not avenge yourselves, but rather give place to wrath; for it is written, "Vengeance is Mine, I will repay," says the Lord. Therefore "If your enemy is hungry, feed him; if he is thirsty, give him a drink; for in so doing you will heap coals of fire on his head." Do not be overcome by evil, but overcome evil with good. (NKJV)

That is the power of love. Here you have a wisdom of God, which the world is not naturally inclined to understand but nevertheless hungers for since each person is designed to receive and give love well. Of course, power has been perverted, but hope is at hand.

A general assumption is that great power automatically brings great corruption. But what set Superman apart? He had not only great power, but the greatest, rarest power of all: helping people with what he had. That is what Christians do—they help people. Profusely but joyously.

As new creations in Christ, we have been dressed with power from on high to love like Jesus. Everything He has is ours, including the power to love without preconditions. Therefore, we love people unconditionally from the limitless strength of God's selfless love, which bursts forth from the Holy Spirit within us. What matters most is that we utilize this power for good, doing God's will on earth, as He did Himself in Jesus, and continues to do through His Spirit in His people—people like you.

All of the senses are engaged in love, sometimes literally, sometimes metaphorically. The Holy Spirit trains us in using these special weapons of love to overpower evil by unleashing good.

Ready ... Set ... Love!

It's time to watch and explore the increase of love in our lives as we personally fill out and publicly spread out in selfless, Jesus-driven, Holy Spirit-powered love.

In a short time, spiritual babies become ready to take their first steps. Now that we're gaining understanding and living by faith, we're ready to walk in love. It's time to see love in action—to "walk in the way of love, just as Christ loved us" (Ephesians 5:2). First John 2:5 tells us, "This is how we know we are in Him: Whoever claims to live in Him must walk as Jesus did." John then emphasizes love as the heart of the Christian's calling.

Babies walk because they *are* growing up. A kid doesn't have to try to grow; they just grow. Likewise, a child of God (a believer) doesn't have to try to grow; they just grow. Growth looks like something. For the Christian this is most easily observed in how we treat people better than we used to.

It's time to walk a straight path through the narrow gate (Matthew 7:13–14). Love is the narrow gate (see verse 12). "So in everything, do to others what you would have them do to you, for this sums up the Law and the Prophets" (Matthew 7:12). *In everything ...*

Again, you have what you need to do this. You have the most important "ingredient"—the Holy Spirit—but you also have eyes, hands, feet, a voice, and so on. Anyone can love profoundly.

The new you can do what was once impossible because you now see like you've never seen before. In the physical, our eyes get worse over time. In the spiritual, our sight gets better if we seek to know Jesus above all. "Therefore we do not lose heart. Though outwardly we are wasting away, yet inwardly we are being renewed day by day" (2 Corinthians 4:16). Naturally, we're growing toward maturity because God is with us and we believe His promises.

The Holy Spirit is training our physical, mental, and spiritual health unto godliness with fresh revelations of love. His love is what grows us and changes our perspective and choices down to the tiniest details, yet with no religious detail about it. He does this through prayer, reading Scripture, other believers, church, missions, gifts, food, and so much more.

As we abide with Him, He opens our eyes to a stunning landscape of incredible heights and profound depths of love along with its grand effects and unlimited possibilities and real-life manifestations. Such a clear view maps the way to creatively and effectively engaging the world through renewed spiritual, mental, and physical senses of the highest level—permeated with supernatural, selfless, and unconditional Christlike love.

We're about to get practical about how such selflessness flows through every channel of our lives to love and glorify the Lord by gifting others with the life-changing blessing of His presence and power. Believe it or not, you're all set to love God, love your *new* self, and love every person. The new you is capable of keeping the two greatest commandments. If this wasn't true, Jesus would have said so.

He was asked, "Teacher, which is the greatest commandment in the Law?" Jesus replied:

> "'Love the Lord your God with all your heart and with all your soul and with all your mind.' This is the first and greatest commandment. And the second is like it: 'Love your neighbor as yourself.' All the Law and the Prophets hang on these two commandments." (Matthew 22:36–40)

We've already discussed how to keep the first by committing to abiding with Jesus in consistent communion (T1 & T2), and making this the top priority above all else. Presuming that's what we're doing, we're then prepared to love others naturally as an outflow of our intimacy with God. In this part and the next, we'll step into the second greatest commandment and see how it is indeed like the first, and how it all wraps up with a nice bow in the end.

Chapter 8:

Loving Every Person

It's time to love people like never before.

Christians should be known as the most radical lovers of God and people. And we should be getting worse! That is, to *progress* in love. This will happen if we gain understanding and live by faith. If we know He loves us, we will love Him too. If we do, we will love others as well. And when we love others, we are, in effect, loving the Lord. This is walking in love.

So if it's God we're spending time with, how could we *not* emerge treating others better? Do you think Daniel would have been as successful in public if he didn't pray with thanksgiving in private three times a day? Would he have been better prepared for the lion's den if he didn't have this background? He was prepared for the worst because He had been with the best.

Now is the time to reveal a selfless Christian in the making. If we were talking about baking cookies, this would be the moment they come out of the oven to the delight of others.

This reminds me of the pleasant smell of the bread bakery growing up. I could smell the fresh bread baking from blocks away. In biblical terms, Jesus is the bread of life (John 6:35). When we receive His Spirit, His bread is baking within us, so to speak, and that's why we give off the "aroma of Christ" (2 Corinthians 2:15–16), which smells even better than the bakery. Good smells make people want what they're smelling. We get to play an important role in delivering the goods to people by helping them not only smell but taste and see that the Lord is good (Psalm 34:8).

In less-appetizing but useful terms, if this book is a skeleton, this chapter is the flesh on the bones. We've talked a lot about love, but this is where things really begin to materialize. It's time to get our hands dirty in the real world, where problems happen, people don't like you, and opportunities await. Connecting with God isn't primarily about receiving His love for yourself in the privacy of your bedroom, or simply surviving in public, but becoming love and being a shining benefit to every person in every place.

We reveal our superpowers in public spaces by demonstrating selfless love in action through our eyes, ears, hands, and mouth. We see people, look and listen for opportunities, and reach out to help. We eagerly and cheerfully seek to recognize and make the most of every opportunity we have to uplift people with words, comfort them with touch, and free them from captivity with prayer and the wisdom of God.

How you treat people reveals what you actually believe about God. Consider this: If you're forgiven of your sins, what's the proof of your forgiveness? The great love you show. But little love shows little forgiveness (Luke 7:47). For instance, you may think God is forgiving, but if you refuse to show others mercy, it's fair to say you don't believe God is merciful. In addition, you may say God is love, but if you hate people, God is not in you and what you say is a lie (1 John 4).

First John is my favorite book in the Bible because it's unmistakably clear about how selfless love works. The consistent theme of John's writings is love, and he refers to himself affectionately as "the disciple whom Jesus loved." I'm happy to say you're also one whom He loves. This applies to everyone we see. Love sees people as loved by God and full of potential. We ought to love what He loves and do as He does.

Keep in mind that what you do to others, you are doing to Him, though indirectly (Matthew 25:40). That's why Jesus said the second greatest commandment is like the first. Mother Teresa recognized this.

We should too. God's creation deserves careful handling. We will give an answer to Him for how we managed our lives and relationships. We don't need to worry about this if we're abiding in Jesus. Instead, we get to enjoy going from glory to glory. If you haven't already, you'll soon discover how fun it is to watch God's love impact a person through His power vested in you.

If you currently find it difficult to love people, just keep reading. It'll get easier. Better yet, it gets enjoyable! If you wish to get better at love, it's a good sign: your heart is being purified by the Lord already and a promising future is at hand. There may be some very exciting changes just around the corner. You're filling out—your branches are becoming longer and stronger and your roots are spreading out to make a solid base in preparation for more growth to come. Sometimes all we need for the next big step is a few stories.

Jesus used stories effectively. People generally learn well through illustration; I know I do. Now I'll share several personal, concrete examples of love in action. My hope is that by giving a more vivid portrayal of the love I've been describing, you'll catch a vision for selfless-sufficient living and find the strength to walk the extra mile, in His steps.

Love Illustrated Relationally: Spouse

The Lord has taught me to see my wife as His precious daughter. You wouldn't mistreat the King's daughter, right?

Also, since I'm with her more than anyone else, she just so happens to be my best opportunity at showing love. Especially after being together for several years, when the initial infatuation wears off and you get to know all the things you didn't have time to discover in the beginning. People are complex and evolving, but the more you are with them, the more comfortable you get and the easier it is to be yourself around them. So hopefully we're an in-good-shape kind of tree!

Mother Teresa said, "It is easy to love the people far away. It is not always easy to love those close to us. It is easier to give a cup of rice to relieve hunger than to relieve the loneliness and pain of someone unloved in our own home. Bring love into your home for this is where our love for each other must start."[23]

My wife said something similar: "Usually people you're the most comfortable with, you do the least for."

People who are nice outside the home but bash their spouse when alone make it clear they're play actors in public. The real you is most evident at home in how you treat your spouse and children, if you have them, and in how you choose to spend your time at home, whether you live with others or by yourself.

I've learned that if I treat my spouse right, it's easier to treat everyone else right too. And the more I do it, the easier it gets. However, if I live for myself and ignore or mistreat her, this gradually spills over into how I see or fail to see others. Of course, the deeper root of the problem lies in the failure to connect with God on a deeper level. But as we grow in love, many things begin to change—and continue to change (for the better)—about how we treat those closest to us.

Love makes our many impulses serve as cues to love somebody. For example, if you're thirsty, you're inclined to find a drink, but love takes it further. Let's say I'm with my wife when I get thirsty. *Love* uses my thirst as a cue to gauge whether or not *she* is thirsty, and if she is, I serve her before I serve myself. That is what love does—it isn't self-seeking so much as it proactively considers how it may serve others. If you do this long enough, it becomes a *heavenly habit*. Next thing you know, you're not particularly conscious of the fact that you're doing a loving deed because as far as you're concerned, you're not even trying!

Many opportunities arise. If I want the first bite, I give it to her. If I want the last bite, I give it to her. If I need to put my coat on, I help with hers. If I want to get in the car quickly because it's cold outside, I get her door first so she can get inside sooner. When it isn't cold, I still get the door because love is courteous and kind. If I'm hot, I should ask my wife if I can open the window, but if she's cold, I will compromise. Knowing her, she would insist on opening the window for my benefit, but I would stubbornly insist on what's comfortable for her. This is how love fights.

Sometimes I'm caught off guard by how terribly long it's been since I took a good look into my wife's eyes. It's love that causes this realization and takes the time to look your spouse in the eyes and show that you see them. It reaches for their hand while working through disagreements. Sometimes we *want* a hug to feel better, but love *gives* hugs to melt away the stresses and anxieties of others. It doesn't wait to receive affection; it gives it first, like God's first love for us (1 John 4:19).

Love expresses kindness with words such as *please, thank you*, and *I love you*—without expecting a canned response. It says their name and regularly pours on terms of endearment, ones reserved only for the two of you. Love asks how they're doing and listens to the response. When you actively listen to someone, it shows them you care. That they're worth your time. Love takes notice of opportunities to actively pray, comfort, and encourage. It speaks the truth gently, not aggressively.

Love dines together. It lifts up thanks to God for great company and food. Love moves you to pray with your spouse *daily*. You've probably heard the saying "Families that pray together stay together." In addition, love doesn't *help* with chores, it has a responsibility and privilege to *do* chores. For example, I don't "help" my wife dry the dishes, as if washing and drying was her chore. No, we share our home, therefore we share the work. She might clean the kitchen, but I clean the bathroom because we're on a team that keeps the house clean. We both work hard and need rest, so we share the burdens.

It's okay to have preferences, make compromises, and do self-sacrificial things. For instance, I prefer drying dishes over washing them. My wife would rather wash. So it works out nicely for the both of us. As for compromise or self-sacrifice, let's say cleaning the toilet is not the most desirable duty, but, for that reason, I am happy to do it so my wife doesn't have to. Likewise, I take the garbage out because it gets heavy and stinky; that way she doesn't have to deal with the weight of the stank. This actually brings me joy because it's done in love. Love considers others. Where there's love, there's joy. The problem comes when we're self-serving and expecting someone to do something we won't do ourselves.

Of course, there are certain things love *doesn't* do in a relationship, such as "spouse bashing," whether at home or at work. I hear this so much, and it saddens me every time because it indicates they don't know their worth or their spouse's. Not to mention, it doesn't speak well of the person saying it, and I'm sure their spouse wouldn't be happy to hear it. If this is a struggle for you, take heart. It is possible to say only good things about your spouse.

Long ago, my wife and I resolved to never say anything bad about each other to anyone, and neither one of us have faltered in this. If we have an issue, we sort it out between the two of us. Quite frankly, it's no one else's business. Love is committed to respectfulness, faithfulness, and actively doing what's beneficial to a positively growing marital union.

Recently, my wife's hands have been dry and cracked, so much so that she couldn't wash the dishes. Love takes over. I normally dry, but I washed too until her hands healed. Love goes the extra mile. Love pays attention. I knew she wasn't using lotion regularly enough. One day I called her at work and reminded her to put lotion on. I later found out she forgot. So I tried again, but this time I stayed on the line until she did.

These are all examples of how God is with me, growing me in love, while I'm with my wife. Basically, I'm in communion with Him whether inside my room or outside it because He's with me wherever I go (Joshua 1:9). Furthermore, the Holy Spirit is in me, which means He's portable—not on a six-foot cord! Naturally, this inward reality should be visibly manifest.

My wife and I see God in each other. Many times I have been humbled by her love, support, and encouragement. I have told her I don't know much about a lot, but she says I know a lot about what matters. How adorable is that?

She couldn't be such a sweetheart if love wasn't in her heart. She takes it to the next level and tells me things like how she wishes she'd had a dad like me growing up because she sees the love I show the kids and what a wonderful relationship I have with them. She's told me on several occasions I'm the most loving person she knows, so much so she has been moved to *tears*. I appreciate this. She clearly has the gift of encouragement.

It's a blessing to have a spouse who says such things about you. I'm not looking for applause by writing this, and I realize I may run the risk of seeming pretentious in some ways, but my goal in stating these things is to show that love changes things. It affects people! Love is real, and it makes a merry marriage. It may be an endangered species in your sphere, but it does exist and it can overtake your sphere for God's glory.

If you're surrounded by darkness, even the smallest light will make a huge difference. The power to make a positive difference in a person's life resides within you for the giving. It may be hard or discouraging at first, but it gets easier relatively quickly. My wife and I have both seen how love expressed in our relationship can happen if we remain in Jesus. When we do, love momentum is activated. Not unlike the snowball effect—the more it rolls, the bigger it gets. As we roll with the Spirit, love moves in action and grows in strength.

I could continue, but the last thing I'll say is this: The going may get tough, but love is stronger. When things get hard, touch softens things. I remember a time when my wife and I had a disagreement. I could feel my blood pressure rising, but the Holy Spirit quickly settled me. I was suddenly compelled to wash and massage her feet. Know this: It is impossible to argue when you're getting a foot massage! I think we would all agree that being the recipient of such love generally inspires an attitude of thanks and better behavior (Matthew 5:16).

After her massage, my wife was inspired to give the same service to me. I wasn't looking for it, but I gladly received it. In a sense, this is what "love covers a multitude of sins" means (1 Peter 4:8). Because love begets love. This ended up being absolutely transformative for both of us. Just like that, harmony was restored. Not because I did something great, but because we know God, who does great things. It's His work, not ours, lest we boast and become proud.

Second Timothy 1:6–7 tells us, "Fan into flame the gift of God, which is in you through the laying on of my hands. For the Spirit God gave us does not make us timid, but gives us power, love and self-discipline." Our instruments of righteousness are God's chosen means of powerfully delivering selfless love through super-powered words of wisdom, tender touch, and considerate choices, all of which benefit others to the glory of God.

Love Illustrated Relationally: Children

Children learn to be like Jesus when they're around Spirit-filled believers. If we don't realize this and fail to connect with God, we'll have an identity crisis until we do. The same goes for our children. Furthermore, since our "mini-mes" are heavily influenced by our example, what they see in us will produce *something* in them. In other words, they'll copy some good or bad habits and outright reject others. They're learning to be like us when they're around us. Just the other day, I saw a man worshiping at church, clapping his hands and singing, and his son was observing this and began doing the same.

Being a parent isn't solely about physical reproduction but multiplying *love*—the image of God—on earth. God is love, and we are made to love. Therefore, we have the privilege and responsibility of raising our children in the instruction of the Lord. The apostle Paul says it this way: "Do not exasperate your children; instead, bring them up in the training and instruction of the Lord" (Ephesians 6:4). The purpose or goal of our instruction is love (1 Timothy 1:5).

Our children learn, or don't learn, this from our example. They'll develop physical characteristics and personality traits that resemble ours. It's up to us to give them their best shot at life by demonstrating a life of love. One of the best gifts a child can receive is parents who love each other in front of them. Maybe because it's easier for kids to succeed at growing healthily if they can see love in action on a daily basis between the two biggest influencers of their development.

I had my first child when I was seventeen. It's a long story. Let's just say I was an expert at selfishness, but nothing forced me to get my mind off of myself like a child did. As unprepared as I was, God knew I desired to rise to the occasion successfully. So He blessed me with strength to serve. He drew love out of me through His Spirit. Many things have changed over the years, but increasing love is a constant.

For example, I've gone through a few seasons of swearing in my lifetime. It never felt natural. I refused to do it around the kids, but I knew it needed to stop altogether since it wasn't in line with the godly character I was after. So I stopped. Because love was growing in me, and love doesn't have a reason to cuss.

As a result, my children are predisposed to speaking cleanly. Not only because I don't do it, but because we talk about why it's a good idea not to. It isn't about controlling their actions by force. Love doesn't scare or dominate people; it compels and frees them. The key is to help children *want* what's good for everyone and *freely* choose it. Of course, our instructions won't stick if we lack integrity. If I tell them swearing is wrong but they hear me doing it, I'm probably doing more harm than if I hadn't said so.

This reminds me of a time I went through a season of drinking alcohol. I purposed not to have it around the kids or at home. But I wasn't trying to hide it. My son caught wind of this and asked me if it was true that I drink. I could tell he was concerned. So I explained that it's something you can do more or less responsibly, and I assured him it wasn't an issue for me. But he wasn't having it. I could sense his displeasure. He wasn't convinced it was a good thing.

Come to think of it, I wasn't either. So I reconsidered what I was doing because I was sensitive to my son's concern. I didn't think alcohol was a problem for me, but it was for him, and that was enough to make me stop. Not wishing to make him stumble, I decided to quit drinking. *Love* compelled me. When I told him about my decision, he was delighted. I was happy that he was happy.

Love proactively promotes positivity. It's so important to talk with kids about selfless love, and how to identify opportunities and learn from mistakes. Better than picking on them and never getting real. Might as well share from my storehouse of experiences and show them tried and true ways of being a Christian in this world. That would probably help them grow. A little sound teaching and sincere living goes a long way. Seize the moments.

For years I've trained the kids to express interest in others by asking questions in conversations, because I know the natural inclination of a person is to talk about themselves. I've seen the fruit of this training. I told the kids I don't need them to ask me how my day was. My feelings aren't hurt if they don't. The point of the training isn't to make me feel better or to give me the mic so I can take the stage and finally talk about myself. No, I told them the agenda is to foster love in their lives. To help sharpen the tools they have for the purpose of effectively loving people with Christlike love.

I don't consider these things duties or forced actions because I believe love happens when you've resolved to seek the Lord. After all, love can't help but do these types of things through you when you're following Jesus the best way you know how. When you abide, you don't have to try. You don't worry because love *is* increasing. Just be with Him. Selfless-sufficient living is about His presence, not your performance. Seeking His presence first and living by the Spirit will lead you into many acts of love with your children.

Exactly what this looks like will vary from person to person. This isn't a science, nor is it a religious list of specific duties to be performed. Rather, it's the outflow of intimacy with God. Love has revolutionized everything about my life and relationships. I recognize the presence of His love in my life and the way it touches every detail.

I mentioned earlier how easily we can fall into the trap of inattention with our spouses. Next thing you know, we haven't looked at them—really looked at them—or held them for longer than we'd like to admit. The same thing happens with children too. Sometimes I'm shocked by how long it's been since I took a good look at my own kids or gave them a good squeeze.

Kids love attention because it tells them you see them and they're worth your time. I take advantage of many ways to show them they're deserving of my attention. Such as limiting my cell phone usage around them. They rarely see my phone. Also, I pray with them. At night, we reserve our final moments before sleep for spiritual conversations and prayer. I have thrown in foot massages and ear rubs too. They can't get over how amazing foot massages are. And the first time my younger son got an earlobe massage, he immediately relaxed and fell asleep. I often stay with them until they're asleep. I never want to give the impression that I'm in a hurry to do other things. Love is present.

Your example and teaching affect your children's choices. For instance, my younger son started giving me occasional back massages. He did this because he received them first. He learned how great they are and used that knowledge as a tool for happily expressing his affection for me. This brought joy to my heart. Not only because a massage feels good, but because I understood the revelation of love at work in his life.

Likewise, my eldest son discovered the joy of helping others through the simple act of getting the door. What goes into such a choice? A few things. First and foremost, he is a believer, therefore his spirit is receptive to love. In addition, he has seen love in action; he has seen me get the door for my wife countless times. Also, I explained such an action is a way of paying respect and honor to a woman. Once upon a time, my wife, mother, and grandmother went to a clothing store and brought my son with them. When they got back home, my mom gleamed as she talked about how well-mannered my son was—he got the doors for them! Naturally, I was happy to hear that. The fruitfulness of children is sweet to the soul: "A wise son brings joy to his father" (Proverbs 10:1).

Love protects children, celebrates their successes, patiently guides them through difficulties, and calls out their potential through prayer. Touch makes a difference, but words make a big difference too. Love exchanges complaints for compliments, discouragement for encouragement, and self-centeredness for Christ-centeredness. Love doesn't seek to control through hitting and yelling. If you say mean things to your spouse, whether in front of your children or away from them, your words will create an atmosphere of negative energy. If a parent is caught up in negativity, it will inevitably spill over to their children's detriment—unless love is present.

Love is there when parents are in prayer. Prayer makes a positive difference not only in yourself but especially in the lives of your children. But most things are out of your control. Which is fine because we depend on a competent God. God is in control, and His powers can reach further than our arms. We should be happy about this, not stressed about what we can't control. We have the privilege of participating in spreading love through prayer.

Fortunately, there are too many examples to tell. All of this to say, *love* has given me the best relationship possible with my children. I have seen God work wonders in their lives. After all these years we still tell each other "I love you." They are comfortable talking with me about anything. Rarely have I needed to correct them, ground them, or take away special privileges. We have a great relationship. They know I'm proud of them. I tell them often. I speak the truth in love, teaching them of all the things I've been writing about in this book. They see my passion for God, my love for my wife, and my heart for their welfare.

As much as I may influence the lives of my children, I can't take credit or personal responsibility for the choices they make or fail to make. It is God who grows us in love and guides us through trouble. I can only give them the best shot I can to do what they will. Not to mention, all of us are impacted by more than one person. Hopefully, the biggest impact is the healthiest one. It depends on what we depend on.

Love Illustrated Relationally: Other Family

Ironically, I was reared in a Christian home but didn't have a good grip on the gospel. Growing up, I felt more like a victim than a victorious Christian. My parents raised me the best they could, but my painful perspective was speaking louder than truth. This was one of my biggest gripes: they did foster care for most of my adolescence. I'm not saying foster care is a bad thing, but I thought it was at the time. My parents only sought to make a positive difference. I ended up living with a total of twenty foster kids over the years. Fed up, I finally told my parents it was ruining my life. So they stopped. And I walked away skilled at negativity.

My parents were busy and our schedules were loaded between work, school, church, recreational activities, vacations, and so on. What little time I had at home was spent doing homework, doing chores, hypnotized in front of a TV screen, or hiding away in my room. Time was divided up between all these things and the foster kids, with nothing left but scraps under the table for me. I felt lonely. Jealous. Angry. Anxious. I would self-medicate with sugar, movies, video games, and sports. I would hang out with friends and get into trouble. Though I always felt an undercurrent of spiritual desire to connect with God.

I tried to make strides and sometimes I did, but they were always short lived. The deeper I dove into a variety of spiritual books, the more I felt like I was drowning. Just when I thought one thing was clear, something else made it frosty. I needed a good defrost. I heard about love (rarely), and I could sing "Jesus Loves Me," but I didn't understand. I didn't actually know God intimately, therefore I couldn't comprehend the selfless nature of love. I didn't know how to live by faith, and I didn't experience the power of the Holy Spirit. All I knew was I was unhappy.

I had deep struggles with anxiety and depression, but I don't blame my parents for this. I needed a revelation of truth just like everyone else does in whatever situation they're in with whomever. It's all the same: We need to know the love of God if we'll ever find refuge above the tsunami waves of our circumstances.

When love came into my life, it changed everything, including the way I see my parents.

If I wish to be selfish, I can resent my parents for "what they put me through," as if their goal was to torment me. I can care more about my well-being and care less about the welfare of the foster kids. I can get upset about the time my parents gave to them instead of me, discarding the fact that some of these kids didn't even *have* a parent because they were disowned. I can take it all personally and get offended, but where's the love in that?

My parents have expressed their regrets on several occasions. They have taken many of my poor choices and painful outcomes personally, as if they were the cause of them. This is dangerous for them because nothing paralyzes a person like living under the heavy burden of guilt does. Jesus lightens the load, but selfish people want others under a heavier load. It says, "You brought this upon yourself." Selfishness wants people to feel bad. It feels sorry for itself and says things like, "I can't believe you did this to me." It doesn't want perpetrators to get off the hook, and if they do they must pay every penny first. It says, "You *should* be sorry," and "You broke my trust. It will take me a long time to recover from this."

What does love do? It takes away the burdens just like Jesus does.

185

This means I will refuse to hold my parents accountable to any misdeed. Remember, love says, "You don't owe me anything." It lays down its life to set others free. If the blood of Jesus covers me with forgiveness, what right do I have to harbor hatred toward anyone? Instead, love gives them the benefit of the doubt and sees them for their worth and potential as determined by God.

Selfishness and self-pity make it difficult to see the good in people. My parents have done many things right. But I couldn't fully appreciate that until love came into my heart. Before, I was fixated on things I didn't like. After, I was fixated on Truth. Philippians 4:8 tells us, "Whatever is true, whatever is noble, whatever is right, whatever is pure, whatever is lovely, whatever is admirable—if anything is excellent or praiseworthy—think about such things."

In other words, love is positive! It appreciates what's good and counts its blessings. Love is thankful. Now I readily recognize how my parents have provided for me. They're the most generous people I know—to a fault! They mean well and want what's best for me. No question about it. They have poured out theirs hearts to God on my behalf. They have expressed their concerns and celebrated my successes.

I was happy to release them from the burdens they were carrying by assuring them I forgive them for everything they regret. I've thanked them for doing their best and supporting my interests. I love them no matter what, and as they age I will continue caring for them. I thank God for my parents.

Even if they didn't do all these wonderful things, I wouldn't have a reason to withhold love from them. Jesus didn't withhold His love from us while we were sinners, so how can I possibly justify doing so if He didn't?

Then there is Grandma. Unbeknownst to me, my heart would swell up with love for her. Since my grandparents lived several states away, I didn't see them much when I was a child, but the older I got, the closer they moved. I have fond memories of board games, holiday treats, and sleepovers. I always enjoyed her company but was mostly concerned with myself. When her health started failing, my compassion exploded. Now I see things differently—things I used to miss.

I notice when she has trouble breathing and I gently rub her back. I give her hugs, help her down the stairs, and escort her to the car. When my grandparents arrive in the winter, I manage the snow and ice hazard by laying down the "red carpet" to improve traction. I assist her with her oxygen bag. I pray for her. I enjoy giving handcrafted birthday cards, writing heartfelt messages, and making an occasional surprise phone call.

She knows I can sing a mean birthday song! I've written a poem and a song for her, and she is convinced everyone needs to hear these. She's often moved to tears of gratitude for these things. My grandma is a sweetheart with a big heart, and it's fun to draw that out with gifts. We love each other deeply. I'm happy to help her, and glad to see her walking with God.

But it wasn't always like that. I'm sad to say I wasn't even thinking about loving her for many years. I was stuck in selfishness—only thinking about my life and what I was going through, or what I needed to succeed. Fortunately, when you seek God regularly and get a revelation, selfless love will rise to the occasion and reach out to others. Now I can't help but love her. It's not like I am trying to "do the Christian thing" either. It is unforced; I'm simply learning the joy of caring for and bonding with people.

Of course, my grandpa is also an honorable mention. Grandpa is a gentleman. He cares for my grandma with all he's got. He drives carefully, treats people with respect, and will find a way to make you laugh. I have good memories of him tickling me out of "his chair" and attending many of my golf tournaments. He's a classic example of love.

As we walk with God, His Holy Spirit will teach us how to love everyone.

Love Illustrated Relationally: Coworkers

It all started with what I refer to as "The Orange Story." When all this love stuff was relatively new for me, I was preparing to face off with a coworker who had a rough and tough reputation. I overheard the brash manner in which she threw people around. Quite frankly, I wanted to show her I wasn't intimidated. I knew she would come at me eventually. When she did, I was prepared and fired back a feisty email. I was proud of my clever rebuttal, but my manager wasn't. He had a few words with me but sympathized with the challenge, and encouraged me to respond more carefully next time. Little did I know, God was doing a work in me. In a moment, the light bulb turned on.

She was coming back to her desk from the break room when she told me, "Someone stole my orange. I can't believe it." She said she had been looking forward to it all morning but someone took it from the fridge. "I've been trying to take more vitamin C since my son is sick." Not to mention, she recently came back to work after being on disability due to a serious medical incident that nearly took her life. Who was I to take a defensive stance against her?

My heart quickly softened toward her. I sensed the sensitivity under the hard shell, and was filled with compassion. It occurred to me that I could do something to help (props to the Holy Spirit). Without telling her my intention, I left the office and made a long but satisfying trip to the cafeteria in search of an orange. I gladly purchased it and made my way back to the office and nonchalantly placed the orange on her desk.

She was very pleased and said, "Thank you. You didn't have to do that," but I told her it was my pleasure. And it was true; I felt a surge of strength to serve, with joy, lasting every step. This is a good because "God loves a cheerful giver" (2 Corinthians 9:7). The best part is this wasn't a struggle or an obligation. Rather, a good work sprung naturally from the Holy Spirit, as does every good deed. The cheer comes if you are abiding in Christ.

Later, she told me this made her day. Small things can make a big difference, good or bad. I could have done nothing about the stolen orange. I could have thought, *Serves her right*. Instead, one act of free-flowing love after another proceeded to overtake the walls once standing between us. We became friends.

Not until my blinders were removed could I see how clearly lovable she is to God. Not because of things she did or didn't do, but because love is without condition. She owes me nothing. All I know is God loves her, His Spirit lives inside me, and she has great potential in Him. Do my actions prove this to her? Perhaps not at all times, but getting my point across, being acknowledged, and finding appreciation isn't the point. It's all about love—giving love unconditionally, without expectation of return or hope for an applause. In most cases, people just so happen to respond incredibly well to selfless love.

Before I was established in such love, few of my coworkers knew I was a Christian. Fast forward several years. Now I have more coworkers than all of my previous jobs combined, and most of them in my department know I'm a Christian. Many outside my department know this too. What changed? Is it because I walk around wearing a Christian T-shirt? No (I don't). Is it because I greet everyone saying, "Hi, I'm Ben, and I'm a Christian"? Nope (I don't). Or is it because I love people? (I do!)

In the past, I didn't know how to get God into the conversation without feeling terribly awkward. Of course, if I failed to "witness," I assumed I was lacking courage and felt guilty as a result. Thankfully, I don't have that anxiety anymore because I understand the "God saves, I love." So I follow the Holy Spirit's lead and timing, and I operate in His power with the boldness He provides. He literally prompts me, as He did in The Orange Story, when it's time to walk through the open door and share my faith with others.

Giving that orange was like planting a seed that led to greater love and prayer. That's witnessing. That's the difference between religion and love. Religion is motivated by fear and feels pressured to act and relieved when it does, but the pressure is off with the easy yoke of Jesus because the driving force is love, in which there is no fear. Love is excited to help somebody and share Jesus. Plain and simple: Love is at the heart of a Christian lifestyle.

People may have heard about God's love, but do they experience it? Have they experienced it through *you?*

Generally speaking, people don't want to hear what you think unless they know you care about them first. Especially if it's God you want to talk about. It's love that opens the door to communicating your Christian faith at work. I understand company policies are in place and they're not usually conducive to talking about such things. But don't worry. The Spirit will guide you in what to say, when to say it, and to whom you should say it (Luke 12:12).

I've learned that love can move like a ninja and maneuver through any obstacle. If Jesus could slip away unscathed from a crowd attempting to throw Him off a cliff for something He said (Luke 4:28–30), we can probably afford to slide in a word or two about Jesus at work. Besides, there's no law against the fruit of the Spirit (Galatians 5:22–23). The important thing is that you recognize the opportunities around you and capitalize on them, without fear. (1 Peter 3:8–22 provides great instruction applicable to the workplace.)

I've had the privilege of experiencing a combination of short-term and long-term relationships at my job, and I can appreciate how it takes time to get to know somebody. I realize it takes wisdom and great care to get closer to a person's heart. That said, the goal isn't to *tell* them as soon as possible that I'm a Christian and they should be too; the goal is to *show* them, through my eyes, smile, words, tone, touch, and so on, that God loves them.

Some people are deceived and need someone to intercede. Some people are in pain and need comfort. Others are stuck in deception and need clarity. There are discouraged people in need of encouragement. Depressed people are thirsty for a kind word. Some are too comfortable, or idle, and need a poke. Some are stressed and could use a laugh. And some are stuck in pride and need humbling and prayer. Whatever it is, love is here to help free people from anything threatening to keep them out of God's presence. There is no greater joy and no better future promise than what Jesus offers. But not everyone knows this. That's why we're here, to spread the good news of the gospel of Jesus Christ, and what better way than through Christlike love?

I've been compelled by love in the workplace on countless occasions, and I've had the pleasure of seeing how it shifts the atmosphere. It's love that produced qualities in me that my coworkers compared to none other than Mister Rogers. (Well, okay, maybe the cardigan had something to do with it ...)

Anyway, when you let love happen in your life, people will take notice. For example, I had someone come up to me and say, "I noticed you don't gossip. I'm learning from you." I had another person approach me and ask, "How do you stay so calm?" Several have commented on my calmness and how I never get upset. I've had people apologize for swearing around me because they know I don't do it. Someone said, "My whole world would fall apart if I heard you swear.

Everything I know about you would go out the window." That statement makes a strong case for the importance of a consistent witness.

People have said a lot of nice things about me and how happy, positive, and kind I am. When they could do their work with others, I was their first choice. I have been told, "I'm thankful for you," and "Everyone loves Ben." In the face of the most minor "infractions," people get protective of me and say things like, "Don't talk to him that way!" I've even heard this one: "I hate all of you! Except Ben."

I think most of my coworkers have these feelings toward me because I show them respect and kindness. I listen to them, give compliments, and make them laugh. I give gifts, whether food, gift cards, prayers, or Post-it notes with Bible verses. I tell stories about things God has shown me. I pray for coworkers and their dreams.

I even pray for them *in* my dreams. Some of these were intense dreams of deliverance, and others issue a warning sign. I taught one of my coworkers how to pray in an unpleasant dream, calling on the name of Jesus, and she recently reported that she had a bad dream and couldn't say His name at first but eventually did and the dream stopped.

Then there was my former coworker who wanted the peace I had, and I taught her how to ask Jesus into her heart and she did that night at home. I've shared tears with others and helped a few through panic attacks. I've given hugs and friendly pats on the back if one of my guys is looking down. I tell them I appreciate them and their hard work. I've helped a few coworkers navigate through some immigration details with pertinent information, prayers, and referrals. One in particular came through a bind and was very grateful for my involvement, saying, "Your prayers made all the difference," and he gave me a very thoughtful gift in return. I've taken advantage of many opportunities to encourage fellow Christian coworkers in their faith. There are so many stories I could tell, as is the case when you begin to lose yourself to love.

It feels weird writing these things about myself, but I think it's necessary because you have to understand this wasn't how it used to be for me. I didn't like people. I was skilled at making fun of them. People didn't like me at work because I was up and down, cocky and annoying. A few times I got into strong disagreements with coworkers. I used vulgar language and did some things that would have gotten me fired if management knew about it. I pulled off many stupid stunts and almost got myself and others hurt in the process. This isn't an exaggeration.

I know, it sounds like a different person than the one I just described—because it is! In Christ, all things are made new. Most of my coworkers don't know about my caterpillar past, but that's okay because I'm a butterfly now. So what about the caterpillar? I'm not saying I do everything perfectly (I don't), but I am saying *love changes something about everything.*

It is love that stirs up more positivity and less negativity. I've noticed how acts of kindness are contagious; witnessing good deeds inspires others to do the same.

Persistent love is the most persuasive witness and promoter of Christian faith. If your selfless love has stood the test of time, hungry people will take notice and line up for the bread of life. They might not know exactly what they came for or what exactly they're getting, but they receive it all the same.

Most people respond well to Christian love, but some are turned off or avoidant. In my experience, the latter is a rarity. Some people refuse to believe or choose love, but it's not my job to save them; God saves (2 Timothy 1:9–10). In addition, for those who do believe, it's not my job to sanctify them; that's what the Holy Spirit does (Romans 15:16). It is my job, however, to love people and trust God with the rest.

Christians are in the business of scattering seeds of love, but sowing seeds doesn't guarantee a healthy crop (Matthew 13:1–18). This doesn't mean we did something wrong by sowing. Rather, the problem comes when we don't sow at all. How will love grow if we don't sow? A famous quote by former hockey legend Wayne Gretzky says it well: "You miss 100 percent of the shots you never take."[24] Likewise, if we never spread love, there will be a crop catastrophe. We've been given seed to sow wherever we go, especially in the workplace, where most of us spend a considerable portion of our lifetime.

Love Illustrated Relationally: Strangers

Once I started growing in love, I began seeing people I normally would have missed. A new normal was unfolding.

For instance, love has opened the door to many interactions within the apartment complex. One time I had a dream about our beloved maintenance man. He was in a motorcycle accident a few years back and his body suffered the consequences, but he was healthier and doing well in my dream. I ran into him early the next morning and told him about it. I often encourage him with a kind word and a friendly touch on the back. Maybe he thought this was a bit odd, but that isn't bad; he often tells my wife and me that we're his favorite. This must mean he appreciates the attention. People *love* love.

I told another one of the maintenance guys how much I appreciated his hard work when he was dealing with the messy garbage area. I always smiled and said hi when I saw him. One day, my car battery died and I didn't know how I was going to get to work. It isn't the job of the busy maintenance guys to help with resident car maintenance, but this guy did; he jumped my car. I was surprised when he told me, "I wouldn't have done it for anyone else."

Then it clicked with me: his sentiment was due to our previously positive interactions. I thought, *Wow, that is amazing.* We've had several maintenance-related issues in the past, but my wife and I committed to treating staff kindly at all times. They have to hear a lot of complaints; we take this into consideration and do what we can to make their jobs more enjoyable.

In addition, I've met people and prayed for them in the laundry room. It's amazing how extraordinary things happen in ordinary places when you do life with God and walk in love. In the past, it was only going to the laundry room and doing a chore. Now it's like a mission field in there.

This just isn't the kind of stuff most of us are expecting when we go about our daily duties, but love changes everything. Jesus said, "It is more blessed to give than to receive" (Acts 20:35). The emphasis is on giving, but, at the same time, what He said also qualifies receiving as a blessed thing too. Love is a blessing all around, whether you're giving it or receiving it.

I know what a blessing it is to be on the receiving end of love. Not only through God in the secret place, but also through his people in public places. Of course, there are many examples, but the earliest, most powerful example that comes to mind is when I was a teenage dad, taking my son out to a restaurant. Money was tight, but I wanted to do something special for him. After eating, we were informed someone paid for our meal! That, my friend, is the tangible love of God.

Loving the Vulnerable

Another story, from years ago, comes to mind in which my wife is the starring lover. We were exploring the city and had just stepped off the train when we took notice of a blind woman. She seemed lost and confused. I was ready to pass her by just as so many others did, but my beautiful wife immediately moved in to assist her. It turned out the woman was trying to get to a certain bus but wasn't sure where to go.

We helped her find her bus. My wife's sincere love and gentleness dazzled me as she locked arms with this woman, guided her to the bus, and confirmed with the driver it was the right one.

The woman was grateful for the help. I was convicted of my inaction, but I was proud of and inspired by my amazing wife. A simple act of care and compassion does wonders. Not only for the one cared for, but the person caring and the people witnessing. Compassion shifts the environment and seasons life with the good stuff.

Matthew 5:14–16 tells us, "You are the light of the world. A town built on a hill cannot be hidden. Neither do people light a lamp and put it under a bowl. Instead they put it on its stand, and it gives light to everyone in the house. In the same way, let your light shine before others, that they may see your good deeds and glorify your Father in heaven." We are "the salt of the earth," but if salt loses its saltiness, what is it good for? Nothing! (Matthew 5:13).

We were made to love. To shine as lights in a dark world (Matthew 5:14). When the light is turned on inside us, selfishness can no longer hide our potential. We are carriers of light dispelling the darkness.

The Son of God appeared and destroyed the devil's work (1 John 3:8). Now we get to join Him in reminding darkness daily that Jesus won. As God's children in this world, we have an insatiable desire for our Father's love to be known through what can be shown. Therefore, above all, we love each other deeply (1 Peter 4:8).

Loving Those Discriminated Against

These are difficult times for many in America. I can't address them all, but I will mention a few: African Americans, Hispanics, and the LGBT, and issues related to them such as racism, immigration, and sexual orientation.

I grew up in a small, predominantly white city, though my best friend was biracial. Once I moved to the metro area, the demographics changed drastically. This was new for me. Growing up, my friends and I made some stupid comments and cracked some bad jokes. We were ignorant. As an adult, I knew better. With love in my heart, I didn't have any trouble making friends. I'm privileged to experience first-hand the magnificent and fascinating diversity of cultures and people that God has created equally in His image. I enjoy having a variety of friends because it's a slice of heaven on earth. Revelation 7:9 says, "There before me was a great multitude that no one could count, from every nation, tribe, people and language, standing before the throne and before the Lamb," worshiping God.

Sadly, in this present hour of darkness, many are lacking love and expressing hatred. Many of my friends could tell you several stories about times they were oppressed. Evil stirs up fear and chaos, but love drives out fear by actively making peace (1 John 4:18; James 3:17; Romans 12:18).

Once upon a time, I was in a retail store and made my way to the restroom. As I passed by the customer service counter, I noticed a young African-American man working at the counter. As soon as I entered the bathroom, I received a strong impression to bless him concerning the racism issue. I knew the Holy Spirit was telling me this, because I've learned to discern His voice.

After washing my hands, I approached the man and he asked how he could help me. I put my elbows on the counter, lowered my head below his eye level, and looked at him with sincerity as I emphatically expressed, "Hey, I just wanted to say sorry about all the racism stuff in the news …"

He looked surprised.

"I just want to say I love you, man." We shook hands.

He was like, "Wow. Thank you. I needed that. Seriously."

I replied, "Yeah?"

He said, "Yeah, more than you know."

I continued, "It just came on me and I needed to say it. I know we don't even know each other, but I know I love you, man."

He said, "I love you too, man. It took a lot for you to come up here and say that."

We exchanged names. He wanted some more brotherly love, so we shook hands again. I could tell this gesture meant a lot to him; God knew it would.

When I got back to my wife, she wondered why I was beaming. I told her what happened. She said she was so happy I'm her husband and that she was proud of me. That she would have loved it if someone came up to her to say that.

I did something similar when I called a customer service line and spoke with a middle-aged African-American woman. I addressed the racism issue and apologized. I told her I wanted her to know that some people really care. I prayed for her. She was very pleased and even said, "God bless you."

It's not just customer service, and it's not just a phone call. There's a person at the other end of the counter, or the other end of the line, and God loves them and so should I. I may be the customer, but I'm here to serve too. And it's such a joy to bless others. People love being respected and appreciated.

What if Mister Rogers didn't wash an African-American man's feet on national TV (twice) because it wasn't popular? Then François

Clemmons (Officer Clemmons on *Mister Rogers' Neighborhood*) wouldn't have had "one of the most meaningful experiences"[25] he ever had, and thousands, if not millions, would have missed out on a powerfully unifying act of love. Love is the right thing to do.

Earlier I mentioned growing up in a small town. At that time, I didn't see much diversity, but I had zero exposure to the gay community. Once I was living in the city, seeing people from the LGBT community became rather commonplace. I used to pick my wife up from a job she used to have, and she had a gay coworker who used public transportation, but his bus stop wasn't very close and it was winter. We gladly drove him to his stop on several occasions. Everyone should know Christians care. But if we're not caring, how will they know?

My wife and I became friends with a worker at a local grocery store who was gay. Over the course of a few years, we ran into him regularly. We were always happy to see him. Sometimes we would chat for ten to fifteen minutes. We would talk, listen, and laugh together. He learned of our Christian faith, but it didn't scare him away. I suppose it helped that he knew we cared for him.

In fact, he came into tough times, going through a divorce and trying to survive on one income. The day we learned of this was the same day a more lucrative job was posted where I work. This piqued his interest, so I gave him my information, showed him how to apply, and told him to put me down as a reference. We agreed it was a sign from God that we crossed paths that day. In the end, he got the job! He messaged me saying, "I'm so thankful that you guys told me about the position, and I don't know how I will ever convey my gratitude!"

After several months of working in the same office space, the Holy Spirit decided it was time I had a conversation with my friend. When we crossed paths, the Spirit prompted me to tell my friend that I was working on a book addressing the question, "Why aren't

Christians more loving?" He replied, "I ask myself that every day." I proceeded to explain my desire to become love and encourage other Christians to do the same since love is at the heart of our faith. He knew about the centrality of love to the Christian faith, and applauded me for getting after it.

In particular, I brought up the tension between the religious and gay communities. I expressed my desire to listen to his perspective and navigate through these issues together. He told me, "If it was anyone other than you and your wife, I wouldn't talk about this because I'd have nothing to say." That was an interesting comment. Apparently, care creates conversations. In other words, this discussion wouldn't have happened if he hadn't experienced our care for him on several occasions prior to it.

Like me, he grew up in a mostly white and Christian demographic, with little to no exposure to the gay community. Having many traumatic experiences with the church and his family led him to move several states away from them. I could tell he was pleased we were having this conversation; I voiced my intent to go deeper with it. He thought this was great and agreed to talk more. He said, "It would be therapeutic. I have *never* had a Christian approach me like this and just ask how I am feeling."

I couldn't believe it. After all these years, he was obviously carrying a lot of pain. Burden upon burden was piling up. Isn't it my Christian calling to care for people, listen to them, and introduce them to the love of God, which removes heavy burdens? Why would I come at him with the Bible minus love? I don't need to straighten him out; I need to love him. Love pursues, cares for, talks, asks questions, listens, prays, and never stops.

He was concerned he would say some things that might offend me, but I assured him I would be fine. I told him I also was concerned about having a negative effect on him. We admitted some prejudices might get brought into the conversation but agreed that talking about it and listening to each other was the mature thing to do. The book of James supports this: "Everyone should be quick to listen, slow to speak and slow to become angry, because human anger does not produce the righteousness that God desires" (James 1:19–20).

Love listens. It helps when you have a shared desire for peace and unity.

This was an emotional conversation for both of us. His eyes watered a bit at one point, and I was filled with compassion. At the end of our conversation, I said, "Come here," and gave him a hug. The first thing the Holy Spirit wanted my friend to know is this: God loves him, and He has filled me with His Spirit to prove it.

Love doesn't withhold affection from anybody (Romans 5:8; 2 Corinthians 5:15).

Loving Your Enemies

What better way to start a section on enemies than to talk about driving? We've all probably experienced some degree of road rage. I can't explain exactly how this works, but I can say "fits of rage" are a sort of "twitch," or involuntary spasm, resulting from the death of the old nature (2 Corinthians 12:20; Galatians 5:20). Living by faith quickens the process and produces strength to love. Maybe driving is an opportunity area for you. I know love has capitalized on many opportunities behind the wheel for me.

I got pulled over for reckless driving on the first day of having my license. I could mention loads of incredibly stupid things I did while operating motor vehicles, but I won't go into all the details. Suffice to say, love has transformed the way I drive and interact with other drivers.

Consider car-driving etiquette. Common courtesy is a thing of the past. Perhaps for many of us, love growing cold is most evident on the road. We all know how aggression and inconsideration manifest. No blinkers are used, and people cut you off, prevent you from passing, weave in and out of lanes, ride your bumper, flick you off, and, in rare but increasing cases, even fight or kill other drivers.

It seems like everyone I know has road-rage stories, some of which as the victim and some as perpetrator. (Funny how we tend to justify what we do either way.) But love makes a considerate driver and wins the respect of many. A lover drives peaceably and is mindful of the speed limit, blinker usage, and keeping a safe following distance. It allows others to pass, makes room for merging, and would rather stop its own cruise control so someone else doesn't have to slow. They think of safety first, wishing to protect themselves and others.

Ironically, some people get mad if you drive mindfully. For instance, I can think of many times people were not happy to be behind me when I was driving the speed limit. And I know what that's like, because I've been the frustrated person behind the "slow" driver. But a kingdom mindset ushers in a new perspective, not about surviving the battle on the road, but thriving in it.

Not long ago, I was driving the speed limit in the center lane on a major highway during rush hour when I noticed a man was following me closely for some time. Eventually, he abruptly shifted lanes and passed me (wisdom told me not to look at him to avoid upsetting him more). When he pulled in front of me, in my line of sight, he held his arm out the window with an extended middle finger and sped off to a nearby exit.

I was casually talking with my wife about other things when this incident occurred. I hardly noticed the man, and my lack of reaction caused my wife to inquire and see if I was aware of what happened. She didn't feel good about it. I agreed it wasn't nice to see, but said we must pray for him. So I proceeded to pray, asking God to send peace, protection, and presence after this man.

I told my wife his actions demonstrated his need for help—he probably hasn't seen much love if he freely acts that way. Or maybe he had a bad day and even regrets what he did, so why not give him the benefit of the doubt? Of course, I could get mad. But what good would it do if I became enraged, giving him the finger back or driving after him? That's a good way to put lives in danger. Basically, he simply needs the love of God, just like we all do. And, as Christians, we have what we need to help people in times like this: prayer.

Another time, a guy was yelling at me in a parking lot. I wished I was who I used to be, for just that moment, so I could really give him a piece of my mind. I also thought about the things I should have said to this guy's face. After he sped away, I resented my passivity.

Fortunately, the Holy Spirit is my Teacher and Counselor. It didn't take long for Him to remind me of what He was showing me the night before regarding radical kingdom thinking and what love looks like in real-life situations. I quickly realized I was bothered in two ways. One, I was plain offended. Two, I was bothered that I was offended! Suddenly, I realized this wasn't a problem, but an opportunity to grow in the kingdom way. Truth overtook me, so I began to pray according to it.

I thanked God for that man and asked blessing to shower down on him. I acknowledged he is no less worth the blood of Jesus than I am. I forgave him as I've been forgiven. I affirmed his potential and destiny. I prayed blessings of protection upon his children and their future with him. I thanked God for forgiving me and fashioning new responses free of anger. Afterward, I could feel an atmosphere shift in and around me. The tight grip of anger loosened under the power of joy in the Holy Spirit. Just like that, the Lord taught me an invaluable lesson in kingdom heart, and how opposite it is of the way that seems right to a man.

The mindset of the kingdom causes a dramatic shift in perspective. According to the world, these guys are my enemies, but in the kingdom, they're my brothers. Sometimes our captivity is obvious, but we can access freedom by the power of God through prayer. I know the Spirit moves to make a difference when we pray. We accomplish his will, for us and others, through prayer. If you don't approve of something someone is doing, please don't let that prevent prayer for them. Love always prays.

> "You have heard that it was said, 'Love your neighbor and hate your enemy.' But I tell you, love your enemies and pray for those who persecute you, that you may be children of your Father in heaven. He causes his sun to rise on the evil and the good, and sends rain on the righteous and the unrighteous. If you love those who love you, what reward will you get? Are not even the tax collectors doing that? And if you greet only your own people, what are you doing more than others? Do not even pagans do that? Be perfect, therefore, as your heavenly Father is perfect." (Matthew 5:43–48)

Perfect? Yes, perfect in love—showing no condemnation, partiality, or precondition (James 3:17).

You probably have many of your own examples about how God's love is at work in and around you. It's fun to grow in love, and encouraging to see the changes. However, as you'll see in the next chapter, we must keep our progress in check by maintaining a humble perspective, lest we become prideful about what we're becoming.

Chapter 9:

Who Is the Greatest?

Transformation is fun! Just as branches become longer and stronger, our selfless love increases in strength and reach. Just as a tree fills out with twigs and leaves, we fill out with Christlike character. And just as roots spread out in the ground to provide a more solid base, we, likewise, are rooted, established, and built up in the love of Christ (Colossians 2:7; Ephesians 3:17). His love is our firm foundation (Perhaps no song puts it better than "Build My Life," by Housefires). Pretty soon, we look back in awe at how far we have come, and we see how God is moving through us more powerfully than ever.

Luke 9:1–2 tells us, "When Jesus had called the Twelve together, he gave them power and authority to drive out all demons and to cure diseases, and he sent them out to proclaim the kingdom of God and to heal the sick." They "went from village to village, proclaiming the good news and healing people everywhere" (v. 6). Imagine how powerful they felt, watching all of this happen through them. They must have been having a blast delivering people.

That said, as fun as it is to grow in love and the gifting of healing, we must beware of danger. Namely, "performance pride," which will attempt to sneak in and contaminate our mind with subtle thoughts of self-importance, judgments about out-loving others, and feelings of entitlement to a greater reward. We'll get blindsided by pride if we don't continue to abide. We need love to put progress into perspective. Only the humility of the kingdom, or being "amazed at the greatness of God" (Luke 9:43)—not our own so-called greatness—can keep us on the path to spiritual maturity.

How Great Is Our ...?

The aforementioned verse refers to the reaction of all, after watching Jesus heal a demon-possessed boy. The father told Jesus, "I begged your disciples to drive it out, but they could not" (Luke 9:40).

Keep in mind, the disciples were riding high on the miracle wave when this happened. After all of their successful healings, I can see how this was probably confusing and disheartening to them. They must have wondered, *Why isn't this working?* I can imagine them trying to heal this boy as though they were trying to open a tight lid on a stubborn jar. The first one tries and gives up. The second one says, "Here, let me try," to no avail. A few down the line are probably waiting for their chance to prove themselves powerful enough. The ones who already failed were likely wishing the same fate upon the others in order to save face and not be "that guy" that couldn't open the lid.

But *none* of them could do it. Jesus blamed this on unbelief and perversity (v. 41). Then He stepped up and "opened the lid" with ease. Who knows, maybe the disciples were so heady at that moment, they thought Jesus opened it easily because they loosened it with all their hard work first. But Jesus knew what was going on. He knew they wouldn't be talking about how great God is, but arguing about how great they are and who is the most deserving of a promotion.

Shortly thereafter, the disciples' lack of faith in *God's* greatness became painfully evident as they argued about which one of them would be the greatest (v. 46). This probably arose from a spicy combo of frustration after what had happened mixed with pride from previous healings. Maybe they compared records. I'm sure each of them was recounting their successes to build a strong case for their campaign to seal the number-one spot in Jesus' kingdom. They may have been tearing each other down, trying to get to the top, in true political-ad fashion.

Even the mother of James and John was campaigning for their prestige (Matthew 20:20–28). She wanted one to sit at the right hand of Jesus and the other at His left. The ten were indignant when they heard this. But Jesus diffused the situation and gave them a valuable lesson by reminding them greatness is about serving, not being served. It is about denying yourself and walking in love, "just as the Son of Man did not come to be served, but to serve, and to give His life a ransom for many" (v. 28).

The other James (the half-brother of Jesus) must have known this, as the following passage strongly indicates: "What causes fights and quarrels among you? Don't they come from your desires that battle within you? You desire but do not have, so you kill. You covet but you cannot get what you want, so you quarrel and fight. You do not have because you do not ask God. When you ask, you do not receive, because you ask with wrong motives, that you may spend what you get on your pleasures" (vv. 1–3).

In verse 6, he quotes Proverbs 3:34: "God resists the proud, but gives grace to the humble." Humility is about acknowledging God's greatness. He continues, "Therefore submit to God. Resist the devil and he will flee from you. Draw near to God and He will draw near to you" (vv. 7–8).

In other words, submit to God because He is the great one—not you. Faith is a gift that comes in greater measure the more we praise Him as number one. In addition, we're resisting the devil in doing so. Rather, when we submit to God we *are* resisting the devil.

We submit to God in our prayers, choices, and perspective. "Humble yourselves in the sight of the Lord, and He will lift you up" (v. 10). "Do not slander one another" (v. 11). "There is one Lawgiver, who is able to save and to destroy. But you—who are you to judge another?" (v. 12).

James concludes the chapter by saying boasting is evil when it's about what you think you control and what you think you'll accomplish. After all, this doesn't acknowledge our fragility, nor does it acknowledge the great strength of God. Boasting should not be in the works of the flesh, but in the finished work of Jesus. "God forbid that I should boast except in the cross of our Lord Jesus Christ, by whom the world has been crucified to me, and I to the world" (Galatians 6:14 NKJV).

I'd like to point out that John made incredible strides despite his mishaps, eventually writing extensively about love. Hard to believe he came so far since he once attempted to destroy people in the name of God by calling fire down from heaven (Luke 9:51–55). Jesus turned to rebuke him (and John's brother), because Jesus was all about destroying the works of the devil—not the people who needed Him most. We need Jesus, but the devil doesn't want us to have Him. The devil came to steal, kill, and destroy, but Jesus came to heal, fill, and deploy. He set us free from the eternal hopelessness of self-driven world-based systems of godliness.

Rank, Reputation, and Reward

As Christians, we're supposed to grow in love. If we do, doesn't that make us greater? I admit I love more now than I ever did before. This is good, right? Is it something I should be proud of? Wanting to become greater at loving, and doing so with some success, isn't necessarily a bad thing, is it?

Becoming greater is nice, but if you're in awe of everything *you* have built, and attribute it all to *yourself*, trouble lurks around the corner. If I think I've disciplined myself well, and I'm doing a fine job in many areas, I'll be tempted to believe I've achieved freedom, in large part, by myself—independently of God. Of course, I would have to tag on "I couldn't have done it without God" to make sure I sound Christian about it. Yet, this mindset coupled with casual lip service will only get me so far.

Rank

When King Nebuchadnezzar, who had everything a man could ever want in this world, was walking on the roof of his royal palace, he surveyed the area and said, "Is not this the great Babylon I have built as the royal residence, by my mighty power and for the glory of my majesty?" (Daniel 4:30).

Look at what happens next: "Even as the words were on his lips, a voice came from heaven, 'This is what is decreed for you, King Nebuchadnezzar: Your royal authority has been taken from you. You will be driven away from people and will live with the wild animals; you will eat grass like the ox. Seven times will pass by for you until you acknowledge that the Most High is sovereign over all kingdoms on earth and gives them to anyone he wishes'" (Daniel 4:31–32).

Pride equals destruction (Proverbs 16:18). It was Lucifer's fallout, and the downfall of multitudes throughout human history. Fortunately for Nebuchadnezzar, he finally repented and turned from his pridefulness:

> At the end of that time, I, Nebuchadnezzar, raised my eyes toward heaven, and my sanity was restored. Then I praised the Most High; I honored and glorified him who lives forever. His dominion is an eternal dominion; his kingdom endures from generation to generation. All the peoples of the earth are regarded as nothing. He does as he pleases with the powers of heaven and the peoples of the earth. No one can hold back his hand or say to him: "What have you done?"

At the same time that my sanity was restored, my honor and splendor were returned to me for the glory of my kingdom. My advisers and nobles sought me out, and I was restored to my throne and became even greater than before. Now I, Nebuchadnezzar, praise and exalt and glorify the King of heaven, because everything he does is right and all his ways are just. And those who walk in pride he is able to humble. (Daniel 4:34–37)

Reputation

People make systems of ranking, which typically suggest one person is better than another. Nebuchadnezzar was at the top of that system when God reminded Him who's in charge. For a time, even the twelve disciples of Jesus were fighting for the top spot.

But God is the Most High, and everyone is equally made in His image—one person is not better than another person. The world might say so, but what does God say? When you receive the Holy Spirit, you don't receive more or less of Him than anyone else. When you receive the righteousness of Jesus, you don't receive more or less righteousness than anyone else. It's not like some people get to hug Jesus but you don't because you're not good enough to be in His inner circle. One is not below or above the other; we're all beside each other, equally in need of a Savior.

Of course, there are differing appearances and abilities on this earth, which the world is quick to segregate and categorize. But God doesn't have favorites among us, and He certainly isn't impressed when we give someone of greater reputation the special treatment. In the book of James, favoritism is exposed as sin, and we learn that love is without partiality. He explains that if we have faith in God, we will love this way. Reputable people in the world are not entitled to preferential treatment in the kingdom. Everyone honors everyone in the kingdom of God.

Consider James 2:1–4:

My brothers and sisters, believers in our glorious Lord Jesus Christ must not show favoritism. Suppose a man comes into your meeting wearing a gold ring and fine clothes, and a poor man in filthy old clothes also comes in. If you show special attention to the man wearing fine clothes and say, "Here's a good seat for you," but say to the poor man, "You stand there" or "Sit on the floor by my feet," have you not discriminated among yourselves and become judges with evil thoughts?

As well, he makes it very clear in verse 9: "If you show favoritism, you sin." But: "Mercy triumphs over judgment" (v. 13).

Lofty thoughts of oneself is dangerous business because it causes you to think higher of yourself than others. In other words, you think you're a better person than someone else. As soon as we think we're better—at anything—than others, judging by our works compared to theirs, we run the risk of becoming egotistical or self-righteous. Do we say hi to the CEO but not the account rep? Do we talk to an attractive person but ignore someone we consider unattractive?

Also, if placed in a higher position of society, we're responsible for remaining humble and showing great mercy and honor to those under our rank or management, because we understand there's no difference between us in the kingdom of God. This means we don't judge by title and appearance or alter our actions accordingly. Rather, we act in love, which consistently sees every person as made in the image of God and deserving of His love through us.

Like Nebuchadnezzar, we would do well to esteem God's rank and reputation over ours, and to honor others by putting their interests above our own. This is the humility of Jesus. Not trying to grasp the number-one spot but making Himself nothing and taking on the nature of a servant. Yet He is sovereign, and all good things come from Him. In fact, we owe Him all the credit for making us, sanctifying us, saving us by His power, and giving us Himself as our eternal prize.

Reward

I think some people have this idea that once we get to heaven, we'll get a bunch of presents for all the great things we did. Here's what I do know: Everyone in the early church shared everything and distributed things equally so no one had too much and no one had too little. In fact, no one had any unmet needs (Acts 4:34). There was no rich-and-poor gap. Sounds like heaven on earth.

If, on the other hand, one of them held onto 99 percent of the wealth and the rest of them had 1 percent, I wouldn't necessarily consider the "richest" person blessed. Because the blessing isn't in the getting so much as it is in the giving, and not because you did a good job by giving, but because you've blessed others as a result. In other words, *they* get the blessing—you get to enjoy giving! We don't give to get more; we give to help others more.

Let's say the 99 percent person was once in the 1 percent, but they gave what little they had and miraculously received an enormous amount of wealth. Is that their reward? Or is it an opportunity to give more? In the world, we're accustomed to thinking about what's in it for us, only to forget it was never about us.

Here's what I'm driving at: expecting rewards is detracting us from seeking The Reward.

The story of the prodigal son illustrates this point well because both of the father's sons were reward focused. The prodigal son, who ran off and used his sizeable inheritance to live wildly, soon emptied all he was given and found himself depleted and alone. His brother, who we'll call the jealous brother, stayed home with their father, and became enraged when his father warmly welcomed and celebrated the return of his prodigal brother, even throwing a party in his honor.

Why was he upset? Because he didn't think his brother deserved it, especially not more than he did. He was jealous because his father never threw him a party for staying, which was more honorable as far as he was concerned. He felt right in his judgment and expressed his righteous indignation to his father. But his father reminded him that it isn't about the inheritance, good or bad choices, or who gets a better party, but being with each other: "'My son,' the father said, 'you are always with me, and everything I have is yours. But we had to celebrate and be glad, because this brother of yours was dead and is alive again; he was lost and is found'" (Luke 15:31–32).

It wasn't about the jealous brother. It wasn't about the prodigal. It was about the love of the father.

However rewards shake out in the end, the most important thing for me is to forget about rewards. I think religion seeks a medal, but relationship seeks a Person. I'm convinced that love doesn't seek a reward because love shared between the Creator and His creation *is* the reward. God is love. When Jesus comes again, He will bring our reward, the best reward of all: Himself. "And behold, I am coming quickly, and My reward is with Me, to give to every one according to his work" (Revelation 22:12 NKJV).

All throughout the New Testament, we find our "work" is to believe in Him, and our reward is to be with Him. I don't see Him coming like Santa Claus with a knapsack in tow and gifts for the masses to boot. Separating the naughty from the nice. He will not be sitting on a sleigh with reindeer either, but on a white horse (Revelation 19:1). I'm not dreaming of a white Christmas, I'm dreaming of a white horse with Jesus on it. This will be awesome and terrifying. The fear of God to the max. Though His reward is with Him, He's not carrying a gift for you, but He is carrying a *sword*. You don't want that. With it he will "strike the nations" (Revelation 19:15 NKJV).

Here's the hope of the believer: "For the Lord Himself will descend from heaven with a shout, with the voice of an archangel, and with the trumpet of God. And the dead in Christ will rise first. Then we who are alive and remain shall be caught up together with them in the clouds to meet the Lord in the air. And thus we shall always be with the Lord. Therefore comfort one another with these words" (1 Thessalonians 4:16–18 NKJV).

As we fight the good fight and run the race, Jesus will come at the perfect time just as the father of the prodigal son ran out to meet his child. When we see Him in all His glory, I'm sure we'll forget about any reward besides Himself.

It's Not Fair

One time my kids were doing the dishes and one of them did more work than the other. The one who did more said, "It's not fair." I've heard this before, from both of them. In fact, I've said it a few times myself. If you haven't said it, you've probably thought it or said something like it. The problem is, "It's not fair" isn't the language of the kingdom. So this became an opportunity to "train up" my children in the way they should go (Proverbs 22:6 NKJV).

I had the kids come with me and sit down in the office. They knew I was up to something. As they awaited in suspense, I said, "I'm going to read you a story," and I opened the Bible to the Parable of the Workers in the Vineyard (Matthew 20:1–16). My son who did less work said to the one who did more, "You're about to get roasted." It's true that the words of Jesus are often like a slow roast, but I reminded the kids we're equally in need of biblical refreshment.

In this parable, Jesus describes how the kingdom operates differently from the world:

> "For the kingdom of heaven is like a landowner who went out early in the morning to hire workers for his vineyard. He agreed to pay them a denarius for the day and sent them into his vineyard. About nine in the morning he went out and saw others standing in the marketplace doing nothing. He told them, 'You also go and work in my vineyard, and I will pay you whatever is right.' So they went. He went out again about noon and about three in the afternoon and did the same thing. About five in the afternoon he went out and found still others standing around. He asked them, 'Why have you been standing here all day long doing nothing?' 'Because no one has hired us,' they answered. He said to them, 'You also go and work in my vineyard.' When evening came, the owner of the vineyard said to his foreman, 'Call the workers and pay them their wages, beginning with the last ones hired and going on to the first.' The workers who were hired about five in the afternoon came and each received a denarius. So when those came who were hired first, they expected to receive more. But each one of them also received a denarius. When they received it, they began to grumble against the landowner. 'These who were hired last worked only one hour,' they said, 'and you have made

them equal to us who have borne the burden of the work and the heat of the day.' But he answered one of them, 'I am not being unfair to you, friend. Didn't you agree to work for a denarius? Take your pay and go. I want to give the one who was hired last the same as I gave you. Don't I have the right to do what I want with my own money? Or are you envious because I am generous?' So the last will be first, and the first will be last."

The first group of workers, who did the most, naturally expected more pay than those who did less work. Sounds fair—in the world. But Jesus is talking about the kingdom. So when the others got paid the same amount, their anger surfaced and their selfishness was exposed.

What right do we have to receive more from God than others? He gives as He pleases. Our job is to do the work cheerfully unto the Lord, and to be content with what we have or are given. Also, we don't resent the blessing of others, we celebrate them!

So, if my coworker gets the promotion I wanted, I should celebrate their success, not resent it or envy them. The real tragedy would be for me to think they don't deserve it as much as I do, and to desire their failure and gloat if it happens. Don't I trust God's timing? Aren't I content with the circumstances? Can I appreciate how this blessing might benefit another person? Am I willing to sincerely congratulate them and thank God, in prayer, for their success? Won't I declare my trust in His provision and thank Him for it? Love will.

The kids got the message. Actually, I haven't heard either one of them say, "It's not fair," ever since. If it happens again, we will revisit this story, talk, and pray about the matter. Apparently, not even the disciples got it the first time around. Not long after Jesus shared this parable, they had an argument about who would be the greatest. The disciples were comparing too. But there's no room for that kind of thinking in the mind of a lover.

Jesus ended the parable with the classic line, "The last will be first, and the first will be last." In other words, those fighting for the front of the line, or the first serving, are moved to the back in the kingdom. However, the first in the kingdom are the ones who take the back so someone else can be ahead of them, or eat first. On a bus, the last compete for a seat, but the first gladly give it up. The last say, "First come, first served," and they are relieved to receive. But the first sincerely say, "You can go first," and they are happy to give.

But it goes even deeper, beyond the action itself. The first don't harbor a motive in which they secretly plot to be first. This is important. If I move myself to the back of the line because I want to be noticed and invited to the front, that's just as selfish as racing to the front. My error will appear less obvious, but it's still an error nonetheless.

I'm not saying we can prevent every errant impulse that comes up. A selfish reaction isn't the problem, but a refusal to have a self-sacrificial response is. To put it simply, using the food-line analogy, the last in the kingdom impulsively rush to the front due to *immaturity*. Whereas the ones who wait or look out for others do so because of their *maturity*. Really, this talk about first and last is a way of describing the growth process we all go through in the kingdom from seed to tree. The point of these distinctions isn't to say who gets the highest position on the podium in the end. Rather, it's to illustrate how the selfless mind and actions of the kingdom should operate now.

Don't Envy Other Believers

If we're spiritual babies, we shouldn't be discouraged about our lack of maturity, nor should we envy the mature. Instead, we ought to garner inspiration and encouragement to be faithful in our calling as the mature were in theirs. Chances are some people are not more mature than you, but you think they are because you consider their calling more glamorous than yours. Maybe you heard a missionary speak at your church about all the wonderful things God was doing on their mission field, and you began to feel condemned because you aren't putting your life in danger for His namesake. As if God doesn't want you where you are, or as though your sphere of influence is less important than the missionary's.

If you feel like a poor excuse of a Christian, like you're not doing good enough *compared* to other people, it's time to forget yourself, embrace love, and experience freedom from condemnation. Because "there is now no condemnation for those who are in Christ Jesus" (Romans 8:1).

The body of Christ has a variety of members for different purposes, but a common good (1 Corinthians 12). There's a reason you have the role you do at work, in your family, and at church. It is for His goodness' sake. What makes you think your work, family, and talents matter any less in your sphere than those getting more attention in the public eye?

Sometimes we admire others so much that we get ourselves into trouble. Trying to be someone we're not. Pursuing a man or woman more than we're pursuing the heart of God Himself. Wanting to do the right thing is great, but feeling like I'm a loser, and justifying it on the basis of how I pale in comparison to someone else, is no better than thinking I'm the greatest Christian. Ironically, this "pure-heartedness" can become envy in disguise and manifest as false humility and discouragement.

The best way to guard against this trap is by simply celebrating God's work through His people. We should appreciate where He put us and thank Him for it and bloom where we're planted! When we understand all of the things we previously explored, we can rest easy about this issue. Love doesn't concern itself with comparisons, and it certainly doesn't feel sorry for itself.

In the Parable of the Workers in the Vineyard, Jesus posed the question, "Are you envious because I am generous?" This strikes at the heart of our performance-related insecurities. If I'm envious about the good things God chose to do in setting apart certain people for good works, I'm off in my understanding and in need of experiencing the love of God in communion with Him. Only then will I celebrate the goodness of God and marvel at the ways His generosity benefits us all.

God does great things through believers, even administering the gift of healing. In particular, physical healings have gotten a lot of attention in recent years. Miracles are entertaining, but without love we're still missing the heart of God (1 Corinthians 13).

Miracles of Love

Love fuels healing, but it's a bigger deal than physical miracles. In John 13, Jesus washed His disciples' feet and predicted His betrayal and Peter's denial. In John 14, the disciples were troubled, so Jesus comforted them. He told them they would be together again. He said they knew how to get to where He was going. Though there were doubts, He encouraged them to believe in Him. Even if only on the evidence of the miracles themselves. He said if people have faith in Him, they'll do what He was doing. In fact, they will do "greater things" or "greater works."

What are these greater things? Multiplying the food at your church potluck? Praying for a missing limb to regrow and watching it happen before your own eyes?

Jesus says "miracles" once in both John 14 and 15 (in the 1984 NIV), but the NKJV and updated NIV don't use "miracles" but "works." The first occurrence refers to miracles as a sort of tool for helping people believe. But the second mention admits works aren't enough for some: "Now they have seen these works, and yet they have hated both me and my Father. But this is to fulfill what is written in their Law: 'They hated me without reason.'"

Only *love* is enough. In between the two mentions of miracles, Jesus says *love*, *loves*, or *loved* nineteen times (ten times in John 14, and nine times in John 15, again in the 1984 NIV). Naturally, in the thick of all this love, Jesus teaches about the Holy Spirit (chapters 14–16) and He prays for everyone (chapter 17 and 18)—including you (John 17:20–26). He ends it beautifully: "Righteous Father, though the world does not know you, I know you, and they know that you have sent me. I have made you known to them, and will continue to make you known in order that the love you have for me may be in them and that I myself may be in them" (John 17:25–26).

He said we will see Him again, and it's for our benefit that He goes away for a time (John 16:7). In the meantime, this is His command: "Love each other as I have loved you" (John 15:12). He recognizes we can't do this without His Holy Spirit, which is why He sends us "another Helper, that He may abide with you forever" (John 14:16 NKJV). He said, "If you love me, you will keep my commandments" (John 14:15). His command is to love each other (John 15:17). If we love Him, we *will* love people (as John describes at greater length in the book of 1 John).

What does this have to do with miracles? Putting them into perspective, I hope. It's all about love. If we're not careful, we'll pursue miracles instead of our Maker. "Not everyone who says to Me, 'Lord, Lord,' shall enter the kingdom of heaven, but he who does the will of My Father in heaven. Many will say to Me in that day, 'Lord, Lord, have we not prophesied in Your name, cast out demons in Your name, and done many wonders in Your name?' And then I will declare to them, 'I never knew you; depart from Me, you who practice lawlessness!'" (Matthew 7:21–23 NKJV).

I'm not saying miracles are bad—I understand believers perform them—but they should never be our primary focus. Jesus always put the emphasis on love. Denying yourself and selflessly loving somebody is the greatest of miracles, requiring nothing short of divine superpower.

When it comes to "miracle workers," or those walking in power, who is a poser and who is the real deal? Jesus said there are wolves in sheep's clothing but they can't hide because we will know them by their fruit (Matthew 7:15–16). In discerning this, the question is, did they love?

There's a powerful illustration of this in Matthew 25:31–46, when the Son of Man comes to judge the nations in what is famously known as "The Sheep and the Goats," or separating the believers from the unbelievers. I encourage you to read this entire passage.

Here's a snapshot:

"When the Son of Man comes in His glory, and all the holy angels with Him, then He will sit on the throne of His glory. All the nations will be gathered before Him, and He will separate them one from another, as a shepherd divides *his* sheep from the goats. And He will set the sheep on His right hand, but the goats on the left. Then the King will say to those on His right hand, 'Come, you blessed of My Father, inherit the kingdom prepared for you from the foundation of the world: for I was hungry and you gave Me food; I was thirsty and you gave Me drink; I was a stranger and you took Me in; I *was* naked and you clothed Me; I was sick and you visited Me; I was in prison and you came to Me.' Then the righteous will answer Him, saying, 'Lord, when did we see You hungry and feed *You,* or thirsty and give *You* drink? When did we see You a stranger and take *You* in, or naked and clothe *You?* Or when did we see You sick, or in prison, and come to You?' And the King will answer and say to them, 'Assuredly, I say to you, inasmuch as you did *it* to one of the least of these My brethren, you did *it* to Me.'" (Matthew 25:34–40 NKJV)

He didn't say, "I was blind and you gave me sight," or "I was deaf and you gave me hearing." When He said, "As you did to the least of these," none of His examples included dramatic healings but plain old-fashioned love (being fed, clothed, and visited). Again, I'm not saying healing eyes and ears doesn't happen or shouldn't happen, but we must have a firm foundation of love (1 Corinthians 13:1–2).

Of course, the aforementioned deeds, such as feeding the poor, can be done without love too (1 Corinthians 13:3). A good deed is a good deed, but God isn't interested in the action alone but the heart's motive behind it. So we should be on guard lest we become prideful about our good deeds. I think it's interesting that the "sheep" in the story were not particularly aware of the love they had shown. This reminds me of the times I've read through old journal entries only to discover something I did that I had since forgotten. I think some level of secrecy—not letting your left hand know what your right hand is doing—is a noble thing. I think it indicates our mind is on God and people, hence with no vacancy for self.

Doing things out of obligation, drudgery, and dread instead of privilege, pleasure, and passion smells like religion, not love. So we need the Holy Spirit to purify our motives in whatever we are doing, which is why we must "plug in" on the daily if we'll ever live a life of love. When we stay connected, supernatural love will happen in every situation.

Just look at Nick Vujicic. He was born without arms and legs, but he has used his "disadvantages" for tremendous kingdom advantage. Having realized he didn't need to get a miracle but be one. Like he said, "If God can use a man without arms and legs to be His hands and feet, then He will certainly use any willing heart!"[26]

God wasn't displeased with Nick, or punishing him for things he or his parents had done. Rather, God's will is that His love would be known, and shown through his people, despite the worst or most desperate of circumstances. Then people can see how freedom in Christ overcomes every hardship in the world.

Love is a miracle!

Look Out for Out-Loving

In the early stages of learning to live a life of love, before regularly communing with God, I worked hard at doing love. However, when you commune, love will be more like breathing than a workout. Yet I treated love like going to the gym—something I had to do to stay in good shape. Inevitably, I would break down under the weight of the challenge due to the impossibility of genuinely loving apart from consistent communion. I was getting fashioned by circumstances instead of faith. Fortunately, God is with me.

Once upon a time, my wife and I had a basket full of clean laundry to put away, and I thought she should do it. Since I was busy working full time during the day and she was working part time at night, it only seemed fair (remember that word?).

She agreed to put them away, but failed to do so on the first day. The day after, she assured me she would do it. But when I got home from work, she was gone and the laundry was still sitting there. When she called me from work, I didn't hide my disappointment. After all, we had an understanding. I could feel the pressure of tiredness and frustration building up while I tried to keep the lid on. I reminded her this kind of thing had happened before, saying one thing and doing another, and I would like it to change. I had such cases well documented.

However, my "logical genius" led to a verdict I wasn't prepared for: I was guilty of not loving.

This was both confusing and refreshing. Confusing because I thought my initial approach made sense, and refreshing because I realized it didn't and there was a better way that made more sense: love.

Love isn't about doing this if you do that; it doesn't require a compromise, nor does it have any expectations. Like Dan Mohler says, "It isn't 'I love you … Do you love me?' It's just, 'I love you.'" Because love takes no account of a suffered wrong (1 Corinthians 13:5). I know I'm talking about laundry, but this verse applies to the whole spectrum of things we get upset about. Sometimes we get upset about wrong things that don't even exist. (While driving, have you ever seen someone make a wrong move and get mad at the other person as if they were the one in error?)

Anyway, once this fresh revelation of love came into me, guess what I did? I joyfully put away the laundry. My wife didn't have to ask me, and I didn't do it begrudgingly. On the contrary, I decided to operate in the energy of the Lord.

I turned a few of her shirts right side out, praising and thanking God that I had this opportunity to care for His daughter in such intimate detail. Love gives and gives and gives and doesn't expect to get. God's "love tank" is always full, and since He's in us, we're never lacking either.

I realized love doesn't keep a record of what she said or did. Therefore, I didn't need to hold her accountable; she is accountable to God—not me. Love moved me to lead by example and do a selfless deed. When love is freely given, it's freely received because it has nothing to do with, "If you scratch my back, I'll scratch yours." So when my wife does put laundry away, I can express gratitude because I know she didn't have to.

Furthermore, if it happens again where she says she'll put it away the next day and she doesn't, I have the opportunity to say, "I know you've been tired, honey, and I so appreciate all the ways you help me around the house. It would be my pleasure to lift this burden from you. It is an honor for me to lay down my life for you in all the ways that are presented. You're a daughter of my King and the love of my life, and I thank the Lord for this opportunity to serve a royal princess."

These words reflect a heart filled with kingdom love, which beats and bleeds with selflessness and lays down its life for others. Maybe this "language" of love seems impossible, but take heart in knowing it develops naturally in communion with God. We have the most to give when we know we're full in Him. Then we won't sweat the small stuff. Rather, we'll embrace it as an opportunity and reveal the depth of our intimacy with the Lord. Whether it's putting away laundry, doing the dishes, cleaning up the house, responding kindly to insult, cooling the hot air of an argument or overlooking mistakes, we have so many privileges to release the love of God. There are so many dark corners we get to shine His light into.

This example came out of a season when God was helping me navigate through the exhaustion of legalistic living (i.e., self-sufficient Christianity). I was convinced I was out-loving my wife. There was so much I was doing. I knew she wasn't putting the same level of effort in, and I tried not to let it bother me, but over time I just couldn't stuff my frustration any longer. This preoccupation with my "love" not being reciprocated became a seemingly justified grounds for resentment.

This is when my guard came down. Slowly but surely I started doing things I had been actively fighting against. I thought, *If my wife isn't working hard at our relationship, why should I?* But on what biblical basis is that justified? Isn't love unconditional?

In my deception, I got dangerously comfortable with idleness and immorality. That is, until God clarified my vision and invited me into deeper communion with Him.

Ironically, once I started communing with Him, and resisting the urge to control my sanctification, some bad habits were resurfacing. This perplexed me for some time, until the Holy Spirit granted me wisdom to see this reality: my willpower was no longer busy hiding my problems under the surface, so they floated to the top. Turns out I wasn't as great as I thought I was. Finally, I could admit my weakness and draw on the strength of the Lord by coming to God "just as I am" and inviting His grace to truly transform me.

From Your Goodness to His Greatness

In our zeal to do well, we might look great in the eyes of others. We may even recognize our own improvement and be tempted to think more highly of ourselves than we ought. If you think you're good, remember, there will always be someone better. This is okay, because the Bible doesn't say you need to be the best.

That's a relief!

Maybe God *has* done a great work in you and you've gotten the reputation of having the best slugging percentage on the team. Does the assessment of others persuade you it's true? Here's the thing: considering yourself the top slugger is problematic. After all, do we keep stats in the kingdom? Or is such analyzation a worldly measurement used in assessing if I'm higher or lower than someone? The thing is, sanctification in the kingdom of God is not a competitive, or even measurable, matter.

Say you were batting .275 and you improved to .350, and another person was batting .200 but improved to .325. Are you doing better since your average is higher? According to that measurement, you improved by .75 point but they improved by .125 point. So even though your average is higher, they improved more than you. But this isn't how it works in the kingdom of God.

We're not competing against each other; rather, we're on the same team—Team Jesus. He picked us. In the world, people are recognized and awarded for outperforming others. On Team Jesus, *we all win*. There are no MVP awards in the kingdom because all are equally valuable to God, regardless of performance level. We each play a necessary part in the health of the whole team, or body. In the body of Christ, one part isn't thought of as better than another (1 Corinthians 12:12–31).

Consider the Parable of the Pharisee and the Tax Collector:

To some who were confident of their own righteousness and looked down on everyone else, Jesus told this parable: "Two men went up to the temple to pray, one a Pharisee and the other a tax collector. The Pharisee stood by himself and prayed: 'God, I thank you that I am not like other people—robbers, evildoers, adulterers—or even like this tax collector. I fast twice a week and give a tenth of all I get.' But the tax collector stood at a distance. He would not even look up to heaven, but beat his breast and said, 'God, have mercy on me, a sinner.' I tell you that this man, rather than the other, went home justified before God. For all those who exalt themselves will be humbled, and those who humble themselves will be exalted." (Luke 18:9–14)

If we struggle with performance pride, our attitude most likely has legalistic underpinnings. Should I thank God when my batting average isn't as low as the guy next to me? Or would that make me a Pharisee?

I can thank God that I know Jesus in a world of people who don't, but the problem comes when I think I'm okay because of *my work* as opposed to *His finished work*. I can't work my own salvation. Our confidence and boasting should always be centered on Jesus, not how well we're behaving.

Due to differing levels of spiritual maturity, it's worth noting the possibility you're more loving than many others. But this isn't an occasion to think God loves you more than them, or that you deserve a better reward because you've been so good. (Remember the prodigal son?) When more growth is given, more is expected (Luke 12:48), and vice versa—it all evens out in the end. The only reason you grow is because God grows you in proportion to your faith in Him (1 Corinthians 3:6–7; Mark 11:22). Our success is in relationship with God; He doesn't measure us the way people do. It isn't about what we've done, but whether we believe in what Jesus did that we couldn't do. Believing in Him will change what we do, but our doing doesn't come before faith.

Let's pose the question again: Who is the greatest? Jesus is the greatest! God is The Great One to be praised!

As for us, out of all the things we could become, *love* is the greatest of them all (1 Corinthians 13:13). Mature lovers don't concern themselves with being the best of the best, but with becoming love, making themselves nothing, and taking on the nature of a servant, just as Jesus did (Philippians 2:7). They understand they're all hell-bound sinners without the redeeming love of our Savior. They realize His example is the best one to follow:

> When he had finished washing their feet, he put on his clothes and returned to his place. "Do you understand what I have done for you?" he asked them. "You call me 'Teacher' and 'Lord,' and rightly so, for that is what I am. Now that I, your Lord and Teacher, have washed your feet, you also should wash one another's feet. I have set you an example that you should do as I have done for you. Very truly I tell you, no servant is greater than his master, nor is a messenger greater than the one who sent him. Now that you know these things, you will be blessed if you do them." (John 13:12–17)

We ought to humbly receive the love of God into our hearts by putting our faith in Jesus and serving others. That is how we walk in love.

Stage Three Summary

In this stage of growth, we saw the proof of love. This volcanic flow of love erupts from an active knowledge of truth and thankfulness, and brings transformation into our social spheres. Now our roots have spread out farther in support of this ever-growing love.

All of these things happen over time. Your changes will look different from mine. This is fine since we're not attempting to carve out a religious checklist of dos and don'ts. It's not about keeping a checklist and feeling great if you do and bad if you don't. It's about walking in love where the Spirit moves you.

The examples I've shared are a glimpse of how God is at work in *my* life. But love will also prepare *you* to thrive in your social situations and relationships. The new you, a workmanship of Christ (Ephesians 2:10), is at hand. Therefore, you now carry the power to make an exceedingly positive impact right where you are and beyond. Each act of love releases a chain reaction of power.

In the next and final stage, we'll discover, develop, and distribute the riches we've been given for the advancement of God's kingdom to the glory of His great name. We'll let our light shine, be fruitful, and multiply His image on the earth. And we'll sow seeds of love in preparation for the final harvest.

Here we go. Onward to maturity!

Stage Four:
Maturity

(T4: Thoughtfulness—Serving Others)

*"Maturity is the final phase in tree growth and is the time when substantial bark develops and, in some cases, when the **fruit** cycle begins. Another sign of maturity is when the tree begins to produce **seeds** for **reproduction**. The energy of the tree focuses on reproduction during this stage, and the tree reaches its **full** size. Growth begins to spread more **outward** than upward at this point. Another sign of maturity is when the trunk reaches 1 foot in diameter."*[27]

Chapter 10:

Coming Out of Hiding

Love is thoughtful.

If *you* are thoughtful, you're "showing care and consideration in how you treat other people."[28]

The love of God is thoughtful. He cares about our life and destiny and treats us with great kindness and mercy. In thoughtfulness, while we were still sinners, God sent Jesus to redeem us. Because of His thoughtfulness, Jesus healed the sick, brought good news to the poor, freed those in captivity, and sent the Holy Spirit to seal us with eternal life and the power to live like Him now. Through His thoughtfulness, the Holy Spirit comforts us and gifts us with power and love and sends us out to comfort and encourage others with what we have received. This means those of us inhabited by the Spirit of God will, like our Father, show creative thoughtfulness in what we do.

God has thoughtfully made provision for us to spread the good news of His love through our talents, or gifts, and testimony to the profit of all. But we must discover, develop, and distribute this power we've been given, lest we remain or become ineffective in helping people and making disciples.

Called to Service

The Bible makes it clear that Christian living is a lifestyle of serving others. Just consider these verses, to name just a few:
- For though I am free from all men, I have made myself a servant to all, that I might win the more ... for the gospel's sake. (1 Corinthians 9:19, 23 NKJV)
- For you, brethren, have been called to liberty; only do not use liberty as an opportunity for the flesh, but through love *serve* one another. (Galatians 5:13 NKJV)
- Do not forget to do good and to share with others, for with such sacrifices God is pleased. (Hebrews 13:16).
- Each of you should use whatever gift you have received to *serve* others, as faithful stewards of God's grace in its various forms. If anyone speaks, they should do so as one who speaks the very words of God. If anyone *serves*, they should do so with the strength God provides, so that in all things God may be praised through Jesus Christ. To him be the glory and the power for ever and ever. Amen. (1 Peter 4:10–11)

Gifts and Talents

God gave us various gifts to prepare us for works of service (Ephesians 4:8, 12). Why?

> So that the body of Christ may be built up until we all reach unity in the faith and in the knowledge of the Son of God and become *mature*, attaining to the whole measure of the fullness of Christ. Then we will no longer be infants, tossed back and forth by the waves, and blown here and there by every wind of teaching and by the cunning and craftiness of people in their deceit-

ful scheming. Instead, speaking the truth in love, we will grow to become in every respect the *mature* body of him who is the head, that is, Christ. From him the whole body, joined and held together by every supporting ligament, grows and builds itself up *in love*, as each part does its work. (Ephesians 4:12–16)

This passage beautifully encapsulates the growth we're after: maturity in love. Look at all the references to progress in Christ: reaching, becoming, growing, and building up. Clearly, we are not supposed to be a "wicked, lazy servant," hiding the gift of God and making nothing of it, as was the case in The Parable of the Talents (Matthew 25:14–30).

In this story, the man in charge gives three of his servants differing amounts of talents. Two of them invest their talents and give the man a greater return when he comes back. Even though the amounts were not equal, the man's response was the same: "Well done, good and faithful servant; you have been faithful over a few things, I will make you ruler over many things. Enter into the joy of your lord" (Matthew 25:21, 23 NKJV).

As you can see, there's no partiality or favoritism in his response. This is fitting, considering what we discussed about our equal reward in Jesus as previously explored through the parables of The Prodigal Son and The Workers in the Vineyard. I understand the person with the most talents was, in the end, given an extra talent (recycled from what the lazy servant wasted), but this wasn't a display of favoritism. Nor was it favoritism when the prodigal son got the big party and not the jealous son. Likewise, when the part-time workers in the vineyard got paid as much as the full-time workers, it wasn't technically a better reward since they got paid equally.

Yes, they did differing amounts of work, but our work doesn't make us deserving of a greater reward since we're all equally in need of a Savior. Besides, how could it? There is no greater reward than God Himself. Picking apart these minor details points to the major balancing act of God: Jesus. The cross of Christ bridges the gaps we contrive. In short, we may have differing talents, but this doesn't mean God has favorite children. If my older son gets paid more than my youngest, maybe it's because my younger son isn't old enough to do the work that results in greater pay, and not that I love one more than the other. If one has the strength to shovel a driveway, and the other has strength to shovel a few steps, can't I decide to give more money to the one who did more work than the one that didn't? (Not that I should pay my kids to shovel …)

But here's the point: Isn't it my money to give according their ability as I see fit? Can't I do this while loving them both the same? They would do well to trust me. Just as we would do well to trust God's judgment and be thankful for His unconditional love and our privilege to show it uniquely through the means given to us.

So it is, there are different kinds of gifts, service, and working, but the same Spirit, Lord, and God is at work in them all. He distributes them to each person, as He determines, for our *common good*. Each and every one of us compose one part of the same body—the body of Christ (1 Corinthians 12:1–14):

> Now you are the body of Christ, and each one of you is a part of it. And God has placed in the church first of all apostles, second prophets, third teachers, then miracles, then gifts of healing, of helping, of guidance, and of different kinds of tongues. Are all apostles? Are all prophets? Are all teachers? Do all work miracles? Do all have gifts of healing? Do all speak in tongues? Do

all interpret? Now eagerly desire the greater gifts. And yet I will show you the most excellent way. (1 Corinthians 12:27–31)

This is where it gets really good. This passage sets the stage for the classic chapter on love, 1 Corinthians 13. Leading up to it, Paul asks rhetorical questions (verses 29–30) because he knows not all of us *are* teachers, healers, miracle workers, prophets, and so on. But he says nothing suggesting there are some of us who can't become love, which, according to him, is the greatest gift of them all. So he tells us to eagerly desire greater gifts than what he mentioned. But what is more impressive and powerful than healing and miracles?

This is where we learn that *love* is "the most excellent way" (1 Corinthians 12:31), the greatest of things (1 Corinthians 13:13), and the driving force behind our spiritual gifts. Only with love can our gifts serve to strengthen, encourage, comfort people, and edify the church (1 Corinthians 14:5, 12). With sincere love we prophesy, serve, teach, encourage, give, lead, and show mercy cheerfully (Romans 12:6–9). It's all about love; our gifts are simply a channel of it from one person to another, according to the grace given each of us.

In his article "What are spiritual gifts?" David Nooitgedagt writes,

> I can receive spiritual gifts by faith, I can fight for them and I can practice using them. But if I don't think about helping people and if I am missing care for people, I can quickly go astray. Then it is easy for me to start believing that the spiritual gifts alone give content or value to those who use them. Then I am being motivated by the wrong thing and soon I will start thinking about honor and being great in the church. Then even

> envy and jealousy can become my motivation to use spiritual gifts.
>
> That's why Paul writes: "I will show you a more excellent way," and then comes 1 Corinthians 13. He uses a lot of words to warn us and assure us that we are nothing if all we have is spiritual gifts. And he explains that it is quite possible to use the spiritual gifts without love. You could almost think that all those who use spiritual gifts have love, almost as if they were one and the same. But that's not the way it is!
>
> A more excellent way (better than just receiving the spiritual gifts as gifts of faith) is when love is the motivating factor. Then it is like a person who has found water in an oasis and is desperately looking for a container so he can bring water to someone who is dying in the desert. Spiritual gifts are like such a container. The container isn't terribly useful by itself, but when it is used by somebody who has love and who has themselves found what can give life to a thirsty soul, then it becomes useful. And in this context, it is also stupid to think about getting honor from your fellow Christians.[29]

We were once in darkness, without love, but now we are children of light. The days are evil, but we can shine the selfless love of God through our gifting in Christ, namely, by serving one another. As members of one body, we're called to be useful with our own hands, that we may have something to share with those in need; God knows we all need the light! (Ephesians 4–5).

> Be very careful, then, how you live—not as unwise but as wise, making the most of every opportunity, because

the days are evil. Therefore do not be foolish, but understand what the Lord's will is. Do not get drunk on wine, which leads to debauchery. Instead, be filled with the Spirit, speaking to one another with psalms, hymns, and songs from the Spirit. Sing and make music from your heart to the Lord, always giving thanks to God the Father for everything, in the name of our Lord Jesus Christ. Submit to one another out of reverence for Christ. (Ephesians 5:15–21)

In other words, be thoughtful about glorifying God by serving Him through loving others. You can probably hear how this passage echoes each stage of this book: Not being foolish but understanding the Lord's will concerns *truth* (T1); giving thanks and singing songs to the Lord is about *thankfulness* (T2); making the most of every opportunity through fullness of the Spirit is His resultant work of our *transformation* (T3); and, last, the focus of this chapter: submitting to one another out of reverence for Christ consists of actions compelled by the *thoughtfulness* (T4) of love.

Fundamentally, our gifts and talents are a means of "submitting" to, or serving one another. In the body of Christ, we share many talents for this. In fact, we possess many of the same gifts to some degree. For example, many of us have taught or encouraged somebody in one way or another, though the expression may look different from one person to the next, and no one person looks exactly like another (even "identical" twins can be differentiated). That said, knowing what your gift looks like will help you know how to use it for the profit of many.

What If I Don't Know What My Gifts Are?

Fortunately, we can still serve others without knowing what our "gifts" are. For instance, anybody can say a kind word, give a hug, or volunteer at a soup kitchen. But we're talking about that thing you excel at or desire more than anything else. Most importantly, that thing you're *passionate* about and intensely interested in—that thing you do without anyone asking you.

My dad is known for regularly working sixty- to eighty-hour work weeks. I'm not recommending that, but he's a good example of someone driven by passion. He simply couldn't do what he does if he wasn't passionate about it, whereas a few people have attempted to do half as much as he does and they burn out. They say it's too much. But why is it too much for them and not my dad? Because they don't have the same drive. Passion makes all the difference.

Dad always told me to do what I enjoy, because it won't feel like work (work in the negative sense of the word). Like Mark Twain said, "Find a job you enjoy doing, and you will never have to work a day in your life."[30]

I think most of us want this. We're passionately pursuing something, or, if not now, we were at some point. Everyone enjoys doing something or has an interest in something. What is it for you? Asking yourself what you're passionate about might be your best hint at knowing how you can serve most effectively.

Sadly, most of us aren't even *thinking* about doing what we love. Or if you do, like me, you won't necessarily make a living off of it. The only reason I can write in addition to working a full-time job and having two kids is because I'm passionate about it. What saddens me most is when dreams end, investing stops, and talents are buried, as if having a job, children, or whatever else is dooming us. I know there are challenges, but I also know there's a lack of vision, intention, and purpose. Fortunately, when we know God and understand we're here to become love, we find purpose, discover our gifts, and tap into the tireless energy of our God-given passion.

In this stage of growth, it isn't only about me finding gifts and reaching maturity, but helping others discover their gifts and grow in love too.

Jesus "is the one we proclaim, admonishing and teaching everyone with all wisdom, so that we may present everyone fully *mature* in Christ. To this end I strenuously contend with all the energy Christ so powerfully works in me" (Colossians 1:28–29). Our gifts (i.e., passions and talents) are an avenue of proclaiming, admonishing, and teaching everyone about the love of Jesus.

If we aren't sure what we're passionate about or how our passion is suited to the kingdom, sometimes all we need to do is ask God, and ask a Christian. Having a conversation with God is like having a conversation with a person—because He *is* a person! He will answer you. Sometimes His answer comes through a fellow believer who brings clarity, encouragement, prayer, or maybe even a prophetic word calling out what you secretly suspected.

I didn't understand what my gifts were for many years. Unbeknownst to me, God was pouring in and drawing out my gifting all along, according to His perfect timing. Looking back, I can see how one thing prepared me for another. Ultimately, this culminated in a personal recognition of what my gifts are.

It's okay if your gifts aren't immediately obvious to you. If this is the case, you don't need to worry about it. Sometimes you just have to steep in love a bit longer. Like a spiritual teabag, you need to steep, or rest, in God's love, in order to release your fullest flavor.

Discovering, Developing, and Distributing Your Gifts

Here I hope to assist you in the uncovering, maturation, and dispersion of *your* gifts. I'll explain how my primary gifts of writing and music have unfolded and exploded for kingdom glory. We may share some of the same talents, but there will inevitably be differences; the body of Christ requires such differences. Even if your gifts are opposite of mine, we can still learn from each other in principle.

Writing

I didn't do well in school, but I excelled in language arts. I was taught to keep a journal in sixth grade. That's when I was trained to actively write about life events. Eventually, in high school, my imagination found a fun playground in creative writing class. As for college, I took only one class—Interpersonal Communication—but I remember enjoying the writing assignments. As my independent spiritual interests grew, I did a lot of reading and notetaking, and I kept a journal.

I found this therapeutic throughout the tumultuous times of my first marriage, which ended in divorce. Before the fallout, God planted a seed in my heart in the form of a strong desire to write a book. This was around twelve years ago. Jon, my friend and mentor, encouraged me in writing, as he was the first one I told about my desire to write a book. I remember sitting down and trying to write it but feeling frustrated because I could sense I wasn't ready but I wanted to be. Little did I know, it would take many years of life experience and spiritual education to prepare me for this moment: publishing my first writing assignment.

After divorce, I continued reading and writing. When I was remarried, I wrote even more. This is also when my highest heights, spiritually, began. Writing was exploding out of me. Fast forward to now, and I have a variety of Word documents with thousands of words, stacks of journals and moleskin notebooks, and piles upon piles of loose notes. If I laid each piece out, one next to another, I wonder how many miles long it would be.

My wife helped me understand this is God's gift to me. I was privately receiving insight from Him all along, and the time had finally come to make it public. Years ago, she said, "The book is already written." She was right. It just wasn't organized yet.

This was an overwhelming task. As far as I was concerned, it was like putting together a million-piece puzzle (I'm still putting it together). All of this to say, God was doing a work in me, slowly but surely, and I simply couldn't stop it. This book is evidence of that. Not to mention, there's much more in my heart, desperate to come out in future projects, but all in God's good timing.

All along the way, I received encouragement from others, whether family, friends, or coworkers, some of whom are writers themselves. When I shared the manuscript for this book with my pastor, he said, "This is your gift to the kingdom."

There was a time, several years ago, when I was approached in a new church by a big and friendly young Southerner named Danny. We didn't know each other, but he asked me, "Are you a writer?" I was taken aback because this was off the cuff. I hadn't given any indication I was a writer; I wasn't writing during the service and I wasn't carrying a notebook. I told him, "I am," and he proceeded to speak prophetically over my calling. He told me I could mention him in the book, and I said I would, so I did. This uncontrived, supernatural word from Danny encouraged me immensely in the writing process.

These are a few examples of many undeniably divine-led initiatives to encourage me in writing. I've had *dreams* about such things. Even other people have. I recently had a coworker share a vivid vision she had about this book while drifting asleep: "I was holding your book. There were colors and trees, and wind was blowing through the pages. It was like the Bible, but not the Bible—something that belonged in every home." She said it was going to help a lot of people. I took her words seriously because she knew very little about the book but her dream said otherwise. She especially got my attention when she said "trees." Since she is a believer, I knew God was addressing me through her.

In the earlier stages of discovering and developing this gift from God, I also noticed what a positive impact my writing was making through simply distributing letters or greeting cards to others. For instance, after reading the birthday card I gave my grandma on her eightieth birthday, I remember my aunt looking up with a surprised and sincere expression, and saying, "You are a writer." I don't know how many tears I had to see and how many confirmations I had to hear until I finally believed it was true: I'm a writer. I had so many reasons to talk myself out of it, but there were even more to believe it is true.

Here's the key: Over all these years, I've been seeking God. In some seasons more than others. But no matter how far I might get away, His magnetic pull drew me back into His presence. Now that I know how to commune with God, I don't feel the magnetic pull because I *am* staying close.

In seeking Him, you'll discover your gift. In being with Him, you'll develop it. In participating with His will, you'll distribute it.

Music

When I was in middle school, I bought a bass guitar with hard-earned money from my paper route. Then I joined a few of my friends in a talent show to perform a popular song in the school auditorium. For whatever reason, my bass had no sound during the performance, but I acted like it did and hoped no one would notice. No such luck.

After the song, my best friend's brother called it out. This friend was taking guitar lessons and getting pretty good at it. We entertained the thought of having a band, so we fiddled around and attempted to create some songs. But I didn't take lessons, and I wasn't any good at it. So I lost interest in bass rather quickly, eventually selling it to one of my brother's bandmates and taking up golf.

My brother became a traveling rock-and-roll musician, and did it for many years, doing lead and backup vocals, songwriting, and playing guitar, bass, piano, and drums—pretty much everything. He claims I inspired him when I bought my bass. This surprised me. Especially when he took it further and said he thinks of me as more of an artist than himself; he sees himself as a performer. I can appreciate the distinction, but I know he's a gifted artist. Yet he admitted his struggles with authenticity and how he was drawn to the genuineness of my work, even finding it refreshing and therapeutic to simply read my lyrics. I was touched he found them meaningful.

This conversation came twenty years after my middle-school stunt. Oddly enough, after getting rid of the bass and committing to golf, I eventually stopped playing golf and picked up the guitar. Having kids was a big part of the change, but going through divorce was the biggest game changer.

The circumstances surrounding my divorce were incredibly vexing. With vulnerability running high, I needed a healthy outlet. My brother's guitarist gave me an acoustic guitar. Divorce is not God's will, but He supplies us with strength to overcome it through whatever means He chooses. In my case, guitar played a tremendously supportive role.

My brother is a self-taught guitar player. I remember watching him practice growing up. So I went to my parents' house and found the old book he learned from and diligently practiced a handful of major and minor chords. It was much easier than I anticipated. Not that I became an amazing guitar player, but I did realize you only need to learn a few chords to play many songs. This was a relief because I wanted to write songs and play them as soon as possible. I didn't have the time, money, or interest to obsess over techniques, take formal lessons, or delve into music theory. I needed to express my emotions through song straightaway.

This began as an irrepressible form of therapy, until I discovered just how much I enjoy it. As I healed from divorce, I continued improving at playing the guitar and expressing my thoughts and emotions through songwriting. Then things really took off. When God drew me to my wife, love caused an explosion of music creation. She became and remains my number-one fan.

Eventually, I branched off into writing more songs to God, and some for friends and family. The positive responses were overwhelming. In these songs, I went from focusing on myself to focusing on others. I progressed from hurting and healing to helping and honoring. Some of these songs were directed at my brother and some were not, but he still found profit in them. Many are expressions of my unconditional love for my wife, which she finds reassuring. Many are for God alone; I know this pleases Him. And many are for friends and family who feel honored and receive their gift with gladness.

I learned that music is about worshiping God and connecting people with His love. Ever since God delivered that guitar into my hands, I have amassed a collection of more than 140 songs. I love worshiping God with spiritual songs, honoring my wife with love songs, and blessing people with thoughtful music.

In stage three I mentioned a song I wrote for my grandma—the one she requested for her funeral. I gave her a CD of it on her birthday, although I almost didn't get it recorded in time. But I knew I couldn't sit on it any longer; one year had nearly passed since I wrote it. Once she listened to it, I was blessed to see how meaningful it was to her. In a Christmas card, she told me she listens to it often, just as I envisioned. That's what these gifts are all about: serving God and serving people.

The night my grandma received the song, my parents and the kids had left, but my wife and I stayed to chat with my grandparents. My grandma was still in mild shock because she didn't know I could sing or write songs (in hindsight, I'm surprised I never told her!). She told me I have a gift, and I need "to come out of hiding." Hence, the chapter title—thanks to Grandma.

I explained how long I've been writing and songwriting and how, in recent months, the Lord was urging and preparing me to go public and share what He has given me. When Grandma encouraged me to come out of hiding, her phrase stuck with me. I knew I had to do it—especially since Grandma said so!

Later, I realized I have a role in The Parable of the Talents story because *I* have been entrusted with talents. The question is, will I hide them and keep them all to myself? Or will I invest them in the lives of others so the Lord finds greater love on the earth when He returns? It didn't take long for God to reveal this biblical parallel to me.

Here's the message: Don't bury what you've been given. It is not time for burying; it's time for sharing. It's time to come out of hiding so you can bless people with your talents by encouraging them in the Lord.

I don't know what the future holds, but when we live by the Spirit, He will guide every step. When you're at the center of God's will, you *will* discover, develop, and distribute your gifts for His glory. But be patient, because it may take more time than you want it to. Take heart: You *are* being prepared for the mission God has for you. Maybe you haven't realized it until now. Maybe you haven't reached a particularly fruitful stage yet, but don't be so sure—chances are we can't properly recognize the impact we're having.

Basically, being in the growth process doesn't mean you're not currently making a positive difference in people's lives. A positive influence can happen not only through your actions, or talents, in whatever measure you have received, but also with your secret weapon: your unique, God-glorifying testimony.

His Testimony in Your Testimony

Gifts are powerful tools of love, but so is your story—how you came to Christ, how He changed your life, how you've seen His hand overcome your troubles, and how His Spirit fills you with love and joy in the face of it all. You might be four months saved, four years saved, or forty years saved—whatever it is, your story is for His glory.

When you abide in Christ, the worst of what you've been through becomes the best of what He overcomes through you: "The light shines in the darkness, and the darkness has not overcome it" (John 1:5).

John the Baptist "came as a witness to *testify concerning that light, so that through him all might believe.* He himself was not the light; he came only as a witness to the light" (John 1:7–8). In the next verse, John refers to Jesus as "the true light that gives light to everyone." Jesus is the source of light from whom we derive ours.

We all have the potential to shine the light of Jesus and testify about Him, but until we receive His love, and believe (John 1:10–13), we will remain a dry wick. Only a baptism of love will set us aflame. Then we've become light carriers, or "children of God" (John 1:12).

"In him was life, and that life was the light of all mankind" (John 1:4). Jesus came to share His light with all of us, and He wants us to share it with everyone we can too. At the Sermon on the Mount, He said His followers are "the light of the world" (Matthew 5:14 NKJV). He continues by saying, "A city that is set on a hill cannot be hidden. Nor do they light a lamp and put it under a basket, but on a lampstand, and it gives light to all *who are* in the house. Let your light so shine before men, that they may see your good works and glorify your Father in heaven" (Matthew 5:14–16 NKJV).

We're called to share the light we've been given. Our life came through Jesus (John 1:2–3), and everything we say and do should point to Him (Colossians 3:17), whether directly or indirectly, depending on the guidance of the Holy Spirit at any given moment.

We're not supposed to bury our talents or hide our light under a basket. We already discussed the uncovering of our talents. But how do we ensure we're giving off light to all "in the house," or around us, that is. We can take our light out from under the basket by actively loving people and manifesting our testimony.

What Is My Testimony?

Simply stated, your testimony is the proof of God's love making you pure and holy. It's your personal narrative concerning how His love has changed the details of your life. It demonstrates how your life has become less of a stumbling block (1 Corinthians 8:9; 2 Corinthians 6:3) for others and more of a lifesaver and motivator.

Maybe some key components of your story involve pulling out weeds, like drug addiction, pornography, or gossiping, by the power of Christ. In the process, perhaps some promising seeds of love were planted, inspiring the drive to form a new church, write a book, or finally pray consistently, with passion. Throughout this book, I'm describing the effects of God's love in my life. As for you, your testimony expresses His life-changing love from your unique angle. Some areas of our lives have probably changed more than others; these are usually the points others can benefit from the most.

For instance, one strong point in my story started with what became my "life verse." Since discovering it, the Holy Spirit has used it, through me, to guide many people into the light of God's love for them; I consider it the bright shining star of my testimony. When I first saw it, the circumstances were ugly, but the outcome was beautiful—not unlike my primary gifts of writing and music, which became my greatest pleasures, but not before they were discovered through my greatest pain: divorce.

Thankfully, in the kingdom of God, our greatest challenges become our greatest opportunities for growth, and our biggest victories afford us the strength to serve others selflessly. Whatever we may come up against, God delivers believers and gives people and places into their hands (1 Samuel 17:37; Joshua 10:8, 19). We ought to remember what He has done, and give Him all the glory (Psalm 77).

My Life Verse

It happened when I was seventeen. I found out my girlfriend was pregnant. The news gripped me with fear. I doubted my readiness and dreaded the thought of telling my parents. In preparation, I talked with my youth pastor before I told them, and I began praying fervently.

When the time came, my heart was beating frantically. I approached my dad and placed his hand over my heart. He looked at me with grave concern and asked, "What's wrong?" I told him. He clearly felt compassion, but I could see the grief come over him as we both wondered what we were going to do about this. He got my mom. She was devastated. Fortunately, the conversation ended with them affirming their commitment and saying, "We will love this child." In spite of my guilt, this brought tremendous peace to me.

As much as I appreciated the commitment of my parents, being a father was my responsibility. This was a frightening thought. I felt unprepared and restless.

Late one night, I turned on the lamp in my bedroom and took out some Christian literature. Then the unexpected happened. I was reading a prayer commanding evil spirits to leave my presence in the name of Jesus, but as soon as my eyes locked onto "evil spirits," I felt a rush of overwhelming fear and panic. It was a terrifying sensation unlike anything I'd ever experienced. I felt out of control and afraid of what was next. I had to move. I didn't understand what was happening or how it would end.

Eventually, I either passed out on the couch or crashed in exhaustion. The next morning I was relieved it was over but absolutely terrified it would happen again. Since it had come upon me suddenly, without notice, I was afraid the next episode could be lurking around any corner.

Interestingly, my mom perceived something was wrong. She asked me if everything was okay, because she woke up praying for me at the late hour when this happened. Without me volunteering any information, she explained she was awoken and prompted by the Spirit to pray for me because I was under attack. So she did. We figured that was around the time I conked out on the couch. This was encouraging, but I was still afraid because I didn't understand what was happening or if it would happen again.

What was I supposed to do now? I felt like I was up against an unbeatable monster. Like a six-foot man versus a nine-foot-six Philistine (1 Samuel 17). I needed five stones but didn't even have one. Not until my mom showed up again, this time with a weapon: the Bible. Like David, I found five stones but only needed one. My life verse has five lines in one verse. This verse was the only "stone" I needed.

I had been sulking in my room, paralyzed in fear and anxiety, when she walked in with her Bible, wanting to play "Bible roulette." The idea is opening the Bible and randomly placing your finger on a verse. But I wasn't happy to see my mom or her Bible. I wanted to be left alone.

I needed help. My mom thought she could bring it, but I didn't. So I told her to go. Leave it to a stubborn Norwegian to refuse. My mom didn't like to see me oppressed. She wasn't going to let me get crushed under the weight of it all—not on her watch.

Back to Bible roulette.

There I was, lying in a state of panic, my body shifting uneasily as if it wanted to get away from itself but couldn't. When I saw her Bible I thought, *Oh, great.* She opened it up, sitting on the edge of my bed, and instinctively placed her finger on an unidentified verse. She said, "I want you to read this. I never do this, and I don't know what verse it is, but I want you to read it."

"Why should I?" I asked.

"I feel led to do this."

"You just read it, then," I said.

"I want *you* to read it."

"No, Mom, I don't want to. Please leave."

"C'mon, Ben. I know you can do this." She still had her finger fixed on the same spot.

"No. *Please* go." I was tossing and turning, adamant that she leave. I was getting upset. Yet I also felt starved for attention but without strength to receive it.

She persisted, her look softened with compassion, sincerity, and genuine concern. Tired of my resistance, she made a desperate plea. "Please?" she said.

We both paused.

Like the persistent friend in Luke 11:5–13, she would not relent, and I gave in. I said, "Okay."

Just as I was about to read it to myself, Mom said, "Out loud."

I didn't want to, but I also didn't want to put all that effort into resisting her again. So I began to read. "Fear not ..." I stopped. Not like stopping at a stop light; more like crashing into a force I couldn't contend with.

Seeing my struggle, she encouraged me to keep on reading. "Keep going. You can do this."

I tried again. "Fear not ..." Then, trying to compose myself again, "Fear not, for *I am with you* ..." At that moment, it was as if God Himself whispered into my ear and wrecked me. My fear and anxiety were instantly collapsing under the weight of His glory. I couldn't hold the tears back; I was completely undone. It was as though God was pulling me in closer and wrapping me in the warmth of His presence, as a parent swaddles and consoles a needy baby in a warm blanket. I felt assured. He was telling me he was right there right *now,* and I *knew* He was.

Staying composed took a valiant effort, but I was strengthened, by His touch, to continue reading. So I choked back my tears, fully convinced I was hearing God speaking to me, and I finished the entire verse. "Fear not, for I am with you. Be not dismayed, for I am your God. I will strengthen you, yes, I will help you, I will uphold you with my righteous right hand." (This is Isaiah 41:10 NKJV.)

Never before had I *felt* the presence of God as intensely as I did in that moment. It was like I could actually *hear* God. His voice was no less real to me than my mom's was. I was cradled in His loving arms, and provided with a strong sense of security and peace far beyond anything I knew. My room was no longer my "safe place"—His presence was.

My mom was crying too. She reverently said, "Thank you, Jesus," praising God through her tears. She was proud of me for completing the verse, and touched by how moving this was.

If she hadn't stepped into my room and followed His lead, this wouldn't have happened. But she did, effectively playing her part as an instrument of His peace. She encouraged me to hold on tightly to this verse, and I did—memorizing it, and recalling it in many times of trouble.

In finding this verse I found a priceless treasure. I would continue to prosper in this revelation, unpacking the abundance and prophetic importance of it for many years to come. It became a thread—a *golden thread*—winding through and weaving together the fabric of my life. God was creating a masterpiece, a quilt I could use to enwrap others in His comforting presence.

A day or two after my Isaiah 41:10 experience, I knew it was my life verse. I was in my room again, standing in front of my window and looking outside. Light was beaming through the window and illuminating my room, and a curiosity popped up in my mind. This prompting came from none other than God Himself.

I was reminded of the wallet-sized name card I had in my wallet—one of those wallet-size verse cards with a name and a verse, that I'd received months if not years ago. Things are pretty easily taken for granted, overlooked, and underappreciated. However, I do believe there are some cases when things are hidden until their appointed time to be revealed, as was the case here in my room. I suddenly felt like I needed to know what verse was on my name card. Digging for it like a hidden treasure, I found my well-worn wallet and unfolded it with eager anticipation.

Here's what I saw:

Benjamin
"Fear not, for I am with you;
Be not dismayed, for I am your God.
I will strengthen you,
Yes, I will help you,
I will uphold you with My righteous right hand."
Isaiah 41:10 NKJV

I was rocked! I quickly realized, without a doubt, this whole thing was a divine setup. Like an "Easter egg hunt," I found something special God had hidden for me. This was a thoughtful act of love, as if receiving flowers from God.

It was all so wonderfully amazing. I initially got the card as a gift, not thinking anything of the verse on it, but rather keeping it as a sentimental Christian decoration for my wallet. Then all of this happened? It was so touching, humbling, and encouraging to know—to *really* know—God was undeniably with me through all things to come. For me, this was a critically needed affirmation in that moment, and God knew it.

I was about to be a father, and I had to get my bearings on the situation at hand. I was afraid I wouldn't be in shape for fatherhood since my recent struggles left me feeling hopeless and in despair. *Can I even do this father thing?* I wondered. *How am I supposed to make it work when I'm feeling this way?* I had a month to figure it out, but that was a lot of pressure considering how devastated I felt.

I remember how hard it was to fall asleep at night. I dreaded bedtime. Lying in the dark was unnerving. It was like I was being suffocated in a blanket of blackness. To offset this, I started using a softly lit night light. Seeing my surroundings gently illuminated gave me a sense of control among the chaos. I'm not sure exactly why, but maybe it simply alluded to the upcoming sunrise, serving as a small reminder that light overcomes the darkness (John 1:5). I was beginning to realize what a big difference such little light can make.

This is where Isaiah 41:10 came in. Just as kids like sources of comfort at bedtime, Isaiah 41:10 was my warm and cozy blanket, my plush teddy bear, my inner night light. I held onto it tightly, memorizing it (as my mom suggested) and falling asleep doing so.

It wasn't long before I was sleeping quite peacefully every night, though the surges of anxiety had not completely dissipated. Any time I felt a rush of panic, I would deflect it with Isaiah 41:10. In this way, I was "taking every thought captive to the obedience of Christ" (2 Corinthians 10:5).

Ever since the first panic attack, I knew momentum was building in the right direction. I had new weapons in my arsenal. I carried Isaiah 41:10 like a sword (Ephesians 6:17). I kept it with me at all times, using it as needed, whether I was feeling anxious at the grocery store, in bed, or on a road trip. Little did I know, an important part of my testimony was being written, and it would later serve to help many people. God was effectively leading me in freedom from fear, and constantly reassuring me of His presence.

In teenage pregnancy, "Fear not, for I am with you."

In child rearing and panic, "Be not dismayed, for I am your God."

In divorce, "I will strengthen you."

In remarriage and becoming love, "Yes, I will help you."

In discouragement, "I will uphold you with my righteous right hand."

Indeed, I was comforted by God's Spirit and growing in the strength of His love and the power to serve. If I'm going to be honest, any time I'm feeling anxious, afraid, and so on, I'm thinking for myself, and I think it's all about me. But having a child got my mind off myself. Dwelling on Scripture got my mind off myself. The list goes on, but here's what I'm driving at: When we're weak, God is preparing us for service to showcase His strength.

My focus was shifting from self-serving to serving others. Abiding in Christ won't leave you stuck in self-centeredness and all the junk that comes along with it. Love changes your life and supplies the power you need to help others find the freedom they need.

When you live by the Spirit, it gets fun because you get into the good stuff: helping others find freedom from what binds them. You have a story, and you can help people with it. For example, not only did Isaiah 41:10 see me through many difficulties; it also served to comfort many people around me going through similar challenges. One person in particular, Becca, was touched in dramatically divine fashion.

Becca's Story

Becca is like a sister to me. I have an extra-soft spot for some people, and she is definitely one of them. She is kind, hard-working, and funny, and her laughter is infectious, but she entered a scary season of things spiraling out of control. Her anxiety was off the charts (something I can relate to).

Coming to work became a dreadful thing for her. One day, it was too much—she couldn't hide it any longer. She wasn't a Christian; in fact, she seemed to despise religion. But God wasn't about to leave her hanging, so He sent me after her when she needed Him most. What happened next was supernatural. Becca kindly agreed to share the story from her point of view.

> Words echoing, tunnel vision, walls closing in. My body is clenching. I'm losing the ability to move. It's suffocating me. I can't think. I can't breathe. I feel so alone. These are the beginnings of a panic attack I know all too well.

This particular day started like any other day. Unfortunately for me, that consisted of two panic attacks before I even got to work.

I was in a room working on documents when I felt the onset of another panic attack. I started rocking back and forth, chanting my now daily mantra, "You're okay, you'll be fine, you are safe," over and over to myself. I was able to calm down enough to reach out to my coworker Ben to come and help with my remaining documents. As he sits down and sets up, I start to feel my body tense. My heart starts racing, and I can't recall if I even started processing the documents with Ben.

My whole body starts to clench, my hand has a death grip on my pen, I'm crying, snot is dripping from my nose, and I am paralyzed. Staring forward, the room empties. It's just Ben and me. Ben's talking to me, but I can't fully make out what he's saying until I hear him ask me if he can touch me. Normally, I cannot handle being touched when I'm over-stimulated by a panic attack or emotions, but in that moment for whatever reason, I nod yes. He then reaches his hand over and touches my arm, and that gave me something to start focusing on.

Ben then asked me if he could pray for me. I am not a religious person; most days I would have been annoyed by someone asking me that and I would have told them no. The approach Ben takes with me during this time disarms me, and before I know it I'm nodding yes again to him. I can hear that he is talking, but I can no longer understand the words and focus only on his touch.

Eventually, I start to calm down, and I think Ben can see that because I can hear him tell me to look at him. I shake my head, not wanting him to see me. The shame and humiliation I can only imagine I'm wearing on my face, but most of all I was afraid to see pity in his eyes. Ben says, "Please look at me, Becca." I find myself turning my head and I look at him directly in his eyes, and it's not pity I see—it is love.

I don't remember exactly what he said to me in that moment, but I do remember him telling me I'm safe, I'm loved, and I believe him.

People were around, but she couldn't see them—we were in God's safe zone and the "fear of man" was absent. I hardly noticed the other coworkers myself because I was in the zone with the Spirit. I began praying Scripture—Isaiah 41:10. When it comes to the energy of God that "so powerfully works in me" (Colossians 1:29), I can't think of a time I felt it more than in that moment, when I asked her to look at me. My eyes felt like they were ablaze, and I could feel warmth, compassion, and boldness. Slowly, she began to settle. She commented on her clenched hand—she couldn't open it at all. But I continued praying for the tension to leave and her hand to loosen, and it gradually did. Her countenance was getting brighter. Soon she recovered enough for us to resume our work.

Afterward, I wrote Isaiah 41:10 down on a sticky note and gave it to her. She stuck it to the side of her computer monitor. It wasn't long before I felt inspired to write a song for her with lyrics based on this experience and some things she said about it.

When I told her I had a song I wanted to share with her, she didn't know it was about her at first. So while she listened to it for the first time, she soon realized it was about her and she started getting emotional. She loved it and wanted to share it with some people, so I told her to go for it. It was fun to see how receptive she was to all of this. Eventually, the time came for her to leave the company, but she came back several months later. She seemed like a new person too. I remember commenting on her handwriting. I know it sounds funny, but her writing looked less like the Richter scale and more like a graceful brushstroke. She later left the department, but we still keep in touch. She told me she talks about our experience to this day.

Big Things Happen

As you can see, Becca experienced the love of God through me. The important thing isn't that you have a life verse or a song, or that you "save" a person, but that you acknowledge the presence of God in your life and manifest His love to everyone through whatever it is He has given you. *Show it* through your actions and talents, and *tell it* through your unique testimony. In this way, you'll glorify God by touching others with love, thereby encouraging them in their growth toward spiritual maturity.

Diseases and insects, or the Enemy and lies, may threaten to harm the health of our tree, but God intends to use it all for good, to take the terrible stuff and flip it in order to accomplish the saving of many lives (Genesis 50:20). We ought to speak of His faithfulness and use our stories in favor of redemption.

By introducing me to my life verse, God delivered me, and eventually several people, from the clutches of teenage pregnancy, panic attacks, fear of flying, insomnia, general stress and anxiety, and so on. Some even found salvation! But I couldn't help free others until I was first free myself.

Sometimes we have nothing to give. But when you're growing with God, you'll get something to give, and it will help many people if you share what He has delivered into your hands. We don't boast about what we've been through, but how He brought us through it. His grace is sufficient for strengthening us through weakness. We should be glad His power is at work in our life (2 Corinthians 12:9 NKJV).

When I was going through teenage pregnancy and panic attacks, I had nothing to give. When I made it through victoriously, I did. The problem isn't that I had problems. The problem is that I had little faith. I needed intimacy with God. What matters most is having consistent communion with God, loving Him, and loving people. If we seek Him in prayer, meditate on His Word, and boast in His ability to successfully guide us through troubles, we will find the strength to serve others.

What makes our testimony of His light the "secret weapon" of our influence? The manner in which it serves as a subtle but powerful, sometimes shocking, introduction to the overwhelming outflow of God's love.

No matter what you've been through or what you've done, your life is not a waste. Your past, present, and future are not too much for God to contend with. With God, our troubles are like firewood, fueling the fire of His presence and making His glory bigger and brighter for all to see—if only we would release our firewood to Him. Then each problem we encounter becomes another log in the fire. So we go through the temporal pains and trials of life marked by the warmth of His love.

Next thing you know, we walk through this life with a brightened countenance armed with a great story to tell! Like Shadrach, Meshach, and Abednego, we put our trust in God and walk through life revealing God reality, and those who will acknowledge His power at work in our lives will give glory to God. He has put us where we are with what we have for the purpose of redeeming all creation. God forbid we shrink back, hide our light, bury our talents, and refuse to sow His selfless love on earth.

Your light is for shining atop a hill so all can see. When you shine brightly and invest heavily, others will reap greatly and God will be glorified. Your talents are for sowing generously; you've been made rich in every way so you can give generously on every occasion (2 Corinthians 9:11). Not in the least by sharing your inspirational stories. Christians give what they have been given for the benefit of others.

When you come out of hiding, big things will happen. One thing is for sure: the love of God through *your* life can make a *big* difference in a person's life, whether they're a Christian or a non-Christian. A person's salvation is between them and God. God saves—we love. If I didn't come out of hiding, who would have helped Becca in that moment?

There are people around you who desperately need the light of God's love. Fortunately, you carry it. But people won't benefit from it unless you let it shine. We can't predict the impact of love, but we can hope for the best and pray fervently. This is what a disciple of Jesus does. They depend on God and show His love. In reality, when we draw people in with love, we're drawing them near Jesus because His Holy Spirit is in us. Therefore, if they receive our love they are receiving His because they are one and the same.

When Jesus saw Peter and Andrew fishing, He said, "'Follow Me, and I will make you fishers of men.' They immediately left *their* nets and followed Him" (Matthew 4:19–20 NKJV). Likewise, we are all called to follow Jesus *immediately*. There is no time to waste, lest we miss a critical moment. We are all desperately in need of His redeeming love. Those of us who know Him have a special responsibility to show the love of Jesus and to invite others into a relationship with Him.

In the next chapter, we'll look at how love seizes the moment and makes disciples of Jesus.

Chapter 11:

Making Disciples

To make a disciple, you have to be a disciple.

A disciple of Jesus is a follower of Him—someone possessed by His Holy Spirit and living a life of love. When did Jesus' disciples really start discipling others? When did they begin teaching others how to follow Jesus? After they spent three years with Him (the book of Acts) and learned to follow Him for themselves, after much trial and error. In the Gospels, it's evident they had power and authority to perform some miracles, but they didn't fully walk in selfless, non-reward-seeking love and preach the gospel until after the resurrection. They couldn't effectively minister to others until the Holy Spirit came upon them with power. Only then could they give what they got through prayer by the laying on of hands (Acts 8:17–18).

Once upon a time, when I spoke with the late Dallas Willard on the phone, he told me to look at all the references in Acts concerning the laying on of hands (because it's a big deal). Apparently, he wasn't trying to hide himself because I had found his phone number with ease. I was at home, it was nighttime, and I was scared. Isaiah 41:10 always comforted me, especially in those dark and quiet moments when I was alone in bed, kids asleep, and left to wonder what would become of those chaotic circumstances.

But I wasn't holding onto this verse the same way I did in the past when overcoming panic attacks. This time it wasn't just about me; I was scared for someone dear to me. I wanted them to find peace the way I did through this verse. Were they going to come out of this okay? What could I do to help? I felt like my entire family was in a spiritual battle and I had to fight to protect them. I tried to fight, but I felt like I needed help. At the time, I was reading Dallas's work, so I thought calling a wise Christian ally like himself would help.

I dialed his number and listened intently as the phone rang until the answering machine sounded. I figured it was unlikely I would get a hold of him since he probably got so many calls on a regular basis. Even so, I decided to leave a message. As quickly and clearly as possible, I told him who I was, where I was calling from, and what was going on.

That's when Dallas picked up the phone. "Hello?"

I was elated but trying to keep cool. "Hi, Dallas. Thanks for answering."

"I get a lot of phone calls and I don't answer most of them," he said, "but I was listening to your message and thought I should answer this one. So what's going on?"

"I know you're a busy man, so I'll try to be quick. Thanks again for taking my call. I feel bad for calling, but things have been really hard lately." I felt uncomfortable, like I was imposing on him. He was a man of few words, and the harsh voice of my inner critic tried to fill the quiet.

"Well, here we are now," he said, as if to say, "Let's talk. We don't need to worry about the time."

I felt more at peace about calling, and I explained everything. Dallas embodied a James 1:19 response; he was "quick to listen and slow to speak." He asked me, "What do you know about the laying on of hands?" I said I didn't know much. He explained the frequency of its use in the New Testament, and said, "There's healing in the hands." He encouraged me to spend some time reading through the New Testament to find these instances. To look at the Gospels, and especially the book of Acts, so I could observe the biblical significance of healing hands in action. He emphasized, "It's a very biblical thing."

The laying on of hands was an unfamiliar concept to me. Frankly, I thought it was a fanciful notion. I wondered, *If it's so easy, or if it's real, why isn't it happening more?* At the same time, I was fascinated by the supernatural possibility of healing others by expressing love through the hands as a supernatural channel for God's power to flow from His Spirit in me to another person.

I knew Jesus could do it, and His disciples, but me? Or people I knew? I doubted it. Yet I trusted Dallas's authority and spiritual wisdom on the subject; he had already profoundly influenced my life through his writing. Prior to this, I hadn't considered this kind of healing a realistic option, but I was desperate for anything that might help.

He asked me, "Do you have three close friends or mentors, maybe a pastor, whom you can trust—people who are mature in the faith?"

I explained I wasn't sure about their comfort level with this kind of healing approach. They were from a conservative-Baptist-type background, like me, and I remember thinking of anything remotely charismatic as highly suspect behavior. He thought it was important for them to have confidence in God's ability to heal, but he thought it was important that they just "get their hands on" this person too. "God can work through this," he said.

I told him I could think of a few people I would reach out to. He suggested they gather around and put their hands on this person's shoulder, hands, and head, and pray, commanding healing by "the power of the blood of Jesus." While the professionals say some things are incurable, Dallas would disagree. He said, "I have seen many, many people healed of afflictions, and even a few who were suffering from this."

He went on to explain that, for reasons he cannot fully comprehend or explain, people have different results: some are not healed, others show some signs of improvement, and yet others are completely healed. The important thing is that we learn to put our faith in God, trusting in His ability to heal right here, right now—to believe it's His will to heal. He assured me that praying with boldness and the laying on of hands is powerful and effective, if you believe. As he spoke, I could feel my enthusiasm and confidence growing; my increasing faith was beginning to curb my skepticism, thanks to Dallas simply taking the time to pick up the phone and talk with me. Before we ended the call, he prayed for strength, protection, and the wisdom of my spiritual friends to help deliver this person from the grip of disorder by the "blood of Jesus."

The prayers I was exposed to growing up seemed mostly passive and weak, devoid of power and relegated to defeat, but Dallas prayed with authority. I found this refreshing. It rang true with my spirit. I may have had doubts about my own level of belief, but I didn't doubt his; I was confident his bold prayers would make a positive difference. This, in effect, strengthened my own belief—simply by witnessing his example. I thanked him again for taking the time to listen, talk, and pray with me. He could've just said goodbye, but he wanted me to keep in touch with him: "Let me know how things go."

This is a glimpse of a mature believer (Dallas) encouraging an immature believer (me) in the faith. In a sense, He was discipling me. He was teaching me how to live by faith in God according to the truth of His Word. He prayed for me and my family, and I have seen the fruit of his prayer over the course of many years since then.

Prayer doesn't positively impact believers only, but non-believers too—or, as I like to think of them, soon-to-be believers. There's a special place in the heart of God for every single person, non-Christians included. He is patient, and persistently after us all because He doesn't want anyone to perish (2 Peter 3:9). As Christians, we have the privilege and responsibility of loving others into the kingdom of God through kindness (Romans 2:4). Therefore, Christians show kindness through their actions, whether in person through care, or in privacy through prayer. In this chapter, I wish to emphasize making *new* disciples of Jesus, as opposed to building up existing ones (addressed in the next chapter).

What can happen when we love non-Christians and pray for them? Here are a few personal, true stories to illustrate.

Luke's Story

I regularly pray for the salvation of my non-Christian coworkers. For a long time, I didn't realize how important and effective this is. Luke is one of my coworkers, whom I affectionately and playfully refer to as Bromeo. This is the guy who told me he was learning from me and noticed that I don't gossip.

We tinkered with a few spiritually geared conversations. One time I invited him on a walk during break to help cool him down after an altercation he had with a coworker. I found out he had a lot of other stressors going on behind it all, so I prayed for him. Despite a few instances of his vocal opposition to religion, he appreciated the gesture (people love when you're thoughtful toward them).

We agreed we should hang out sometime, but it took three years for us to finally meet *outside* the workplace for the first time. During my nightly prayer, I regularly ask God to draw people to Himself through me, and to empower me to help them receive His Holy Spirit. My meeting with Luke was an answer to prayer. For several months preceding our meeting, I had several visions of being with him in a party room and praying.

SELFLESS-SUFFICIENT

Eventually, I knew it was the right time to invite Luke out for pizza—*free* pizza. This was a big deal for him because he was a single dad, having a hard time making ends meet, and living on scraps for food. Not to mention, money was tight for me, and I literally had just enough extra money for that pizza and nothing more. (Coincidence? I think not!) He happily agreed to hang out and grab a free meal. I reserved a party room.

Of course, I prayed for God's blessing on this throughout the day, and my kind-hearted wife was praying about it too; I didn't even have to ask her! She also said a prayer with me before I left. Her prayers always make a positive difference.

I was more tired than usual that day. I don't normally yawn, but I was yawning a lot. I hoped I would feel more energized that evening, but I didn't fret about it because I trusted God would show up and do what needed to be done. This put me at ease and opened me up to His energy, which so powerfully works within us (Colossians 1:29). Actually, as soon as my friend arrived, it was like a switch was flipped in me. I felt great! Energetic. Alert. Happy and centered.

Luke was glad to be there. To his delight, I brought him some extra food. It was good to see him smiling because he went through a nasty divorce, and divorce has a way of robbing people of their smiles. I could tell my friend was having a hard time getting through the aftermath of its destruction. With all the hardships and chaos in his life, it appeared he was under a curse. I know how lonely, confusing, and painful divorce is. I also know how therapeutic and healing it is to talk things through and receive prayer.

Once the pizza arrived, I asked him how things were going. He didn't have any trouble opening up. Even telling me things he had "never told anyone before." I got candid a few times too, in an effort to benefit him. I felt completely guided by the Lord in all of this, whether I was speaking or listening.

This conversation was a divinely orchestrated opportunity to bring healing into Luke's heart. God loves my friend, and He chose to love him through me. I have been through divorce and found complete healing in Jesus, and I can confidently say I've never been happier. This means I have hope and encouragement—a testimony—to give to those going through the fires of life, such as divorce. I know people can come out clean and purified if they go through it prayerfully, with confidence in our Lord. We have a lot of problems, but there is only one answer: Jesus.

Suddenly, I saw a door open to talk about the love of God, and I walked through it without hesitation. I gushed about the love of God and called out Luke's readiness to receive it. I asked him if he had ever asked the Spirit of Jesus to come and live inside him. He said not to his knowledge, but he does pray sometimes. I described how the Holy Spirit works, and I told him I could give him what I have through prayer and the laying on of hands. I asked him if he would let me pray for him to receive it.

He said yes! So I placed my left hand on his back and hovered my right hand above his chest, sometimes gently landing a touch, and invited the Holy Spirit to come and rest upon him. Then I guided my friend through prayer, having him repeat after me, admitting his sin, receiving forgiveness, confessing Jesus as Lord and Savior of his life, and thanking God for sending His Spirit to inhabit his body. I also guided him in praying by faith concerning certain things that were troubling him. I could tell it wasn't natural for him because the truth has a way of exposing the dark spots.

Afterward, he thanked me and said it felt good. He looked like he felt good! I told him I had to give him a hug, so we rose to our feet and hugged. I remember starving for such brotherly love when I went through divorce, so I said, "You probably haven't had many of these," and I just held it for a while.

After hugging him, I told him he is loved by God, and how he has so much potential in Christ. I assured him that God is proud of him. That God loves people Luke has a hard time loving. That he doesn't need anyone other than God because no one else can meet his needs. I said God's love and forgiveness isn't just for receiving but giving too. No one is better here—we are all equally in need of God. Speaking the truth in love in this way helps guard us against holding grudges toward others, such as an ex-spouse. God shows mercy toward people and forgives them, as should we (Luke 11:4; Luke 23:34).

As we continued our conversation, I spent time attempting to sharpen his perspective by teaching him about spiritual matters and encouraging him to read the Bible, pray, and go to church. His sister (a Christian) had already invited him to church several times, and he went (even bringing his kids) on several occasions. Clearly, God had been wooing him.

It was a heavenly evening with Luke. I know the angels were rejoicing (Luke 15:10). We said our goodbyes and he thanked me again for everything. Back home, I went into my room and praised God for the way His Spirit moved through me to help my friend. I acknowledged how God answered my prayers, and thanked Him for His faithfulness.

Don't be one of the nine out of ten who don't give thanks for healing *or* praise to God (see Luke 17:11–19). I asked Jesus to give further revelations and wisdom to my friend, and I broke off every curse by the power and authority of Jesus's name. I passionately prayed with a heavenly tongue. I was quite possibly the happiest I've ever been in prayer. I couldn't resist jumping, dancing, and lifting my arms. It was a true celebration.

After all this progress and a promising new beginning, I was caught off guard when I noticed Luke was upset and swearing—the next day. Feeling confused, I began reflecting in prayer. I was immediately faced with the temptation to question the legitimacy of his conversion. Just as quickly as the doubt was raised, the truth shot it down. The Holy Spirit quickly reminded me of how the growth process works. It begins with a seed—which takes *time* to grow, so be patient. Think of how patient God is with us! What right do I have to not be patient with others?

Sometimes it might take three or more years of planting and watering until the Spirit of God can take root in another person's heart. Equipped with this understanding, I thanked God and acknowledged the good work He did and continues to do in Luke.

I remember my pastor saying God accomplishes His will through prayer. We can promote good only through prayer—we ask, He does. This story is evidence of that. My friend's salvation is not my doing. God has always been after him.

Just like He was after Nia.

Nia's Story

Nia is the one who announced to the room that, "My whole world would fall apart if I heard Ben swear. Everything I know about him would go out the window." This was said with an air of whimsy, but I sensed there was some truth behind it. She said this before she was a Christian, which tells me the purity of our example can make a significantly positive impact, as she graciously shares in the following statement about our relationship and her conversion experience:

> People say God works in mysterious ways. I would say God has worked perfectly and poetically in my life. When I look back on my journey with God over the past few years, I am in awe of how flawlessly he has moved in my life. Many small interactions have

brought me to an entirely new understanding of myself in Christ. It's been beautiful, completely transforming, and overwhelming in the best way possible. Although in many ways I do feel I've been made "new," I am also who I have always been.

Before meeting Ben I was uninterested in a relationship with God. I associated religion with judgment and condemnation. I never understood the difference between God and religion, I thought the words were synonymous. Ben was the first person who piqued my interested in God simply by observing the way he lived his life. He seemed to be truly at peace, and not because his life circumstances were ideal or easy. He appeared to have a peace that came from within. I was not at peace in my life, however, and I also didn't know what I was missing. I decided a long time ago that some feelings and actions were assigned to me by way of biology. I was anxious. I was a worrier. I was restless. I was up and down emotionally. While I felt I deserved peace, I also fundamentally believed the above described adjectives would always be part of who I was—as integral to my identity as any other descriptive word one could say about me.

Then, about three and a half years ago I met my partner in life, Jon. I was immediately drawn to his kindness and commitment to his children. We shared a lot about our kids the night we met at a random Halloween party. It was one of those funny stories where both people should not have been in a place, but they were, and when they met, it was more than chemistry, it was immediate mutual understanding. At the time I might have described it as "meant to be"; now I would say "by God's design."

During one of the first conversations I had with Jon, he asked me when the last time I went to church was. I was immediately disappointed. This was obviously not going to work. He was a self-described Christian. I was not. I was certain he would find out who I really was, and judgment and condemnation would follow. Eventually he did find out who I really was. Thank you, God, Jon never pushed his views on me. He reminded me of Ben in that way. He was just a kind, helpful, loving person who seemed very at peace. He seemed so together. I would eventually come to realize that his life circumstances were not easy or ideal either. His peace came from within—from God.

Eventually I embarked on my own spiritual journey, starting with an open-minded curiosity. Along the way God would draw me in by dropping these little bread crumbs. He would send me messages using a language that only I spoke. It was unmistakably God letting me know I was loved and protected. To find out much later that Ben prayed for my salvation, and that I would meet a man of God, is so special to me. I would have never necessarily wanted that. But as I continue to learn, God doesn't make mistakes. Thank you for your prayers—they changed my life.

Why the Credit Is Not Mine

I didn't save Luke or Nia—God did. It would be foolish of me to seek a reward for my service since I've only done my duty (Luke 17:7–10). Furthermore, "What do you have that you did not receive? And if you did receive it, why do you boast as though you did not?" (1 Corinthians 4:7). Paul's thought-provoking, pride-killing questions remind us we can do nothing without God, therefore all credit is due Him. In other words, when it comes to the stories I told, I was building on a foundation already laid. People planted seeds and watered them before me, and people will continue planting and watering after me. Sometimes we plant, and sometimes we water.

Like the apostle Paul said:

> I planted the seed, Apollos watered it, but God has been making it grow. So neither the one who plants nor the one who waters is anything, but only God, who makes things grow. The one who plants and the one who waters have one purpose, and they will each be rewarded according to their own labor. For we are co-workers in God's service; you are God's field, God's building. By the grace God has given me, I laid a foundation as a wise builder, and someone else is building on it. But each one should build with care. For no one can lay any foundation other than the one already laid, which is Jesus Christ. (1 Corinthians 3:6–11)

What is our "one purpose"? God-glorifying *service*. Remember what the reward was for the workers in the field? Some worked harder than others but they all got the same reward. A denarius. Remember the prodigal son story? His brother, who stayed with his father, didn't get a better reward; rather, they both got the same reward—being with his father (it was never about the fattened calf). In other words, when you drink the "living water," you won't want anything else to drink (John 4:1–26).

We're supposed to serve God by loving people, expecting nothing in return (Luke 6:35), and celebrating the spiritual successes of others. Disciples don't take credit or look for promotion and honor. That's what I'll call *spiritual security*—when you know the love of God is enough, and being with Him is all you need, as opposed to jockeying for false securities. Instead, we're made to humble ourselves by serving others. Until we learn to thoughtfully serve God and others, we cannot effectively make disciples of Jesus.

The Makings of a Disciple Maker

If you're going to bake something, you need the appliances, tools, and ingredients necessary to do so. If you don't have an oven, kitchen utensils, the recipe, and *all* ingredients, you can't make cookies. Likewise, how can I make disciples if I don't have all the things we've been talking about (namely, love)?

The church, in large part, appears to have most of the ingredients but seems to be missing the most important ingredient of all: love. And without love, you can't make disciples. Jesus saved people through love, and He continues to save people through His love by the power of His Holy Spirit within us.

Jesus said, "This is to my Father's glory, that you bear much fruit, showing yourselves to be my disciples." (John 15:8).

Is the world a better place because we're Christians? It should be, but if we're fruitless, probably not. We need the fruit of the Spirit to make disciples. Then you can help people going through what you went through. This is how we use what we have to testify about Jesus and offer hope. When you have love, your fruit is good for the taking. Disciples have spiritual food for spiritual needs, and they give it generously.

A *food bank* is "a place where stocks of food, typically basic provisions and nonperishable items, are supplied free of charge to people in need."[31] A committed disciple is like a walking ~~food~~ fruit bank, with all nine fruit of the Spirit to go around: love, joy, peace, patience, kindness, goodness, faithfulness, gentleness, and self-control (Galatians 5:22–23). The more mature you are, the holier you will live, and the greater the impact you will have. People generally notice when they're freely given something of great value. In which case, they're typically filled with gratitude, which honors the Lord. A disciple maker seeks to honor the Lord by seeking Him first in all things.

Witnessing through Holiness and Purity

Todd White has created a powerful, free documentary called "Pure and Holy."[32] He wisely confronts this "cheap grace" I-don't-need-to-live-transformed idea by reminding us we are called to live holy lives (1 Peter 1:13–16; 1 Thessalonians 4). Near the beginning of the documentary (14:11) he eloquently and biblically explains his avoidance of alcohol as a personal conviction—not a judgment upon others. He avoids it as a witness to others, so as to remove the possibility of it being a stumbling block to them. He mentions a time he was asked to drink alcohol in Europe because it's part of their culture, but he said he wasn't willing to sacrifice his conscience for the sake of being relevant to their culture.

Then he tells a sobering personal story (16:40). For about the first five and a half months he was a Christian, he said he "lived as a hypocrite, drinking, and partying." He would party together with a good friend and tell him about Jesus. They were in a band together, and everyone ended up quitting except this guy. He believed in Todd, but he didn't believe in Jesus, his "imaginary Friend." Todd said he was living "real bad in front of him, for five and a half months, partying with him, getting drunk with him, still getting high and talking about Jesus."

Then he went to rehab because there was no change in his life. Three days in, he was radically changed, but this best friend of his had a brain aneurism, was in a coma, and died a day later. "And my best friend that I could have witnessed to with my life, I lived as a hypocrite, confessing one thing but living another way." And he told Todd the day before he died that Jesus wasn't for him. So Todd wanted to emphasize the importance of living a holy life and avoiding the appearance of evil (1 Thessalonians 5:22) as a witness to others.

Of course, this doesn't mean his friend would have believed in Jesus if Todd wasn't drinking at that time. I think the noteworthy point isn't feeling guilty about missed opportunities, but letting them fuel our initiative to take our biblical mandate for holy living seriously. Because a pure witness is a more convincing and effective witness. Living maturely is an important facet of making disciples.

I highly recommend watching this documentary. I saw it with my wife and kids; we were all powerfully moved by the Holy Spirit. After seeing it, we talked and prayed about what we learned, and we all walked away with increased faith and a greater desire for holy living.

Our choices that glorify God the most just so happen to serve us and everyone else the best. There's something to say about the wisdom of love, which not only seeks to avoid the appearance of evil but also serves to preserve your life and protect the lives of others. Since disciples are lovers, they serve and protect. Jesus came not to be served, but to serve, and set captives free (Matthew 20:28; Luke 4:18). As His disciples, we get to do the same by the power of His great name. We see a strong example of this Holy-Spirit-empowered ability at work in the beginning of Acts 3. Peter's mature example of a loving disciple of Jesus shows us how he was involved in making a disciple.

"Look at Us," But Look at Him

I once heard Pastor Satise Roddy, of Oasis Church (Minnetonka, Minnesota), give a moving sermon on Acts 3, where Peter heals a lame beggar.[33] It occurred to me that he didn't only heal someone; he opened a door to their discipleship. If you read it, you'll see how a true disciple and previous Jesus-denier made a disciple of Jesus (after Jesus was resurrected).

> Now Peter and John went up together to the temple at the hour of prayer, the ninth hour. And a certain man lame from his mother's womb was carried, whom they laid daily at the gate of the temple which is called Beautiful, to ask alms from those who entered the temple; who, seeing Peter and John about to go into the temple, asked for alms. And fixing his eyes on him, with John, Peter said, "Look at us." So he gave them his attention, expecting to receive something from them. Then Peter said, "Silver and gold I do not have, but what I do have I give you: In the name of Jesus Christ of Nazareth, rise up and walk." And he took him by the right hand and lifted *him* up, and immediately his feet and ankle bones received strength. So he, leaping up, stood and walked and entered the temple with them—walking, leaping, and praising God. And all the people saw him walking and praising God. Then they knew that it was he who sat begging alms at the Beautiful Gate of the temple; and they were filled with wonder and amazement at what had happened to him. (Acts 3:1–10)

I won't go into all of the details here, but a few things from Pastor Satise's sermon got the most of my attention. First, Peter told the downcast man to "Look at us" (v. 4). This reminded me of the time I asked Becca to look at me. Clearly, there is power in a look of love. Second, Pastor Satise emphasized the fact that when the lame man was healed, Peter helped him up, and then the man "received strength" (v. 7). Moments prior, he couldn't even move, but now he was praising God, walking—even jumping—while doing so. Peter not only helped this man up; he made a disciple of him.

It's great when people look at us, receive our help, and experience life-changing love as a result, but we need to keep ourselves in check, as Peter did. In verse 12, Peter says, "Why look so intently at us, as though by our own power or godliness we had made this man walk?" The attention was on Peter, but he pointed them to Jesus since all the glory is to God (Acts 3:13–26). Peter and John proceeded to teach the people about the resurrection of Jesus, but as they spoke, the religious leaders arrested them because they were greatly disturbed by all of this. So the two taken into custody, but not before approximately five thousand people were saved having seen this miracle and hearing the word (Acts 4:1–4).

Here we have a biblical example of one Spirit-filled person (Peter) giving one act of love and making a five-thousandfold difference—minimum! Who knows how much love multiplied from there? I wonder what those five thousand people did, who they influenced, and how families and societies were changed as a result. Here's what it comes down to: Disciples make disciples, who make disciples, who makes disciples, and so on.

The beggar thought he was just going to get paid, but Peter didn't have money; he had something better. At this point, Peter must have been living a pretty holy life. After all, he had learned his lesson about denial, gotten the church started off on the right foot (Acts 2), and emphasized the importance of living a holy life in 1 Peter (his letter to Christians scattered throughout the Roman Empire).

Even though Peter was a proponent of holiness, he certainly wasn't perfect (Galatians 2:11–21). I'm sure he wasn't participating in orgies and killing people, but he was still a work in progress, and so are we. That said, our holy actions, or lack thereof, don't warrant our ability or inability to perform miracles (Galatians 3:5); rather, our faith in Jesus releases His power to perform miracles through us.

Keep in mind, even if you don't see physical deliverance in yourself or those you pray for, it doesn't mean you're doing something wrong, and it certainly doesn't mean you can't make disciples in spite of a "limiting" condition. Such things aren't all bad. After all, Paul's "thorn in the flesh" remained, but this didn't stop him from being mighty for the kingdom. The lame man had his limitations, and so do we, but were just as qualified as anyone else to make a positive difference in the face of adversity. Helping people follow Jesus is our God-appointed mission.

In what is famously known as The Great Commission, Jesus says to His disciples, "All authority in heaven and on earth has been given to me. Therefore go and make disciples of all nations, baptizing them in the name of the Father and of the Son and of the Holy Spirit, and teaching them to obey everything I have commanded you. And surely I am with you always, to the very end of the age" (Matthew 28:18–20).

But we can't do this on our own. We need to come together and help each other out. That is what the church is all about.

Don't Forget About the Church!

Jesus not only taught Peter how to fish for people (Matthew 4:18–20), but eventually, "God used Peter greatly in the foundation of the church. It was Peter who first proclaimed the gospel on the day of Pentecost, and he was also the first to take the gospel to the Gentiles."[34] Believers make disciples, and churches make disciples too. Christians in a church are like teachers and students in a school. We start as a student and become a graduate, maybe even a teacher. Teachers help students, and some students help other students. As they grow, their knowledge and responsibilities increase. To those given much, much is expected. This is not a curse, but a privilege and blessing.

Basically, we have the opportunity to receive help from the church *and* to help those within it. In an age of declining church attendance, let's give the church the attention it deserves. I've heard, for years, that church attendance is declining, but Spirit-filled worshipers are quickly on the rise and filling the churches with the power of the Holy Spirit like never before. Let's not worry about church attendance, but use our time, talents, and resources to care for the bride and body of Christ. Besides, only love can trigger a blast of attendance anyway.

Of course, the following verse shows us attendance isn't God's goal: "His intent was that now, through the church, the manifold wisdom of God should be made known" according to what He accomplished in Jesus (Ephesians 3:10–11).

Jesus sent the Holy Spirit to inhabit people and build the church, beginning with Peter (Acts 2) and quite possibly ending with us. If you've had bad experiences at the church, I'm sorry. But things are different now. Find a joyful, Holy-Spirit-filled church that prays and is filled with expressive love, powerful worship, and soundness of mind. But be on guard against falling into the habit of "church shopping." I remember Dan Mohler telling a story about a woman who told him she left a church because it wasn't very loving, but he playfully told her it should have been loving because she was there! Sometimes we find the good stuff at church, and sometimes we need to bring it to the table. Trust the Holy Spirit to guide you in this.

In the last chapter, we'll turn our attention to the "new early church," and how we can be a part of this powerhouse for God in these last days.

Chapter 12:

Love Anthem

In the early church, "all the believers were one in heart and mind" (Acts 4:32). Look at the next few verses and you'll see this meant they were all about Jesus and serving others. Nowadays the temptation is to get distracted by all the other things that go into managing a church. That doesn't necessarily mean these are bad things, but maybe the scales are unbalanced. The thing is, Jesus is the scale by which we should be measuring everything. So hopefully our service to others carries more weight on the balance than our personal entertainment does. If I make it all about me, I won't be able to see. A self-centered church is a nightmare, and only a revelation of love can shake us awake.

My dream is a love anthem in which the body of Christ comes together in singleness of heart about love. Like the early church, we can emphasize Jesus and embrace serving others. We can catch a vision of His selfless love and get ignited with passion to become Christlike love. It's our mission to make delighted disciples of Jesus by spreading His pleasing aroma everywhere. He gave us what we need to live a life of love.

The church is here to help us, and we're here to help the church. In a sense, we are the church because we're members of the body of Christ, which is the church. So we could say, people are here to help us, and we're here to help people—plain and simple.

Our song is love. Ephesians 5:18–21 says, "Be filled with the Spirit, speaking to one another with psalms, hymns, and songs from the Spirit. Sing and make music from your heart to the Lord, always giving thanks to God the Father for everything, in the name of our Lord Jesus Christ. Submit to one another out of reverence for Christ."

Paul told Timothy the goal of our instruction is love (1 Timothy 1:5). Therefore, the goal of the church should be love too. Furthermore, Paul says in another letter, "My goal is that they may be encouraged in heart and *united in love*" (Colossians 2:2).

As many members—universally and locally—of one body, we collectively form what we know as the church. When the power of love is at the heart of any particular church, it changes everything. Even though each believer is a sort of portable church, there's something special about not the literal church building per se, but gathering together in it. When love reigns in the church, it's hard to leave the building and easy to go back. Even if you feel like you don't want to go, you'll be glad you did. There is a soul-striking difference between a dry church and a flourishing one.

The Church's Role in Your Growth toward Maturity

Until I wound up in a Spirit-filled church, I didn't realize how desperately I needed help, let alone how realistically I could find it in such a place. I went through many seasons of going to church and not going to church. By far, my driest seasons in life were happening when I wasn't going. On the other hand, the most productive seasons of growth occurred while I was going. One experience, in particular, kicked things off.

It was my first time setting foot in a Pentecostal church. I was raised Baptist. I won't get into how I ended up in a charismatic church (long story), but I will say I went in with my guard up. Where I came from, you keep a lid on your emotions. I was torn up inside, and I didn't know how to deal with that. I needed answers, but I wasn't getting them there. I believed in God, but I didn't understand what I was seeing in the church; there was nothing desirable, powerful, or life-changing about it.

After getting divorced, I virtually stopped going to church. I tried a few other places and eventually moved to another city. I was skeptical about finding a church I would like, probably because I wasn't aware of any suitable options. Fortunately, it all served an important purpose: I don't think I would be writing this book if I didn't have all the experiences I've had. It's not a waste, and it's no one's fault, but these things will be used for God's glory because that is what He does: He redeems things and grows us up. He shines light in the darkness, brings truth, and sets us free. Thankfully, God is merciful. When He saw I wasn't bearing fruit, He transplanted me into different soil (Luke 13:6–9).

So there I was, going to an evening service all by myself at a Pentecostal church. It was small and cozy, located in a rented business center suite (but has since moved into a much larger space). I didn't hear much about charismatic churches growing up, except, "Don't go there." Like any church, one varies from the other. Either way, I was cautious because I was taught to expect weird things at such a place. Naturally, I was suspicious and on the lookout for my cue to run out of there.

But obviously, I was desperate because I was there. I was in dire need of help, and a network of churches referred me to this particular church. I was trying to put things together after the destructive wake of divorce. I was newly and happily married, but my wife was living in a different country for an unpredictable period of time. Seeing my children so infrequently was still a fresh wound. To make matters worse, I was having a hard time making ends meet, not eating enough, looking for a job, and carrying a whole lot of stress. My knees were about to buckle under the weight of the circumstances and the weakness of my faith. Then it happened—I was strengthened.

The service began with worship. I wasn't used to all the movement, so I had a lot to look at. I was curious. Why all the motion and commotion? People were lifting *both* hands. They were singing *loudly*. I saw genuine *smiles*. Heard the freedom of *laughter*. I was captivated by graceful *dancing* and gently flowing streamers. People were *clapping*. Some were even giving *shouts* of praise to the Lord! (I'd never heard such a pleasantly shocking loud noise!)

There was *prophesying*—the pastor was leading worship when he said, "Some of us came in here with a Spirit of heaviness" (I felt like he could see it on me), but the Lord was about to take that burden away. Just like that, I received the word of the Lord personally, and I began to *feel* His presence all over me. It felt like fire was on me, and I could feel it moving up and down my entire body and I suddenly became very hot. My back and chest felt like they were on fire, but in a good way—as if literally burning the weight of stress off of me.

I held my hand over my heart and cried, and cried, and cried—tears of healing were flowing like a waterfall from my eyes to my shirt (this was the first time I ever cried so much my shirt got soaked). I could literally feel freedom. This went on for several minutes. No one bothered me. I was happy about that because this was between me and God. After all those years, it was like I met Him for the first time. Years ago, I'd heard His voice in the Isaiah 41:10 verse. Years later, in that moment, He held me. And He wouldn't let go. Not until the weight was gone, the tears were out, and a joyful smile formed on my face.

The rest of the service was a blur. Now I knew what it was like to be drunk in the Spirit—filled with His sobering presence (Ephesians 5:18). This was my most powerful encounter with the tangible love of God. How could I not be changed after this? The love of God overwhelmed me on every sensory level. It wasn't just about what I was feeling, but what I was seeing and hearing too. Everything I knew was shattered. This wasn't weird—it was *worship*, true worship.

Just like that, God removed my spirit of heaviness and clothed me with a light garment of free-flowing praise (Isaiah 61:3 NKJV). My spiritual drought was over, and my journey into the heart of God and His life-changing love was launched. Moments ago, I felt so heavy I could hardly move. Now it was like I was floating.

I approached the pastor with a smile and told him after the service that "I'm the one who came in with a spirit of heaviness, and I'm leaving without it." He smiled big. We talked for a bit and I told him about my circumstances. He offered prayer. I welcomed it. He made motions with his hands and touched me. He had me open my palms and admit "God's hands are big enough" to take care of me and my family. He spoke blessings over me. I could see he was sincerely confident in God and passionate about what he was saying.

I felt warmth all over again. In the best sense of the word, I was absolutely wrecked. These weren't powerless prayers either. This was the beginning of many prayers and prophetic words that would produce much fruit in my life personally and circumstantially. After this particular service, I remember feeling more calm, relaxed, and happy than ever as I was wandering around, just soaking it all up and taking it in. I knew things would never be the same.

I came back for more the next week. Again, I was powerfully moved by what I was seeing. This time I saw two young guys (probably late-teens or early twenties) crying and hugging—not a quick hug either but a flat-out embrace. One was praying for the other. They were surrounded by equally passionate young worshipers. I'd never seen anything like this. I saw this church and thought, *It's alive!* They always had a prayer team up front, ready to pray for anyone who had a need, at the end of each service.

SELFLESS-SUFFICIENT

So I went for it. A man and his wife prayed with me. When one prayed, the other spoke in tongues. They shared words and visions, offered encouragement, and comforted me with gentle touch. Again, I was crying profusely. I was used to being preoccupied with what other people might be thinking, but now I didn't even care—because I was being purged of self-consciousness. Not because I was trying to be, but because I was caught up in the thick presence of the Holy Spirit.

The pastor was talking about people struggling with sin in their lives and said some of us just need to get baptized. I had already been baptized several years prior, but things were different this time. In the past, I did it as a public profession of my belief in Jesus, but nothing more than that. Now I knew it was supposed to be about real-life transformation too, so I got baptized again. This and so much more was happening in this wonder-filled first season of overflowing revelations of love in my life.

Then everything came full circle when I found Dan Mohler on YouTube. Honestly, when I first saw him, I was a bit freaked out because he is intense. But I hung in there and kept watching. The more he spoke, the more my spirit awoke. Next thing I knew, I was watching hours and hours of his messages. I'd been inspired before, but never like this. He was unique. He didn't prepare notes or dress up. He didn't have a formal education but was a pastor. I'm not saying it's bad to have an education or dress up, but I am saying Dan Mohler does things differently from what I was used to seeing.

He didn't even set out to become a pastor, but he was asked—three times. He was asked to pray on the matter, so he did and—to his surprise—accepted the call. There are hundreds if not thousands of videos of him on YouTube now, but he didn't put *any* of them up. He doesn't have a computer and only recently acquired a cell phone. He doesn't charge a speaker fee but accepts whatever the church has decided to give. He foots the bill for his plane tickets. I could go on, but here is my point: I don't know anyone else like him, and I've never heard such impassioned and clear preaching.

Sometimes he's quiet and sometimes he's loud (headphones users, you've been warned!), but he wields an effective sword of the Spirit that cuts to the heart. Getting the feels is fun and God approved at times, but that's not all there is to it. We need a renewed mind—a *reshaped perspective* in order to live a holier lifestyle. We need to know about love. The church benefits greatly from such an example.

At the time, a church friend went out to lunch with me and said, "I really think worship is the key for you." This inspired me so much I wrote a worship song about it, and I discovered he was, in fact, right. Worship music used to bother me growing up, especially the Christian music you didn't hear in the church. That all changed with numerous songs by Jesus Culture, Hillsong, Elevation Worship, and others.

So I was soaking in all this creative worship, and I began praying like I never prayed before (the way I described it in T2), even having prophetic dreams. My confidence in the goodness of God was soaring. My heart started pounding with love (as described in T3). In no small part because I was surrounded by this "cloud of witnesses"—this multitude of Spirit-filled people in that church and online.

Hebrews 11 gives several examples of faith in action through various believers, and how they ought to be a source of inspiration to us in our walk with God. The next chapter continues, "Therefore, since we are surrounded by such a great cloud of witnesses, let us throw off everything that hinders and the sin that so easily entangles. And let us run with perseverance the race marked out for us, fixing our eyes on Jesus, the pioneer and perfecter of faith" (Hebrews 12:1–2). In other words, good examples can create good examples. This is what the Bible means by serving, sharpening, and building each other up in love.

The church I currently attend is amazing. In addition to much prayer, worship, power, and gifting, there is soundness of mind, humbleness of heart, and plenty of generosity. The teaching is on point. There are many successful but humble people, not to mention generous people. Our church has given away twenty-three used cars to people who desperately needed them. Furthermore, the leadership team actively calls out and supports the gifts of the people for the advancement of God's kingdom, both inside the church walls and outside.

I realize not all churches are alive or thriving. Many are lukewarm, and some are dry and withering away. Where there's no power or selfless love, there's no soundness of mind either. However, experiencing Spirit-filled church shook me to the core and affected everything—my thoughts and choices, relationships, dreams, confidence in God, prayer life, healing, worship, and so on.

Now I acknowledge and appreciate the role of the church in my life. It has served me well, but it doesn't end there. I am happy to honor God by accepting my role in the church, which is to thoughtfully serve my brothers and sisters in Christ, as they have served me. Whether giving time, talents, teaching, money, a listening ear, prayer, a kind greeting, a word of encouragement, or whatever, we have something valuable to contribute to the overall health of the church.

"When you come together, everyone has a hymn, or a word of instruction, a revelation, a tongue or an interpretation. Everything must be done so that the church may be built up" (1 Corinthians 14:26).

Your Role in the Church's Growth

I have received so much love at church, and continue to, but it doesn't stop at receiving. I must give back! A lot of this entails sharing my testimony and gifts with fellow believers. My pastor told me writing is my gift to the kingdom. I can't say it didn't cross my mind, but it was nice to hear it from him because I value his input; he's a man of

God. His discernment led to my encouragement, and confirmed what I previously suspected. In a sense, his kind word drew it out of me all the more, inspiring me to keep at it. So here I am, writing this book for the church and hoping it will help strengthen my brothers and sisters in Christ, and hopefully even bring some in that are seeking to join the family. Our arms are open!

If you care to become love, you will be an absolutely useful addition to your church in one way or another. Even if you feel like you're in a season of receiving more so than giving, that's not a problem because what you're getting is a blessing not only for you but the person giving to you. In fact, it is more blessed to *give* than to receive—so be thankful you can be a part of someone else's blessing; this is a sort of indirect service in itself. Likewise, it isn't only good for me to receive prayer; it is good for the other person to give prayer. There's a time to receive, and a time to give. And the church is the best place to practice.

"Be shepherds of God's flock that is under your care, watching over them—not because you must, but because you are willing, as God wants you to be; not pursuing dishonest gain, but eager to *serve*" (1 Peter 5:2).

I mentioned my church gives away cars. Well, catching wind of that inspired me and my wife to embrace generosity and serve someone in need. We're about to buy a used vehicle, and we plan to give our current vehicle to the church once we do. This is exciting for us because we know we're a part of something meaningful. There's so much that can be learned from a Christ-centered church.

After all the prayer I received and the things I learned, the Holy Spirit decided it was time He grew a conviction in me to pray for others in unexpected ways. He showed me it's easier to ask for prayer than it is to volunteer it. To demonstrate, instead of seeking prayer from someone on the prayer team, why not approach and pray for them?

For example, after a Sunday service, the youth pastor and his wife were up front ready to pray for whomever came to greet them. They were expecting their first child soon. I can tell you *I* wasn't expecting anything; I was just sitting there, about to leave. But as they were standing and no one approached them, I took notice and suddenly felt great compassion and an irrepressible urge to bless them. I briefly reflected on my past, and hoped they would have a better run than I did. The least I could do was the most I could do: pray.

So I introduced myself (first time we met), and asked if I could pray for them (I don't recommend doing this all the time since we should honor what they are there for, but if the Spirit leads you, follow!). They seemed surprised since they were there to give prayer, but I had to do this. I knew the Lord wouldn't have it any other way. So I prayed, and I could tell it was meaningful to them. This doesn't mean I did a good job; it means we are here for each other. When we live to love and follow the lead of the Holy Spirit, we will look out for our brothers and sisters naturally.

It's fun and satisfying to help someone, because there's no greater joy than serving others with the strength God provides. "If anyone speaks, they should do so as one who speaks the very words of God. If anyone serves, they should do so with the strength God provides, so that in all things God may be praised through Jesus Christ. To him be the glory and the power for ever and ever. Amen" (1 Peter 4:11).

One time I prayed for Chris Quilala (a Jesus Culture label artist, and a worship pastor at Jesus Culture Church in Sacramento, California). I met him after a show and got a picture taken with him. Chris is a chill, kind-hearted man, and I felt the brotherly love instantly. In my spirit, I felt a need to pray for him. He admitted his schedule was grueling. I had compassion on him because I knew how incredibly busy he was touring, and what a strain that must put on his vocal cords. So I asked him if I could pray for him.

He was pleasantly surprised and welcoming of my offer. I gently placed my hand atop his chest and began to pray, imparting strength to his voice. Afterward, he was very appreciative. Many times we don't know exactly what such a gesture means to somebody, but knowing isn't really the point either; the point is showing love. I could have just gotten a picture with him and overlooked what he was dealing with. I could have ignored the prompting of the Spirit to avoid embarrassing myself. I could have asked for his autograph and bounced once I got it. But love has a peculiar way of taking things deeper. I understand not every situation lends itself to such an event. That said, such events will happen when becoming love matters to us.

It is also important to consider how the love of the church affects non-believers, and how our role as a Christian in the church and outside its walls can play a major role in the salvation of non-Christians. Love among believers builds us up and draws outsiders in.

We're meant to serve one another, share our testimony about Jesus, use our gifts for His glory, and have regular fellowship with other believers. In this way, our love will grow beyond what a building or a body can contain, and outsiders will be reached and nourished. That is kingdom reproduction. Maturity is when fruit is out in full force—when all believers are uniting, serving, and multiplying the image of God, which is love.

Unify and Multiply

Remember, "another sign of maturity is when the tree begins to produce seeds for reproduction. The energy of the tree focuses on reproduction during this stage, and the tree reaches its full size. Growth begins to spread more outward than upward at this point."[35] In spiritual terms, every disciple of Jesus who bears fruit *has* seeds for sowing; there are seeds in their fruit. So we bear fruit and scatter seeds in preparation for the final harvest (when Jesus returns). Making disciples is *reproduction*. The church is a sort of reproduction hub, serving as a community maturity maker and personal growth facilitator. If the church was an orchard, we could say it's filled with trees of various sizes and differing needs, nonetheless all are cared for by our good Orchardist in an attempt to bring about our fullest potential.

Jesus equipped us for "works of service, so that *the body of Christ* may be *built up* until we *all* reach *unity* in the faith and in the knowledge of the Son of God and *become mature*, attaining to the whole measure of the fullness of Christ" (Ephesians 4:11–13). He gives us what we need to realize this vision: seeds for sowing.

> *Now he who supplies seed to the sower and bread for food will also supply and increase your store of seed and will enlarge the harvest of your righteousness.* You will be enriched in every way so that you can be generous on every occasion, and through us your generosity will result in thanksgiving to God. This service that you perform is not only supplying the needs of the Lord's people but is also overflowing in many expressions of thanks to God. Because of the service by which you have proved yourselves, others will praise God for the obedience that accompanies your confession of the gospel of Christ, and for your generosity in sharing with them and with everyone else. And in their prayers for you their hearts will go out to you, because of the surpassing grace God has given you. Thanks be to God for his indescribable gift! (2 Corinthians 9:10–15)

"Remember this: Whoever sows sparingly will also reap sparingly, and whoever sows generously will also reap generously" (2 Corinthians 9:6). Want a good example of a professional sower? Look no further than John Chapman (also known as Johnny Appleseed). Legend has it, he didn't want anyone to go hungry, so he tirelessly traversed the land, scattered seeds, and grew countless apple trees. Likewise, we don't want anyone to spiritually starve, so we tirelessly scatter seeds of kingdom love in hope that they will take root in a person and fill them with the joy of abundant and eternal life in Christ (John 10:10).

I see each copy of this book as a seed for sowing. Who knows what churches and whose hands the wind of the Spirit will blow it into? One thing is for certain: we need to seed for a harvest of love because Jesus said He will be back soon (Revelation 22:7, 12, 20).

Why do we need to unite, multiply love, and spread the good news about Jesus? Because we want to be with Him, and we don't want anyone to perish (Hosea 4:6) on the path to our reunion with Him.

Jesus Is Coming Back Soon

In the context of the second coming of our Lord, Paul writes in 1 Thessalonians 5:10–11 that Jesus "died for us so … we may live together with Him. Therefore encourage one another and build each other up." When He appears in the sky, coming on the clouds, a loud trumpet will sound and He'll send His angels to gather the believers (Matthew 24:30–31). We'll be caught up together in the clouds to meet our Lord in the air, and we'll be with Him forever (1 Thessalonians 4:17).

> For the grace of God has appeared that offers salvation to all people. It teaches us to say "No" to ungodliness and worldly passions, and to live self-controlled, upright and godly lives in this present age, *while we wait for the blessed hope—the appearing of the glory of our great God and Savior, Jesus Christ,* who gave himself

for us to redeem us from all wickedness and to purify for himself a people that are his very own, eager to do what is good. These, then, are the things you should teach. (Titus 2:11–15)

Our "blessed hope" is seeing Him come for us. We have faith this day is approaching fast. This is an exhilarating thought for Christians, but terrifying for unbelievers (Revelation 6:15–17; 19:11–21). As excited as we are about His return, I understand it can be hard to wait. However, our concept of time is different from His. Our "clock" is off, so to speak. "The Lord is not slow in keeping his promise, as some understand slowness. Instead he is patient with you, not wanting anyone to perish, but everyone to come to repentance" (2 Peter 3:9).

The temptation of impatience is offset by trusting the Lord's timing and having a heart for those that don't know Him yet. In one of my songs, I say "Please don't come yet. Please don't come yet. There's so much love left to do." That said, despite our eagerness to be prepared, only He decides when the field is ready for harvest.

Have you ever played Scattergories? You do what you can to fill out the entire card, but once the timer stops, you have to put the pen down. I excel at this, but I don't always complete the card. In life, we have all these ideas about things we want to do, but what if we don't have time?

For instance, this book has been on my heart for years, so finishing it and putting it out there is a big deal for me. I'm fully convinced the Lord wants me to do this. But one unsettling thought I've had is what if Jesus comes back before I press publish? Does that mean I sat on it too long and missed my chance because I was lazy? I can't live with that. Fortunately, my wife is a wonderful helper. She's put those insecurities to bed by reminding me that, "Even if you don't accomplish all you wanted to, Jesus won't be mad at you. You just want Him to find you doing His work when He comes." This is true (Matthew 24:45–51).

"And this gospel of the kingdom will be preached in the whole world as a testimony to all nations, and then the end will come" (Matthew 24:14).

John was given this vision of the end:

> I looked, and there before me was a white cloud, and seated on the cloud was one like a son of man with a crown of gold on his head and a sharp sickle in his hand. Then another angel came out of the temple and called in a loud voice to him who was sitting on the cloud, "Take your sickle and reap, because the time to reap has come, for the harvest of the earth is ripe." So he who was seated on the cloud swung his sickle over the earth, and the earth was harvested. (Revelation 14:14–16)

He will come, and we will give an account to Him. He will give to each person according to what that person has done (Revelation 22:12). In other words, did you believe in Him? That is the question, because what we've done can't save us. I don't know about you, but this inspires me to get ready for His return by putting my faith in His power to save and sanctify. What better way than by worshiping Him?

An anthem is an uplifting song, and the song of the church ought to be love: "I will sing of the LORD's great love forever; with my mouth I will make your faithfulness known through all generations" (Psalm 89:1). Therefore, it is time to "live a life of love" (Ephesians 5:2), but we must take our eyes off of ourselves and lift them up to the Lord. He is where our help comes from (Psalm 121:1–2). As ever-maturing plantings of the Lord, let's unite in singing of His love forever.

> *"Let the trees of the forest sing,*
>   let them sing for joy before the LORD,
>   for he comes to judge the earth.
> Give thanks to the LORD, for he is good;
>   his love endures forever.
> Cry out, "Save us, God our Savior;
>   gather us and deliver us from the nations,
> that we may give thanks to your holy name,
>   and glory in your praise."
> (1 Chronicles 16:33–35)

Stage Four Summary

A mature church is a big deal. It's making a hugely positive impact on the earth—starting with individuals. Yes, the church is composed of individuals. Not to mention, a potential-filled individual with a testimony and talents is reading this book (you!). Such people, or disciples of Jesus, are the ones who turn an upside-down world right side up.

Consider the incredible, unstoppable growth of the Christian church since the time of Jesus on earth, beginning with twelve regular people—His appointed disciples—who became supernaturally sold-out to Jesus. Many more disciples like that exist today because the gospel of the kingdom continues to rapidly grow—eventually filling "the whole world," just as Jesus foretold (Matthew 24:14). (That is like a tree filling out completely. Sounds like maturity to me.) With a wide array of technological advancements, spreading the Word of God is easier and happening more quickly now than ever. Many individuals are actively employed in this great commission.

For instance, if you know who Todd White is, you know he's made a tremendously positive impact on thousands upon thousands of people both in person and through his ministry, Lifestyle Christianity. But just think with me: What if his spiritual mentor, Dan Mohler, didn't sow seeds in Todd or water them faithfully? Think of the thousands of people who would have missed out on a transformational encounter with the love of God through a faithful follower of Jesus. Fortunately, since Todd and Dan have both been faithful in sowing generously, many are reaping generously the fruits of their kingdom-oriented labor.

Maybe you're sold-out, like Dan, in which case, there may be a Todd in your life (if not now, maybe later). But wouldn't it be tragic if we hid our light from people when the light is what they need most? What if Dan Mohler never came out of hiding? What if Todd White didn't come out of hiding? What if I don't come out of hiding? And what if *you* don't come out of hiding?

Remember, love through you makes a *big* difference. Every act of love is like a pebble tossed in a pond, causing a ripple effect reaching far beyond its point of impact. We're here to join this far-reaching love revolution by overthrowing lovelessness with selfless-sufficient living.

We can't do this in our own strength. Our trees suffer from attacks and diseases. Thankfully, there is hope in Jesus. If we will find hope and thrive in abundant living on this earth, we must follow Jesus into eternity and love people into His kingdom—now—but not everyone will.

> Jesus went through all the towns and villages, teaching in their synagogues, proclaiming the good news of the kingdom and healing every disease and sickness. When he saw the crowds, he had compassion on them, because they were harassed and helpless,

like sheep without a shepherd. Then he said to his disciples, *"The harvest is plentiful but the workers are few.* Ask the Lord of the harvest, therefore, to send out workers into his harvest field." (Matthew 9:35–38)

Who will rise up?

Conclusion:

Who Will Rise Up?

In the beginning of this book, I quoted Jesus saying the love of many (but not *all*) will grow cold. He was referring to the end times. He said, "Because of the increase of wickedness, the love of most will grow cold, but the one who stands firm to the end will be saved. And this gospel of the kingdom will be preached in the whole world as a testimony to all nations, and then the end will come" (Matthew 24:12–14).

"When the Son of Man comes, will He find faith on the earth?" (Luke 18:8). Will He find us doing His will? I'm convinced we don't have much time before Jesus returns in the fullness of His glory for the final harvest. But are we ready? Do we know Him? Are we sealed with His Holy Spirit and armed with His power to love selflessly? If so, we will have the supernatural strength to stand, on that day, and withstand the judgment coming upon the earth (Luke 21:36). Living a selfless-sufficient life is the proof of His seal upon us, and our guarantee of being caught up with Christ for eternity.

Now that we're at the end of this book, a question is begging to be answered: Who will rise up?

There's a powerful song called "Who Will Rise Up" (I like the Southland Worship version, but credits for the song go to Jason Ingram and Lindsey McCaul). It's about deciding to become love. Who will rise up? *We* will rise up! Don't forget: *You* are part of the "we." Therefore, the question is: Will *you* rise up?

I Am Looking for One Person ...

In a video from Jesus Culture 2006, Senior Pastor Bill Johnson of Bethel Church in Redding, California, begins by saying,

> I am here looking for one person. ... I love to see crowds burn but I know I can shape history if I can find just one ... one person. You hear people say a lot "you know, if we can get a thousand people in unity and prayer over this matter, we'll get it fixed." Yeah, maybe. One prayer of faith will usually do it. One person. Anybody can burn in a crowd. I want to find someone that will burn by themselves. Anyone can burn in a movement. I want to find the one person that will pray when there is no prayer meeting called. That will get up in the middle of the night when there is no crisis. The one person that gets their personal victories when nobody is looking. Defeats their lion and their bears so that when they have their day before Goliath they have all the confidence in the world and it is not arrogance.[36]

Are you such a person? If not, you can be. In fact, your heart was meant to burn for God this way. But you can't do this yourself.[37] Only the Holy Spirit can light your torch. Then we'll burn with love for God and people. Our faith is not supposed to be in men—in our power—but in the power of God (1 Corinthians 2:5).

Remember, Jesus is the power of God (1 Corinthians 1:24). So when I say "growing in love by the power of God" (this book's subtitle), it's like saying "growing in love by abiding in Jesus." And this works, because that's the only way Christlike love can happen.

The four-stages-of-tree-growth model is meant to simplify our pursuit of love in truth, thankfulness, transformation, and thoughtfulness by reshaping our perspectives and informing our lifestyle choices.

Four Stages of Tree Growth Snapshot and Their Spiritual Parallels Simplified

You may have noticed the bold highlighted key words in each tree growth-stage description. If you put them all together, here is what you get:

T1: TRUTH

    RECEIVES

    SUNLIGHT

    WATER

    DEEPER ROOTS

T2: THANKFULNESS

    BEGINS TO MATURE

    DEVELOP

    FORM

    STILL VERY IMMATURE

T3: TRANSFORMATION

    INCREASE

    BECOME

    FILLS OUT

    SPREAD OUT

T4: THOUGHTFULNESS

    FRUIT

    SEEDS

    REPRODUCTION

    FULL

    OUTWARD

Basically, when gaining understanding (T1), we receive sunlight, water, and deeper roots. When living by faith (T2), we begin to mature, develop, and form, but we're still immature. When walking in love (T3), we increase in it, become fuller of it, and spread it everywhere we go. When serving others (T4), we bear fruit and produce seeds for reproduction, which results in a full church of disciples making increasingly outward impact.

Naturally, this growth process accomplishes not only our personal growth, but also serves to assist in the growth of many outside oneself. This multiplication is the overwhelming result of God's incredible power, which causes love to grow in our lives. It's true: If we abide in Jesus, we *are* growing in love by the power of God.

But living in His power depends on our answer to His invitation to follow Him. Since *abiding involves deciding*, we ought to carefully evaluate what we are currently choosing to do and why, and to consider whether or not our choices are glorifying God.

To Love or Not to Love?

We can talk about love all we want, but until we decide to go all-in, we'll only *talk* about love, but not *walk* in love. "I ask that we love one another ... that you walk in love" (2 John 5–6). What is your answer to John's request? Or, to ask it in Shakespearian language: *To love, or not to love? That* is the question.

My answer is my *choice*. It defines where my allegiance lies: Is my commitment to God, or myself?

A rich man came up to Jesus (Matthew 19:16–30), wondering what he had to do in order to get eternal life. (As if there was something he could do other than follow Jesus). Jesus played his game and threw out some commands, but the man said he was already doing them. Then Jesus turned it up a notch, telling him to sell what he owns and follow Him, as His twelve disciples did (verses 21 and 27).

But the man walked away sad because he wasn't willing to make that sacrifice. He liked the idea of eternal life, but he didn't like the thought of following Jesus at the expense of giving up other things. He wasn't willing to go all-in. He was more interested in holding onto stuff and doing the commands versus following and being with the only One who could save him. The disciples had a hard time processing this; they didn't yet understand Jesus was the only way to the Father. Sometimes we get confused too, and our affections become misguided. They were afraid they left their families for nothing (verse 27).

But we're not supposed to love anyone—not even our spouse or children—more than we love Jesus (Matthew 10:37). Honestly, we can't properly love someone without Him anyway. He assured His disgruntled disciples at the end of the rich man story that "everyone who has left houses or brothers or sisters or father or mother or wife or children or fields for my sake will receive a hundred times as much and will inherit eternal life" (Matthew 19:29).

Ask the Holy Spirit to bring your affections and choices into alignment with the will of God. He will show you what you need to see, at the time you need to see it, and He will give you strength to do what you once thought was impossible—"with God all things are possible" (Matthew 19:26).

Presently, how are your choices reflecting your decision to follow Jesus daily? Maybe you're doing some things right but other things need to go. Perhaps you've never treated Jesus or your transformation as seriously as other aspects of your life—until now.

A Day in the Life of a Christian

Now is the day of salvation! (2 Corinthians 6:2). Therefore, "be very careful, then, how you live—not as unwise but as wise, making the most of every opportunity, because the days are evil. Therefore do not be foolish, but understand what the Lord's will is" (Ephesians 5:15–17).

Naturally, Christians make a serious commitment to Christ by living pure and holy lives—progressively getting better, not worse. If we're abiding in Jesus, we're growing, and growth in love means we're continuously losing an appetite for sin. When we commit to glorifying God in everything we do (Colossians 3:17), sin loses its appeal. Because when we're "making the most of every opportunity" (Ephesians 5:16), we are, in essence, "filled with the Spirit, speaking to one another with psalms, hymns, and songs from the Spirit. Sing and make music from your heart to the Lord, always giving thanks to God the Father for everything, in the name of our Lord Jesus Christ" (Ephesians 5:18–20).

Things change when this happens. New desires are formed. I remember my pastor talking about this. How focusing on Jesus instead of ourselves creates new desires within us for greater good. For instance, let's say you have a problem with a quick temper. Focusing on your anger or the nuisance and trying to control it isn't the solution. Focusing on Jesus is the answer. You confess your problem, admit you don't have the power to change it, and ask Him for new desires, His mind, and the power to change completely. When you can't help but seek God in all things, some changes will come more quickly than others, but next thing you know, you can't stand things you used to enjoy.

The more you seek Him, the more you want to. So once you start, it's hard to stop. The more you read about Him, the more you think about Him. So when you do, you run out of time to worry. The more you pray with Him, the more you have to say about Him. So people find help, hope, and healing. However, the less we seek Him, the less we want to. So we're spiritually starving to death. The less we read about Him or hear about Him, the less we will think about Him. So we find time to worry about things. The less we pray, the less we will talk about Him. So people become victims of our selfishness, and they experience hurt and need help, but our lack of encouragement fails to provide hope.

When you live for Him, life gets really fun—yes, *fun!* Because you have reasons to enjoy waking up, going to work, and doing chores. You have reasons to enjoy driving, time with the family, and going to sleep at night. You have reasons to enjoy Bible study, going to church, and praying at home. Furthermore, life with God supplies a wisdom of love that guides you into better health spiritually, physically, and mentally.

I've experienced the joys of freedom in Christ firsthand as it pertains to things like forming a strong personal connection with God; loving alone time with Him more than anything else (people, work, hobbies, money, entertainment, and so on); overcoming depression and anxiety; sleeping soundly through the night—without snoring—sometimes with awesomely vivid and enlightening spiritual dreams (even prophetic ones); having exceptional overall health, stable energy throughout the day, a relaxed mind and body, and a peaceful heart; and never burning out spiritually.

There was a time I couldn't stand going to church and prayer felt like a dreadful chore. When it came to worship, I didn't even want to sing. Reading the Bible was boring to me. But all of this and much more has changed dramatically. Now I love doing these things because I'm not performing religious duties but enjoying relational privileges. I could go on and on. Jesus was right about the abundant life being a life lived in communion with Him. Like He said in John 10:10, "The thief comes only to steal and kill and destroy; I have come that they may have life, and have it to the full."

When Jesus comes, will He find faith on the earth? Fortunately, yes! The final harvest is coming, and you play an important role in it. The workers are few, but there are workers. The love of many will grow cold, but not all. Now isn't the time to bury your talents and cover your light. Life, as we know it, is about to expire, whether the earth or these corruptible bodies we live in. But all things will be made new (Revelation 21:1–8), and our bodies will be raised incorruptible (1 Corinthians 15:35–58). However, like our Father in heaven, we don't want anyone to perish on our way back to Him (2 Peter 3:9). So we ought to put our faith in Jesus and love like Him, for the day of our Lord is quickly drawing near.

> Let no debt remain outstanding, except the continuing debt to love one another, for whoever loves others has fulfilled the law. The commandments, "You shall not commit adultery," "You shall not murder," "You shall not steal," "You shall not covet," and whatever other command there may be, are summed up in this one command: "Love your neighbor as yourself." Love does no harm to a neighbor. Therefore love is the fulfillment of the law. And do this, understanding the present time: The hour has already come for you to wake up from your slumber, because our salvation is nearer now than when we first believed. The night is nearly over; the day is almost here. So let us put aside the deeds of darkness and put on the armor of light. Let us behave decently, as in the daytime, not in carousing and drunkenness, not in sexual immorality and debauchery, not in dissension

and jealousy. Rather, clothe yourselves with the Lord Jesus Christ, and do not think about how to gratify the desires of the flesh. (Romans 13:8–14)

Remember, the world needs to see the love of God in *your* life! But will you rise up?

Only you can decide.

Appendix: If You're Not a Christian

Thank you for turning here. If you're not a Christian, I'm convinced God has lovingly drawn you to this page. Here you'll find the best free gift I can point you to: the knowledge you need to receive the Holy Spirit—sent straight from Jesus Himself.

Why should you want His Spirit?

His Spirit opens a personal line of communication between you and Jesus and keeps you connected. That way you can discover the joy and power of prayer—in a personal relationship with God (this is not a religious thing!). Once Jesus plants His seed within you, a mature tree will be underway. The Spirit of God within you makes it possible for you to overcome sin, live beyond the grave, and enjoy an eternity in the presence of your heavenly family and Father with no more tears, death, pain, or evil.

By accepting His Holy Spirit, you'll experience peace, comfort, and wise counsel all the days of your life. He'll produce good fruit in you. He'll give you hope, miraculous provision, and contentment in troublesome circumstances. He'll bring you out of the dirt and into the sky. His Spirit is a deposit guaranteeing what is to come.

None of us know how much time we have left. But we do know Jesus said He is coming soon. There is no time to waste—now is the day of salvation! A seed has the potential of a tree, and you have the potential to know God and love people when the seed of the Spirit is planted within you. If the Holy Spirit gets in you now, your life will begin to alter dramatically. Maybe you've tried a lot of things in life, but have you done this? Nothing else offers anything close to the hope found in Jesus Christ.

All you have to do is C.A.R.E.: Confess, Ask, Repent, and Engage.

- **C**onfess: We must humble ourselves and admit we have fallen short of God's glory and done Him and people wrong. We must acknowledge our need for a Savior.
- **A**sk: We must invite the Holy Spirit to come and live inside us, thank Him for doing so, and thank Him for forgiving us of all our sins—past, present, and future.
- **R**epent: We must commit to a renewed lifestyle of Christian purpose and turn away from the sins the Holy Spirit convicts us of. Get baptized to signify your new life in Christ.
- **E**ngage: We must read the Word of God, pray, and find Spirit-filled friends and churches to spur us on in our faith. Be proactive, read Bible-based books, and love people.

Jesus wants to save you. Right now, Jesus is alive in His resurrected body, at the right hand of God, praying for you (Romans 8:34). He's also preparing a place for you so you can be with Him where He is (John 14:3). He's coming back to get you—soon! (Revelation 22:7, 12, 20). This is rapturous news if you're a believer sealed with the Holy Spirit, but terrifying if you're not. He stands at the door of your heart knocking; please let Him in and see for yourself that He is the real deal.

Luke 15:10 tells us "there is rejoicing in the presence of the angels of God over one sinner who repents." If this is you, welcome to the family! Things are about to get awesome.

Acknowledgments

Thank you, Lord, for giving me a revelation of love. Nothing compares to the satisfaction of knowing you and showing you in this life. I thank you for planting this book within my heart and making it a reality. It has been an absolute privilege and pleasure to go deep with you throughout the writing process. Thanks for teaching me how to commune with you while writing; it is my favorite thing to do. I only hope this book will glorify you and help people know you and show you. Your will be done, Lord!

It's an honor to say God was stirring up the content of this book in me for years. There were late nights, early mornings, and countless hours spent writing. There were ups and downs, excitement and discouragement, and everything in between. But my dear wife was supportive through it all. I kept this a mostly private project for quite some time, so I had no one to talk to but God and my wife, but that was more than enough. So I extend an eternally heartfelt thanks to my lovely bride for being with me through it all. You encouraged me to no end. There is no doubt in my mind: I couldn't have done this without you. I love you forever.

I would also like to thank Dan Mohler and Todd White for their dedicated service to the kingdom. (Thanks to all the churches and people that posted their videos on YouTube as well!) These guys are incredible men of God. I have benefited immensely from what they are doing. The essence of this book is in no small part inspired by them.

Of course, I wish Loren was here to see this book. He is one of the best examples of a Christlike person I've ever known. Years ago, he gave me many free counseling sessions and helped me through my darkest hours. I don't think he realized how much he helped me. He knew I wanted to pay him back, but couldn't. Thankfully, he never expected it and wasn't worried about it. He said he was sure I would pay it forward in a different way. Hopefully this book fits the bill. I miss him, but the hope of heaven assures me I will see him again soon.

Then there's Dr. Kilde. Thank you for cutting to the heart of the matter during our visit. I hope your role in this book is a pleasant surprise to you. (He won't know about the positive effect he had on me until he reads this because I never told him about it—until now).

Then there's the other Jon. I wish I saw more of you nowadays, but you will always hold a special place in my heart. I think about you often. Like Loren, you were there for me during the good times and the bad. I have always enjoyed your company, and I look forward to seeing you next time.

So many people have helped prepare me for this moment. Thanks to the unwavering love, support, and commitment of my immediate family—my wife, children, parents, grandparents, and brother. You've all taught me valuable things about life, and I appreciate and love you all. Thanks for being excited about the book. And thanks to my sweet grandma for inspiring one of the chapters.

Thank you, Rod, for encouraging me in the craft. You are an incredibly talented writer. I miss our walks, talks, and chocolate chip muffins.

Pastor Jac, you're an inspiration. I admire your wisdom, wit, dedication to prayer, and your confidence in God. I also appreciate your warmth and generosity. Your support means a lot to me. Thanks for blessing this project.

Every time before writing, I worshiped in prayer and song. I found myself gravitating to a select number of songs throughout this project. "Do it Again" and "Give Me Faith" by Elevation Worship. "Thank You Jesus," "I Surrender," and "What a Beautiful Name" by Hillsong. "I Want to Know You," "Miracles," and "My Soul Longs for You" by Jesus Culture (Chris Quilala and Kim Walker-Smith). "What a Beautiful Name/Agnus Dei" by Travis Cottrell feat. Lily Cottrell. And my personal favorite: "Build my Life" by Housefires. Their "This Love" song is right up there too. Also, thanks to the wonderful, calm-inducing musical accompaniment of the *Rest in Him* album by Southland Worship. Not to mention some of their other songs: "Your Word," "Father You Have Loved Us," and "Release Your Spirit." I thank all of the above for the outflow of miraculous, life-changing, Spirit-filled music!

I held a vision of this book cover imagery in my head for years, but Miladinka Milic brought it to life with magnificent detail, exceptional skill, and rare creativity. God bless you, Mila! Thank you for everything.

Thanks to Sarah Pierce and Erik Bell for making my photo shoot enjoyable! I'll admit I wasn't thrilled about getting my picture taken, but meeting the two of you made it worthwhile.

Of course, I cannot forget my dear editor, Christy Distler, owner of Avodah Editorial Services. Out of all the editors in the world, God knew you were the right one for this project. Your kindness, patience, attention, and professionalism are greatly appreciated. Having your help was a gift from God. Thank you for your generous service to the kingdom!

Last but certainly not least, I'd like to thank *you* for taking the time to read this. I hope you find a great return on your investment!

About the Author

Benjamin P. Olson is a former self-centered Christian legalist who used to have little regard for anyone other than himself. Then, many years ago, Dan Mohler came to him as God's messenger and shot an arrow of truth into his heart, which played a central role in the death of Ben's old self. This healing, transformational baptism of love helped bring about his new life in Christ Jesus. Now Ben enjoys intimacy with God and a progressively selfless lifestyle—laying down his life in service to others for the glory of God. He finds inspiration through various loving examples of fellow Spirit-filled believers, such as Todd White of Lifestyle Christianity.

As a longtime private writer (amassing thousands of pages and 140+ songs), Ben eventually received a revelation from the Holy Spirit that it was time to go public and feed the spiritually hungry through his gift of writing. He does so with the goal of using what he has been given to glorify God by scattering seeds of love upon the earth. There is a God-planted mission in his heart to find teachable Christians, and to sharpen, encourage, and build them up in their faith upon the strongest foundation of all: the love of God.

References

1. Ted Marten, "Names of the Stages of Tree Growth," *eHow*, https://www.ehow.com/info_8761441_names-stages-tree-growth.html.
2. Ibid.
3. "Dan Mohler – The Essence of the Gospel," *YouTube*, May 19, 2014, https://www.youtube.com/watch?time_continue=1362&v=fbvAQoKEMeQ.
4. Brother Lawrence, *The Practice of the Presence of God* (London: H. R. Allenson, Ltd., 1906), 11–12.
5. "Brother Lawrence, Practitioner of God's Presence," *Christianity Today*, https://www.christianitytoday.com/history/people/inner-travelers/brother-lawrence.html.
6. Ibid.
7. "Todd White – Including God in Everything," *YouTube*, March 14, 2018, https://www.youtube.com/watch?v=EWZPZROEWRo.
8. Marten, "Names of the Stages of Tree Growth."
9. "Dallas Willard > Quotable Quotes > Quotes," *Goodreads*, https://www.goodreads.com/quotes/1019974-we-don-t-believe-something-by-merely-saying-we-believe-it.
10. "God reality changes your life – Dan Mohler," *YouTube*, April 30, 2016, https://www.youtube.com/watch?v=_NtMB6keCI0.
11. "Go from self-centered to living by faith by Dan Mohler," *YouTube*, July 10, 2015, https://www.youtube.com/watch?v=gPMdBSYPTHI.
12. *English Oxford Living Dictionaries*, s.v. "sorrow," https://en.oxforddictionaries.com/definition/sorrow.
13. *English Oxford Living Dictionaries*, s.v. "merry," https://en.oxforddictionaries.com/definition/merry.
14. The Holy Bible, New International Version®, NIV®, footnote definition of "praise."
15. John Nielsen, "Study: Moths Can Remember Caterpillar Stage," *NPR*, March 10, 2008, https://www.npr.org/templates/story/story.php?storyId=88031220.
16. "Don't let life speak louder than truth Dan Mohler," *YouTube*, June 3, 2018, https://www.youtube.com/watch?v=-Bd_OrCBuZ0.
17. Marten, "Names of the Stages of Tree Growth."

18. John Piper, "Jesus Died for Your Spouse's Sins," *Desiring God*, October 10, 2018, https://www.desiringgod.org/messages/marriage-gods-showcase-of-covenant-keeping-grace/excerpts/jesus-died-for-your-spouses-sins.
19. Sean Martin, "WATCH: This is what happens to your body when you die," *Express*, May 13, 2006, https://www.express.co.uk/news/science/669719/WATCH-This-is-what-happens-to-your-body-when-you-die.
20. Marten, "Names of the Stages of Tree Growth."
21. "Clark Kent," *Wikipedia*, https://en.wikipedia.org/wiki/Clark_Kent.
22. "What Is Mental Health?" *MentalHealth.gov*, August 29, 2017, https://www.mentalhealth.gov/basics/what-is-mental-health.
23. "Mother Teresa > Quotes > Quotable Quote," *Goodreads*, https://www.goodreads.com/quotes/328379-it-is-easy-to-love-the-people-far-away-it.
24. "55 shades of Great: Random facts about Wayne Gretzky on his 55th birthday," *ESPN.com*, January 26, 2016, http://www.espn.com/nhl/story/_/id/14621635/nhl-55-shades-great-facts-wayne-gretzky-55th-birthday.
25. "Walking The Beat In Mr. Rogers' Neighborhood, Where A New Day Began Together," *NPR*, March 11, 2016, https://www.npr.org/2016/03/11/469846519/walking-the-beat-in-mr-rogers-neighborhood-where-a-new-day-began-together.
26. "Nick Vujicic – man without limbs shares the Bible verse that gave him purpose," *Christian Today*, https://christiantoday.com.au/news/nick-vujicic-man-without-limbs-shares-the-bible-verse-that-gave-him-purpose.html.
27. Marten, "Names of the Stages of Tree Growth."
28. *Cambridge Dictionary*, s.v. "thoughtful," https://dictionary.cambridge.org/us/dictionary/english/thoughtful.
29. David Nooitgedagt, "What are spiritual gifts?" *Active Christianity*, https://activechristianity.org/what-are-spiritual-gifts.
30. "Mark Twain > Quotes > Quotable Quote," *Goodreads*, https://www.goodreads.com/quotes/646569-find-a-job-you-enjoy-doing-and-you-will-never.

31. *Google Dictionary*, s.v. "food bank," https://www.google.com/search?rlz=1C1CHBF_enUS824US824&ei=O3mNXNizE-HF_QaX94jABg&q=google+dictionary&oq=google+dic&gs_l=psy-ab.1.0.0j0i10j0i131j0l3j0i10j0l3.7391.8928..10144...0.0..0.116.928.5j5......0....1..gws-wiz.......0i71j35i39j0i131i67j0i67.WGI1tP2ZQzM#dobs=food%20bank.
32. "Todd White – Pure and Holy (FREE MOVIE)," *YouTube*, December 14, 2018, https://www.youtube.com/watch?v=QfldY6ChOuI.
33. Satise Roddy, sermon at Eden Prairie Assembly of God, January 6, 2019, https://vimeopro.com/epag/epag-sermons/video/309958157.
34. "What is the rock in Matthew 16:18?" *Got Questions*, https://www.gotquestions.org/upon-this-rock.html.
35. Marten, "Names of the Stages of Tree Growth."
36. "Bill Johnson – I Am Looking For One Person," *YouTube*, March 28, 2012, https://www.youtube.com/watch?v=iNVINiUaCrA.
37. "Todd White – You Can't Do This in Your Own Strength," *YouTube,* April 21, 2017, https://www.youtube.com/watch?v=v3OEshioSE.

Made in the USA
Columbia, SC
01 May 2019